where LOCALS →hike

✦ ✦ IN THE WEST Kootenay ✦ ✦

{ the **PREMIER** trails IN SOUTHEAST B.C. near KASLO + NELSON }

➡➡ Boot-tested and written by

KATHY + CRAIG COPELAND

hiking camping.com

Heading outdoors eventually leads within.

The first people on Earth were hikers and campers. So today, when we walk the land and bed down on it, we're living in the most primitive, elemental way known to our species. We're returning to a way of life intrinsic to the human experience. We're shedding the burden of millennia of civilization. We're seeking catharsis. We're inviting enlightenment.

hikingcamping.com publishes unique guidebooks – literate, entertaining, opinionated – that ensure you make the most of your precious time outdoors. Our titles cover spectacular wild lands in western North America.

nomads@hikingcamping.com   hiking camping.com

Returning to Sol Mountain, from Pride Rock (Trip 2)

Twin Lakes (Trip 2)

Published in Canada by hikingcamping.com, inc.
P.O. Box 8563, Canmore, Alberta, T1W 2V3
nomads@hikingcamping.com

Maps and production by C.J. Poznansky
giddyupgraphics@mac.com

Cover and interior design by Matthew Clark
www.subplot.com

Printed in China by Asia Pacific Offset

All photos by the authors, except pages 186 & 188
by Dave McCormick, page 215 by Sara Rainford /
Tourism Rossland

Front cover: *Summitting Mt. Crawford, above Plaid Lake (Trip 31)*. Back cover: *Sweet Lake, upper Carpenter Creek Valley (Trip 7); Monica Meadows (Trip 16); Fry Creek Canyon (Trip 48); Retallack Cedars (Trip 45); Reco-Texas Ridge (Trip 10)*

Inside front cover: *Trail to Whitewater Mtn (Trip 11)*
Inside back cover: *MacBeth Icefield waterfalls (Trip 15)*

Library and Archives Canada - Cataloguing in Publication

Copeland, Kathy, 1959-
    Where locals hike in the West Kootenay : the premier
trails in southeast B.C., near Kaslo & Nelson / Kathy and
Craig Copeland. -- 3rd ed.

Includes index.
ISBN 978-1-927462-00-3

1. Hiking—British Columbia—Kootenay Region—Guidebooks.
2. Trails—British Columbia—Kootenay Region—Guidebooks.
3. Kootenay Region (B.C.)—Guidebooks. I. Copeland, Craig, 1955- II. Title.

GV199.44.C22K66 2012   796.52220971162   C2012-902633-6

YOUR SAFETY IS YOUR RESPONSIBILITY

Hiking and camping in the wilderness can be dangerous. Experience and preparation reduce risk, but will never eliminate it. The unique details of your specific situation and the decisions you make at that time will determine the outcome. Always check the weather forecast and current trail conditions before setting out. This book is not a substitute for common sense or sound judgment. If you doubt your ability to negotiate mountain terrain, respond to wild animals, or handle sudden, extreme weather changes, hike only in a group led by a competent guide. The authors and the publisher disclaim liability for any loss or injury incurred by anyone using information in this book.

CONTENTS

Maps

Introduction

A Serene Mountain Enclave 7 / The West Kootenay 8 / Shoulder-Season Hiking 11 /Dayhiking or Backpacking 14 / Trails Not in this Book 14 / Placate the Weather Gods 16 / Rainy-Day Trips 17 / Hiking with Kids 17 / Challenging Trails 18 / Physical Capability 18 / Leave Your Itinerary 19 / Distances and Elevations 19 / Maps 19 / Carry a Compass 19 / Trailhead Access 20 / Ferries 22 / South of the Border 22 / Wilderness Ethics 23 / Hiking with your Dog 25 / Wildlife 26 / Bears 27 / Know Before You Go 29

Above Griffin Lake, Kokanee Glacier Park (Trip 23)

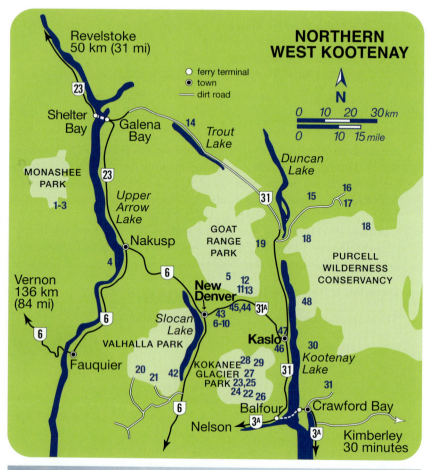

NORTHERN
WEST KOOTENAY

Revelstoke
50 km (31 mi)

23

Shelter
Bay

Galena
Bay

14

Trout
Lake

○ ferry terminal
◉ town
— dirt road

N

0 10 20 30 km
0   10   15 mile

MONASHEE
PARK

23

1-3

Upper
Arrow
Lake

Nakusp

Duncan
Lake

31

15   16
        17

18

GOAT
RANGE
PARK

19

18

PURCELL
WILDERNESS
CONSERVANCY

Vernon
136 km
(84 mi)

6

4

6

5   12
     1113

New
Denver

43
6-10

45,44

31ᴬ

48

6

Slocan
Lake

47

Kaslo

46

VALHALLA PARK

30

6

Fauquier

20
21

42

KOKANEE
GLACIER
PARK

28 29
27
23,25
24 22
26

Kootenay
Lake

31

31

6

Balfour

Nelson

3ᴬ

Crawford Bay

3ᴬ

Kimberley
30 minutes

On Mt. Jardine's west ridge (Trip 13)

Northern West-Kootenay Trips

1	Mt. Fosthall	21	Gimli Ridge
2	Sol Mountain / Pride Rock	22	Kokanee and Kaslo Lakes
3	Mission Ridge	23	Sapphire Lakes / Mt. Giegerich
4	Saddle Mountain	24	Glory Basin
5	Alps Alturas	25	Helen Deane Lake
6	Idaho Peak	26	The Keyhole
7	Prospector Peak	27	Woodbury Cabin
8	Mt. Carlyle	28	Woodbury Traverse
9	Misty Peak	29	Silver Spray Cabin
10	Texas Peak	30	Mt. Loki
11	Whitewater Canyon	31	Mt. Crawford / Plaid Lake
12	Mt. Brennan	42	Slocan Lakeshore
13	Mt. Jardine	43	Carpenter Creek Valley
14	Silvercup Ridge	44	Silver Avenue
15	MacBeth Icefield	45	Retallack Cedars
16	Monica Meadows	46	Kaslo River
17	Jumbo Pass	47	Kaslo Vista
18	Hamill Creek / Earl Grey Pass	48	Fry Creek
19	Meadow Mountain		
20	Gwillim Lakes		

Mt. Crawford (Trip 31)

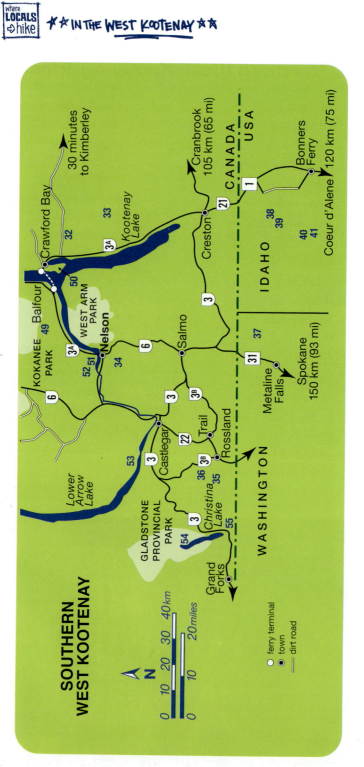

Southern West-Kootenay Trips

photos: *1 Baker Street, Nelson 2 Kootenay Lake's west arm 3 Sandon*

*Mt. Hamill
from Slate Peak (Trip 18)*

A Serene Mountain Enclave

After four years of working in downtown Vancouver office towers and living in a 480 sq. ft. apartment amid the city's West End, one of the most densely populated urban areas on the planet, we decamped to the hinterland. Vancouver is a gorgeous, stimulating city—a yeasty brew with an international flavour that we savoured gratefully and left reluctantly. But we yearned for wilderness. Seeing the North Shore Mountains across English Bay wasn't enough. We wanted to live *in* the mountains. The remote east shore of Kootenay Lake, wedged between the Selkirk and Purcell ranges, seemed as far into the wilds as we could go and still run a publishing company. So we bought a cabin on the lakeshore, chased out the packrats, stuffed our book inventory into the basement, and settled in.

The West Kootenay is a serene mountain enclave. Lightly populated by quirky peaceniks who relish their seclusion. Punctuated by just enough glacier-crowned summits to tantalize a peak freak. It was everything we sought. Just one thing was missing: a hiking guidebook. The only one ever written on the area was out of print long before we arrived. Much had changed since then, as we soon discovered.

During five years of living in the West Kootenay, we hiked like escaped convicts, which in a sense we were. We logged more than 2400 km (1488 mi). Since then, we've returned for several weeks of striding the Selkirks, Purcells, and Monashees nearly every year. Of all the ground we've covered there, we chose 55 hikes to include in this book, making it the resource we needed when we first arrived in the West Kootenay.

Why isn't this an encyclopedically exhaustive volume? Because detailing every wretched, obscure scratch in the dirt would overburden and confuse the vast majority of hikers, therefore failing to guide them. By definition, a **guide**book should winnow and recommend, sparing the reader unnecessary, tedious decision-making. It should also be eloquent. Guidebooks have languished too long as a knuckle-dragging subspecies of literature. So our goal was to write a superior primer—accurate of course, but also lucid, as well as entertaining—that most local or visiting hikers will find helpful and enjoyable.

What's not in this book? Punishing, dreary, sketchy trips, mostly. Their appeal is limited to inveterate explorers and intrepid mountaineers. The average hiker would find these journeys frustrating, disappointing, or overwhelming.

So now you can quickly, easily choose a West Kootenay hike, confident each one in this book offers a transcendent experience. Our opinionated descriptions will help you decide *where* to go and understand *why* you're going. Our precise *by vehicle* and *on foot* directions will ensure you get there and back without difficulty.

We hope *Where Locals Hike* compels you to head outdoors more often and stay out longer. Do it to cultivate your wild self. It will give you perspective. Do it because the backcountry teaches simplicity and self-reliance—qualities that make life more fulfilling. Do it to remind yourself why wilderness needs and deserves your protection. A deeper conservation ethic develops naturally in the mountains. And do it to escape the cacophony that muffles the quiet, pure voice within.

The West Kootenay

Pervasive, beautiful mountains are the distinguishing attribute of the West Kootenay. All else that defines the region is a gift of the mountains. The mild, welcoming, West Kootenay climate? It's strongly influenced by the deep valleys

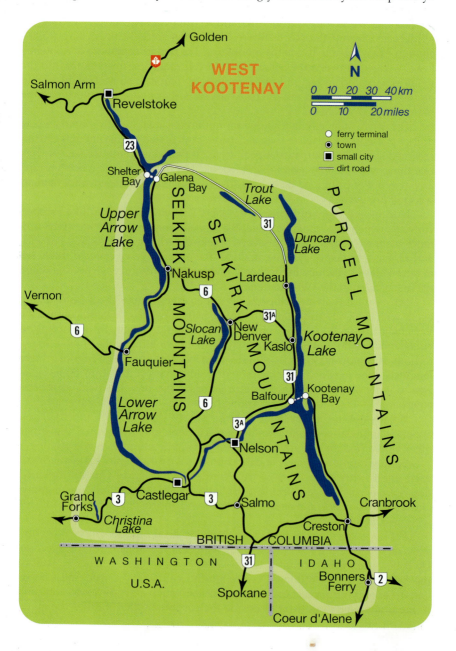

East shore of Kootenay Lake

and huge lakes, both created by the mountains. The wild vastness that envelopes the West Kootenay, fostering serenity, offering solitude, tempering every aspect of daily life? It's protected by vertical topography: the mountains. Even the colourful threads of the West Kootenay social fabric—counter-cultural attitudes, alternative lifestyles—were spun from isolation, which is enforced by the mountains.

Yet there are no West Kootenay mountains as such. Three primary ranges give the West Kootenay its tightly pleated, accordion topography. To the west are the gentle, rounded Monashee Mountains. The spikier Selkirks shoulder their way between the Arrow Lakes and Slocan Valley. Farther east, the craggy Purcells separate the West Kootenay from the East Kootenay and the Rocky Mountain Trench. All comprise sub-ranges. All are subsumed by an even greater mountain system: the Columbia Mountains. The region's tallest peak is 3090-m (10,135-ft) Mt. Cooper, in the Goat Range, north of Hwy 31A. Check out the photo in Trip 19.

During the ice age, the West Kootenay was covered at about 2134 m (7000 ft). Only traces of that ice remain. Even the most stupendous West Kootenay glaciers—Macbeth Icefield (Trip 15), for example—are teensy compared to the frozen sea that once engulfed all but a few islands. Instead of ice, today we have lakes. Glacier-gouged, inland fiords. Great veins of water so deep, cold and clean that lakeshore residents pump it up to their homes and drink it unfiltered.

At 532 m (1746 ft), Kootenay Lake is 110 km (68 mi) long, 2 to 6 km (1.2 to 3.7 mi) wide, and 200 m (656 ft) deep, with an additional 30-km (18.6-mi) tentacle reaching to Nelson. Small only by local comparison are 40-km (25-mi) Slocan Lake and 44-km (27.3-mi) Duncan Lake reservoir. Upper and Lower Arrow lakes are actually a single reservoir dammed near Castlegar. It stretches 230 km (143 mi) to Revelstoke.

If most of the West Kootenay is either vertical or submerged, what's left for human habitation? Not much. So the towns are petite.

Nelson, the region's unofficial capital, is home to 10,230 people; another 10,000 live within a 16-km (10-mi) radius. Castlegar is home to 7816. Creston has 5,380 residents, Nakusp 1,574, Kaslo 1,026, and New Denver 504. The land's skyward tilt limits population growth. Skinny lakeshores, slender valleys, and steep slopes grant livable real estate begrudgingly.

Only trees flourish in great numbers here. Hospitable forests host mountainside parties, welcoming the usual gang: fir, pine, birch, spruce, larch. In a few isolated nooks, single-variety stands of cedar or hemlock spurn the festivities and refuse to socialize.

Sadly, logging continues apace in the West Kootenay, just like it does throughout the province. New clearcuts are continually scalped from the forests, and logging trucks piled high with freshly cut trees keep rumbling down the highways.

Meanwhile, hikers should imagine life without logging roads. Would they endure steep, viewless, all-day slogs to reach most West Kootenay trailheads? Not likely. Consider Mt. Loki. Few hikers attempted it when the ascent began near Kootenay Lake. A recent logging road now allows you to drive within a one-hour hike of treeline, making Loki a reasonable thus popular dayhike and earning it a place in this book: Trip 30.

Before logging, the region's dominant industry was mining. Gold, silver and copper booms began in the 1890s. New Denver, Silverton, Slocan, Sandon and Kaslo were originally mining settlements. The high country was riddled with mines.

Miners' cabin beside historic trail, Carpenter Creek Valley (Trips 7-9)

Relics from West Kootenay mining days, Sandon

Today, mining in the West Kootenay is history. The mineshafts are collapsing, the cabins rotting, the abandoned equipment rusting away. Some of the miners' trails, however, are still in service as hiking trails.

A few facts will help you envision the astonishing magnitude of the former mining industry here:

• More than 300 mines operated simultaneously near Sandon, most of them above 1524 m (5000 ft).

• Entire forests were consumed to provide the timber necessary to build and maintain the Sandon mines.

• Two railway lines were needed to handle Sandon's incoming supplies and outgoing ore.

• Sandon mines produced silver, lead and zinc worth—in today's value—more than $35 billion. That's greater than the value of the ore produced during North America's three major gold rushes—California, the Cariboo, and the Klondike—combined.

Shoulder-Season Hiking

Mid-July through mid-October is prime hiking season in the West Kootenay. That's when alpine trails will most likely be snow-free. Shoulder-season trails are at lower elevations where strong sun exposure allows snow-free hiking earlier and later in the year: perhaps starting in April, often continuing into November. Shoulder-season options are fewer, shorter, and less scenic than the choices available to you in summer. Most are dayhikes. And shoulder-season hiking is almost always in forest, but hey, at least you'll be hiking. Only three West Kootenay trails are long enough to warrant consideration for shoulder-season backpacking: Christina Lake (Trip 54), Slocan Lakeshore (Trip 42), and the Hamill Creek portion of the Earl Grey Pass adventure (Trip 18).

Trips at a Glance

Trips are listed according to geographic location: starting in the north and the west, moving south, then starting again in the north, moving east and south again. After the trip name, the complete-trip distance is listed, followed by the elevation gain.

Dayhikes & Backpack Trips

1	Mt. Fosthall	18.4 km / 11.4 mi	1177 m / 3861 ft
2	Sol Mountain	12 km / 7.4 mi	959 m / 3145 ft
3	Mission Ridge	10.4 km / 6.5 mi	515 m / 1689 ft
4	Saddle Mountain	10.6 km / 6.6 mi	864 m / 2834 ft
5	Alps Alturas	10 km / 6.2 mi	579 m / 1900 ft
6	Idaho Peak	2.8 km / 1.7 mi	146 m / 479 ft
7,8,9	Mt.Carlyle Lodge	10.2 km / 6.3 mi	616 m / 2020 ft
	plus destinations beyond lodge:		
7	Prospector Peak	2.2 km / 1.4 mi	350 m / 1148 ft
8	Mt. Carlyle	3 km / 1.9 mi	305 m / 1000 ft
9	Misty Peak	2 km / 1.2 mi	259 m / 850 ft
10	Texas Peak	10.8 km / 6.7 mi	1067 m / 3500 ft
11	Whitewater Canyon	14.2 km / 8.8 mi	817 m / 2680 ft
12	Mt. Brennan	14.6 km / 9 mi	1525 m / 5001 ft
13	Mt. Jardine	15 km / 9.3 mi	1205 m / 3952 ft
14	Silvercup Ridge	39.5 km / 24.5 mi	1190 m / 3900 ft
15	MacBeth Icefield	15.6 km / 9.7 mi	1198 m / 3929 ft
16	Monica Meadows	8.5 km / 5.3 mi	580 m / 1902 ft
17	Jumbo Pass	8.4 km / 5.2 mi	685 m / 2246 ft
18	Hamill Creek/Earl Grey Pass	64.4 km / 40 mi	2073 m / 6800 ft
19	Meadow Mountain	5.4 km / 3.4 mi	510 m / 1673 ft
20	Gwillim Lakes	11.6 km / 7.2 mi	1164 m / 3818 ft
21	Gimli Ridge	9.8 km / 6.1 mi	765 m / 2510 ft
22	Kokanee & Kaslo Lakes	17 km / 10.5 mi	524 m / 1718 ft
23	Sapphire Lakes	8.6 km / 5.3 mi	347 m / 1138 ft
24	Glory Basin	29.6 km / 18.4 mi	977 m / 3204 ft
25	Helen Deane Lake	5 km / 3.1 mi	162 m / 531 ft
26	The Keyhole	11 km / 6.8 mi	1144 m / 3752 ft
27	Woodbury Cabin	16 km / 10 mi	809 m / 2654 ft
28	Woodbury Traverse	8 km / 5 mi	693 m / 2273 ft
29	Silver Spray Cabin	14 km / 8.7 mi	1052 m / 3451 ft
30	Mt. Loki	10.2 km / 6.3 mi	1151 m / 3775 ft

31	Mt Crawford	4.6 km / 2.9 mi	519 m / 1702 ft
32	Gray Creek Pass Summits	8.6 km / 5.3 mi	796 m / 2610 ft
33	Haystack Mountain	8.4 km / 5.2 mi	976 m / 3200 ft
34	Toad Mountain	8 km / 5 mi	625 m / 2050 ft
35	Seven Summits	30.4 km / 18.9 mi	732 m / 2400 ft
36	Old Glory Mountain	16.8 km / 10.4 mi	1114 m / 3654 ft
37	Shedroof Divide	14.4 km / 8.9 mi	762 m / 2500 ft
38	Trout & Big Fisher Lakes	15.2 km / 9.4 mi	761 m / 2496 ft
39	Pyramid & Ball Lakes	8 km / 5 mi	394 m / 1292 ft
40	Two Mouth Lakes	11.3 km / 7 mi	509 m / 1670 ft
41	Harrison Lake	9.7 km / 6 mi	406 m / 1332 ft

Shoulder-Season Dayhikes

42	Slocan Lakeshore	16 km / 10 mi	150 m / 492 ft
43	Carpenter Creek Valley	14.5 km / 9 mi	loss 376 m / 1234 ft
44	Silver Avenue	4.4 km / 2.7 mi	128 m / 420 ft
45	Retallack Cedars	0.6 km / 0.4 mi	negligible
46	Kaslo River	2.7 km / 1.7 mi	111 m / 364 ft
47	Kaslo Vista	1 km / 0.6 mi	155 m / 508 ft
48	Fry Creek Canyon	10 km / 6.2 mi	208 m / 682 ft
49	Kokanee Cedars	2 km / 1.2 mi	122 m / 400 ft
50	Pilot Peninsula	12.8 km / 8 mi	235 m / 770 ft
51	Pulpit Rock	3.6 km / 2.2 mi	338 m / 1109 ft
52	Sproule Creek	10 km / 6.2 mi	262 m / 860 ft
53	Syringa Park	6 km / 3.7 mi	90 m / 295 ft
54	Christina Lake	12.8 km / 8 mi	306 m / 1004 ft
55	Cascade Gorge	8 km / 5 mi	45 m / 148 ft

Dayhiking or Backpacking?

The West Kootenay lacks truly long trails, so most of the trips in this book are dayhikes shorter than 15 km (9.3 mi). For reasonably fit hikers who maintain a moderate pace, only five trips are long enough to warrant backpacking: Hamill Creek / Earl Gray Pass (Trip 18), Gwillim Lakes (Trip 20), Kokanee Glacier Park (Trips 22, 23, 24, 25), and Silvercup Ridge (Trip 14). But be creative. The Hamill Creek portion of the Earl Grey Pass trip is a premier dayhike in shoulder season, or a worthwhile dayhike in summer. If you're swift, a few backpack trips are hikeable in a day, for example Gwillim Lakes, or Glory Basin. Some dayhikes make excellent backpack trips if you want or need a shorter option, for example Silver Spray Cabin (Trip 29), or Plaid Lake (Trip 31).

Trails Not in this Book

There are many West Kootenay trails we never want to repeat and therefore wouldn't recommend to others. In most cases, the trail and / or access road is too punishing, tedious or sketchy to be feasible for the vast majority of hikers. Here are examples:

A few trails—like those to Fletcher and Wheeler lakes, near the northeast edge of Kokanee Glacier Park—are not maintained because they enter prime grizzly-bear habitat. So the trails themselves pose difficulties, but respect for the bears and concern for your own safety also dictate you not hike there.

Several destinations, such as Copper and Red mountains SW of Nelson, are insufficiently scenic to justify the horrendously long, hideously rough access roads.

Trips that require far more driving than hiking are time wasters, unless the scenery is stellar. That eliminates the 3-km (1.8-mi) trail to Nun Lake (W of Creston), Shannon Lake (1.6-km / 1-mi trail after 15-km / 9.3-mi drive) high above the NW end of Slocan Lake), and the 1.5-km (0.9-mi) trail to Wilson Falls (NW of New Denver).

Nilsik Creek, Lemon Creek Valley

Trail-less destinations, like Ymir Mountain above Whitewater Ski Area, can be attractive. But they usually necessitate bushwhacking, scrambling or routefinding, sometimes all three. These challenges are best left to capable mountaineers who don't need guidebooks.

To gain a better sense of the trips excluded from this book, read a few excerpts from a previous edition that included inferior options but adamantly warned readers away:

Wee Sandy Creek, Valhalla Provincial Park

Objective discernment has yet to illuminate the mysterious aura that shrouds Valhalla Provincial Park. That's because very few hikers have explored it thoroughly. Yet many have heard of Valhalla, and they swoon when it pops up in conversation. They imagine themselves trekking, deliriously awestruck, through an exalted mountainscape. It's an exaggeration—only slightly less mythic than the park's name, which refers to the great hall of dead Norse heroes. Valhalla has dramatic alpine scenery, but less than advertised. And what little it has isn't easy for hikers to appreciate. Of the park's six trails, only one reaches the alpine zone and just two others reach the subalpine zone. All the rest, including Wee Sandy, stay deep in forest. No grand vistas. No peak-studded horizons. No flower-filled meadows.

Sherman Lake, southern Purcells, E of Kootenay Lake

Energy-saving ideas—from gas-powered lawn mowers to escalators—have brought untold ease and enjoyment to humanity. Here's another one: Don't hike to Sherman Lake. Its only remarkable feature is a prodigious mosquito population that will feast on your hot, sweaty, exhausted butt should you ignore this warning and drag it up there.

Bleak Lake, St. Mary's Alpine Provincial Park

"Here there be dragons," was printed on the earliest world maps, indicating the outer limits of human discovery. Today, St. Mary's Alpine Provincial Park is the subject of similar warnings. "Boulders the size of houses." "An epic thrash through cantankerous terrain." "The place brews bad weather like Starbucks brews coffee." But just as the first cartographers were merely retelling ancient mariners' tales, most descriptions of St. Mary's are recycled. No trails pierce the park boundaries, so neither have many hikers. First-person eyewitness reports are scarce. The few who have been there exaggerate the park's beauty in order to rationalize their tribulations. So what's it really like? Forested. Heavily forested. Contrary to its name, two-thirds of this "alpine" park is below treeline. Peaks are few and blunt. The totality is vast and beautiful. But unforgettably awesome? No, at least not if you're well traveled. The drama of St. Mary's is strictly in the doing.

Placer Lakes, southern Selkirks, west of Creston

The mountain god must have started building in the northern Selkirks, because he was obviously pooped when he got down here to the south end of the range. Instead of concentrating on alpine architecture, he was dreaming about an ice-cold ambrosia. And it shows. Boundary Country topography is slapdash—just lumps and bumps.

Dewar Creek Hot Springs, Purcell Wilderness Conservancy

Nearly every Canadian home has several hot water taps. Most have large receptacles, called *bathtubs*, designed for poaching oneself in hot water. And many have hot tubs, specifically for outdoor poaching. So why do the words *hot springs* inspire droves of hikers to journey to this remote

trailhead, then plod the long, mucky, viewless trail through grizzly country, only to reach a couple small, frequently overcrowded pools of tepid water? We've even met hikers at Dewar Creek Hot Springs who'd come all the way (ten hours) from Edmonton in September. They drove through the Canadian Rockies—blowing off all its world-class trails at a time of year when hiking there is so profoundly beautiful it can be a spiritual experience—preferring this tedious slog instead! And theirs was just one of ten vehicles at the trailhead that day. Maybe Dewar Creek Hot Springs has been a bit over publicized and overrated. Do ya think?

Placate the Weather Gods

The volatile West Kootenay climate will have you building shrines to placate the weather gods.

Summer is woefully short. Most trails aren't snow-free until July. High passes can be blanketed in white until later that month. In the mountains, snowfall is possible on any day, and likely at higher elevations after late September. So don't count on more than three months of alpine hiking: mid-July through mid-October. Remember that just one week of clear, sunny weather can greatly increase trail accessibility.

Regardless of the forecast, always be prepared for heavy rain, harsh winds, plummeting temperatures, sleet, hail… the whole miserable gamut. Likewise, allow for the possibility of scorching sun and soaring temperatures. The weather can change dramatically, with alarming speed. A clear sky at dawn is often filled with ominous black clouds by afternoon. Storms can dissipate equally fast, but seem not to do so as often as we'd like.

Charts showing the average monthly precipitation during the West Kootenay hiking season are of little help. June is likely to be wettest. The figures for the driest months—July, August and September—are too close for anyone to

West Kootenay summers can be hot.

reliably predict when your hiking trip is least likely to be rained out. Precipitation increases noticeably after September, though October still tends to be less rainy than June. Keep in mind that many rain-free days are cloudy. So don't waste those precious, clear days. When you wake up to a blue sky, head for a premier trail, aim for a dazzling vista, and go like a gerbil.

Charts showing the average monthly maximum and minimum temperatures in the West Kootenay valleys reveal the following. July and August are hottest, with highs sometimes approaching 30° C (86°F), and lows near 10° C (50°F). June and September highs are just over 20° C (68°F), while lows drop below 10° C (50°F). September is slightly cooler than June, and May is slightly cooler than September. October highs are just over 10° C (50°F), and the lows drop nearly to freezing. Of course, the higher your elevation, the lower the temperature. For example, imagine camping above treeline (near 2287 m /

7500 ft in the West Kootenay) and leaving a half-full waterbottle outside your tent all night. In September, ice will have formed in the bottle by morning. In October, the water could be frozen solid.

Many hikers say fall is their favourite time in the West Kootenay. Bugs are absent, crowds diminish, larch trees are golden. But the shorter days restrict dayhiking, and colder nights make backpacking less comfortable. We prefer the long days and warm nights of mid-summer.

Rainy-Day Trips

Though it's possible to hike most trails in a rainstorm, the peaks you came to see will likely be shrouded. Above treeline, you risk death by thunderbolt. But with the right attitude, on certain trails, a rainy-day hike is a revelation.

Mist cloaking mountains creates a mysterious atmosphere. New waterfalls appear, ever-present ones swell. Forest understory brightens, and the fragrance is headier. When sunlight bursts through tattered clouds, or a rainbow arches suddenly overhead, it's rousing.

So don't sit out the storm: hike it out. The trails below are good choices for a little wet-weather exercise. Some are shoulder-season dayhikes that in summer are insufficiently rewarding. But superior scenery is invisible during a downpour. That's when these low-elevation trips shine:

- Harrison Lake (Trip 41), W of Bonners Ferry
- Slocan Lakeshore (Trip 42), SW end of Slocan Lake
- Carpenter Creek Valley (Trip 43), between Sandon and New Denver
- Retallack Cedars (Trip 45), between New Denver and Kaslo
- Kaslo River (Trip 46), in Kaslo
- Fry Creek Canyon (Trip 48), N end of Kootenay Lake
- Kokanee Cedars (Trip 49), NE of Nelson
- Pilot Peninsula (Trip 50), near Kootenay Bay ferry terminal
- Sproule Creek (Trip 52), W of Nelson
- Syringa Park (Trip 53), W of Castlegar
- Christina Lake (Trip 54), E of Grand Forks
- Cascade Gorge (Trip 55), S of Christina Lake

Hiking With Kids

We hope your hikers-in-training will find these trails manageable and enjoyable. They're the shortest and easiest in the region.

- Idaho Peak (Trip 6), W of Sandon
- Drinnon Lake (Trip 20), SW of Slocan
- Trout Lake (Trip 38), W of Bonners Ferry
- Pyramid and Ball lakes (Trip 39), W of Bonners Ferry
- Harrison Lake (Trip 41), SW of Bonners Ferry
- Silver Avenue (Trip 44), between New Denver and Kaslo
- Retallack Cedars (Trip 45), between New Denver and Kaslo
- Kaslo River (Trip 46), in Kaslo
- Fry Creek Canyon (Trip 48), N end of Kootenay Lake

- Kokanee Cedars (Trip 49), NE of Nelson
- Pilot Peninsula (Trip 50), near Kootenay Bay ferry terminal
- Sproule Creek (Trip 52), W of Nelson
- Syringa Park (Trip 53), W of Castlegar
- Cascade Gorge (Trip 55), S of Christina Lake

Challenging Trails

In the West Kootenay, if you're not bushwhacking, then it's a trail. Anyone whose point of reference is the Canadian Rocky Mountain National Parks will be appalled by some of the scrappy routes called *trails* here.

Deadfall is a common obstacle on West Kootenay trails.

A few, for example in Kokanee Glacier Provincial Park, are superb. But others are steep, narrow, rough, brushy, crisscrossed with deadfall. Many trails (or the overgrown roads that now serve as trails) were hastily constructed by miners intent on wealth, not recreation, so the tread is poorly routed with insufficient switchbacks. New trail construction in the West Kootenay is a seldom-realized fantasy. So expect to be challenged—physically and mentally—while hiking here. And don't complain that most West Kootenay trails fail to meet national-park standards. If they did, you'd be meeting national-park crowds on West Kootenay trails.

Physical Capability

Until you gain experience judging your physical capability and that of your companions, these guidelines might be helpful. Anything longer than an 11-km (7-mi) round-trip dayhike can be very taxing for someone who doesn't hike regularly. A 425-m (1400-ft) elevation gain in that distance is moderately challenging but possible for anyone in average physical condition. Very fit hikers are comfortable hiking 18 km (11 mi) and ascending 1524 m (5000 ft)—or more—in a single day.

Backpacking 18 km (11 mi) in two days is a reasonable goal for most beginners. Hikers who backpack a couple times a season can enjoyably manage 27 km (17 mi) in two days. Avid backpackers should find 38 km (24 mi) in two days no problem. On three- to five-day trips, a typical backpacker prefers not to push beyond 16 km (10 mi) a day. Remember: it's always safer to underestimate your limits.

Leave Your Itinerary

Even if you're hiking in a group, and especially if you're going solo, it's prudent to leave your itinerary in writing with someone reliable. Agree on precisely when they should alert the authorities if you have not returned or called. Be sure to follow through. Forgetting to tell your contact person that you've safely completed your trip would result in an unnecessary, possibly expensive search. You might be billed for it. And a rescue team could risk their lives trying to find you.

Distances and Elevations

There is no definitive source for accurate trail distances and elevations in the West Kootenay. Maps, brochures and trail signs often state conflicting figures. But the discrepancies are usually small. And most hikers don't care whether a trail is 8.7 km (5.4 mi) or 9 km (5.6 mi), or an ascent is 715 m (2345 ft) or 720 m (2362 ft). Still, we made a supreme effort to ensure accuracy.

Maps

The maps in this book are for general orientation only. Our *on foot* directions, however, are elaborate and precise, so you shouldn't find topographical maps necessary. Yet we do recommend them for several reasons: (1) On a long, rough hike, a topo map makes it even easier to follow our directions. (2) A topo map is safety equipment, because it can help ensure you don't get lost. (3) If the terrain through which you're hiking intrigues you, a topo map can contribute to a more fulfilling experience. (4) After reaching a high vantage, a topo map enables you to interpret the scenery.

The Surveys & Mapping Branch of the Department of Energy, Mines and Resources (DEMR) prints 1:50,000 topographic maps covering the West Kootenay. They're sold at outdoor shops and bookstores. We've listed the applicable DEMR topo maps for each trip in this book. They're the most helpful maps for hikers. They can be frustrating, however, because DEMR doesn't update all the information, such as trail locations. Narrower, less popular trails are not always indicated, even though the trails themselves are distinct on the ground. DEMR maps are also expensive, and you might need more than one for a long trip. Hamill Creek / Earl Grey Pass (Trip 18), for example, stretches across three DEMR maps: Lardeau 82 K/2, Duncan Lake 82 K/7, and Toby Creek 82 K/8.

Carry a Compass

Left and *right* are relative. Any hiking guidebook relying solely on these inadequate and potentially misleading terms should be shredded and dropped into a recycling bin. You'll find all the *on foot* descriptions in this book include frequent compass directions. That's the only way to precisely, accurately, reliably guide a hiker.

What about GPS? It might be invaluable if you're trekking cross-country (off trail), long distance. But most hikers generally find a map and compass totally adequate for navigation. Following our detailed directions

while hiking the trails in this book, you won't need a GPS unit.

Keep in mind, the compass directions provided in this book are of use only if you're carrying a compass. Granted, our route descriptions are so detailed, you'll rarely have to check your compass. But bring one anyway, just in case. A compass is required hiking equipment—anytime, anywhere, regardless of your level of experience, or your familiarity with the terrain.

Clip your compass to the shoulder strap of your pack, so you can glance at it quickly and easily. Even if you never have to rely on your compass, occasionally checking it will strengthen your sense of direction— an enjoyable, helpful, and conceivably life-saving asset.

Remember that our stated compass directions are always in reference to true north, which slowly changes. (Visit http://geomag.nrcan.gc.ca/calc/mdcal-eng.php to calculate the current declination). In the West Kootenay, as of the summer of 2012, true north is approximately 15° left of (counterclockwise from) magnetic north. If that puzzles you, read your compass owner's manual.

Trailhead Access

Two-wheel-drive cars can reach many West Kootenay trailheads. But a high-clearance vehicle is sometimes essential. And four-wheel-drive is preferable. That's because trailhead access here is typically via unpaved logging road. Some are abandoned: steep, narrow, rough, brushy. Others are active, which means a monster vehicle carrying a huge load could come rumbling around the next corner. En garde.

Check the *trailhead access* rating in the stats box for each trip. If you're inexperienced at backcountry driving, consider these suggestions before you hit the dirt. A little preparation can increase your confidence and safety.

You'll encounter logging trucks on highways and backroads.

• Before leaving home, look at your vehicle's undercarriage. Get on your knees and really see what's down there. Make note of where you have the least clearance and where you have the most, so you'll know how to straddle rocks.

• Check your vehicle's fuel supply and engine fluid levels before departing the last town.

• Always drive with your headlights on—even during the day.

• Drive cautiously. You never know what's up ahead. It's possible the road has been damaged recently by severe weather or other natural hazards. Fallen trees are common.

• Never block the road. If you stop, pull far enough off to allow a logging truck to pass.

Yield to all industrial vehicles. As soon as you see one, pull as far over as possible and let it proceed.

• Faced with deeply worn tracks on the sides of the road, and a high ridge in the middle that might scrape your undercarriage, drive with one tire on the ridge and the other outside the track.

• Some trailhead access roads have been purposely gouged. These trenches, called *waterbars*, actually help maintain the road by preventing erosion. But they can also prevent wimpy vehicles from reaching trailheads. If you encounter a deep one, don't approach it straight on. You might bottom-out. Instead, slice across at an angle. That way your tires drop into the waterbar one at a time, instead of both at once.

• After heavy rain, expect mud to compound your trailhead access difficulties. If you encounter enough mud that you begin nervously hoping the road will improve, turn back. It will probably get worse. If you're determined to proceed, don't slow to a crawl. You need momentum. If you're not stuck yet, but it appears you will be, reverse out immediately. Trying to turn around can land you in a bigger mess.

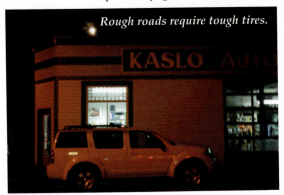

Rough roads require tough tires.

Kootenay Lake ferry

Ferries

Touring the West Kootenay, you'll appreciate the shortcuts that ferries provide across the formidable lakes. But in summer, the prelude to a carefree crossing is usually a frustrating delay in a long line of vehicles waiting to board. You might have to hang out—are you sitting down?—for up to two hours.

On Kootenay Lake, a ferry shuttles between Balfour on the west shore and Kootenay Bay on the east. Departures are every 50 minutes in summer. The Balfour schedule is 6:30 a.m. to 9:40 p.m. The Kootenay Bay schedule is 7:10 a.m. to 10:20 p.m. The 9-km (5.6-mi) crossing takes 35 minutes.

On Upper Arrow Lake, a ferry links Galena Bay on the east shore with Shelter Bay on the west. Departures are every hour. The Galena Bay schedule is 6:30 a.m. to 11:30 p.m., plus 12:30 a.m. The Shelter Bay schedule is 6 a.m. to 11 p.m. The 5-km (3-mi) crossing takes 20 minutes.

South of the Border

Mountains ignore borders. So should you. Though the Selkirk Range is peakiest in British Columbia, it extends into Idaho and Washington. The Kootenay River also flows into the United States. Since the term *West Kootenay* lacks official, designated boundaries, we let the land itself determine the content of this book. That's why it includes five hikes south of the border: Trips 37 through 41.

West Kootenay residents who've yet to hike in the northern reaches of Idaho and Washington will be astonished at the high quality of the backcountry roads and hiking trails. Perhaps they'll realize how undervalued outdoor recreation is in southeast B.C. and how much more our government can and should be doing to support it.

The U.S. Forest Service does an exemplary job. Most backcountry roads are broad, smooth, brush free, and clearly signed. So are most hiking trails, which is even more remarkable. The trails were well engineered to begin with, so they're comfortably graded—ideal for kids. And they remain a joy to hike, thanks to continued maintenance by volunteers and paid contractors. Just be prepared to drive a long way off pavement (25.5 km / 16 mi) to reach the trailheads. The compensation is that two or three trips begin conveniently close to one another—a good reason to come for a couple days instead of just one.

Harrison Lake, Idaho Selkirks (Trip 38)

More than 565 km (350 mi) of developed trails squirm through Bonners Ferry Forest Service district in the Idaho Panhandle. The four trips in this book are just a sampling. You won't need to hike more than that to grok the general theme. The scenery is mildly pleasant, but falls far short of spectacular. It pales in comparison to the B.C. Selkirks, for example in Valhalla, Kokanee Glacier, or Goat Range provincial parks. In appearance, the Idaho and Washington Selkirks resemble the southern Purcells, particularly the area around Haystack Mtn (Trip 33).

Another drawback to these south-of-the-border trails is that they're crowded. Solitude is difficult to find. To avoid the throngs, you have several choices: (1) Go midweek. (2) Schedule your visit in fall, after kids return to school and the flood of vacationers subsides. (3) Probe deeper into the wilds than most people dare, perhaps onto the ridges above and beyond trail's end.

Wilderness Ethics

We hope you're already conscientious about respecting nature and other people. If not, here's how to pay off some of your karmic debt load.

Let wildflowers live. They blossom for only a few fleeting weeks. Uprooting them doesn't enhance your enjoyment, and it prevents others from seeing them at all. We once heard parents urge a string of children to pick as many different-coloured flowers as they could find. Great. Teach kids to entertain themselves by destroying nature, so the world continues marching toward environmental collapse.

Give the critters a break. The wilderness isn't a zoo. The animals are wild. Recognize that this is their home, and you are an uninvited guest. Behave accordingly. Allow all of them plenty of space. Most are remarkably tolerant of people, but approaching them to take a photograph is harassment and can be dangerous. Some elk, for example, appear docile but can severely injure you. Approaching any bear is suicidal. Read our *Bears* section.

Stay on the trail. Shortcutting causes erosion. It doesn't save time on steep ascents, because you'll soon be slowing to catch your breath. On a steep descent, it increases the likelihood of injury. When hiking cross-country in a group, soften your impact by spreading out.

Roam meadows with your eyes, not your boots. Again, stay on the trail. If it's braided, follow the main path. When you're compelled to take a photo among wildflowers, try to walk on rocks.

Leave no trace. Be aware of your impact. Travel lightly on the land. At campgrounds, limit your activity to areas already denuded. After a rest stop, and especially after camping, take a few minutes to look for and obscure any evidence of your stay. Restore the area to its natural state. Remember: tents can leave scars. Pitch yours on an existing tentsite whenever possible. If none is available, choose a patch of dirt, gravel, pine needles, or maybe a dried-up tarn. Never pitch your tent on grass, no matter how appealing it looks. If you do, and others follow, the grass will soon be gone.

Avoid building fires. They're prohibited in Kokanee Glacier Provincial Park. Even where they're allowed, fires are a luxury, not a necessity. Don't plan to cook over a fire; it's inefficient and wasteful. If you pack food that requires cooking, bring a stove. If you must indulge in a campfire, keep it small. Use an existing fire ring made of rocks. If no rings are present—which is rare—build yours on mineral soil or gravel, not in the organic layer. Never scorch meadows. Below a stream's high-water line is best. Garbage with metal or plastic content will not burn; pack it all out. Limit your wood gathering to deadfall about the size of your forearm. Wood that requires effort (breaking, chopping, dragging) is part of the scenery; let it be. After thoroughly dousing your fire, dismantle the fire ring and scatter the ashes. Keep in mind that untended and unextinguished campfires are the prime cause of forest fires.

Be quiet at backcountry campgrounds. Most of us are out there to enjoy tranquility. If you want to party, go to a pub.

Pack out everything you bring. Never leave a scrap of trash anywhere. This includes toilet paper, nutshells, even cigarette butts. People who drop butts in the wilderness are buttheads. They're buttheads in the city too, but it's worse in the wilds. Fruit peels are also trash. They take years to decompose, and wild animals won't eat them. If you bring fruit on your hike, you're responsible for the peels. And don't just pack out your trash. Leave nothing behind, whether you brought it or not. Clean up after others. Don't be hesitant or oblivious. Be proud. Keep a small plastic bag handy, so picking up trash will be a habit instead of a pain. It's infuriating and disgusting to see what people toss on the trail. Often the tossing is mindless, but sometimes it's intentional. Anyone who leaves a pile of toilet paper and unburied feces should have their nose rubbed in it.

Poop without impact. Use the outhouses at trailheads and campgrounds whenever possible. Don't count on them being stocked with toilet paper; always pack your own in a plastic bag. If you know there's a campground ahead, try to wait until you get there.

In the wilds, choose a site at least 60 m (66 yd) from trails and water sources. Ground that receives sunlight part of the day is best. Use a trowel to dig a small cat hole—10 to 20 cm (4 to 8 inches) deep, 10 to 15 cm (4 to 6 inches) wide—in soft, dark, biologically active soil. Afterward, throw a handful of dirt into the hole, stir with a stick to speed decomposition, replace your diggings, then camouflage the site. Pack out used toilet paper in a plastic bag. You can drop the paper (not the plastic) in the next outhouse you pass. Always clean your hands with a moisturizing hand sanitizer, like *Purell*. Carry enough for the entire trip. Sold in drugstores, it comes in conveniently small, lightweight, plastic bottles.

Urinate off-trail, well away from water sources and tentsites. The salt in urine attracts animals. They'll defoliate urine-soaked vegetation, so aim for dirt or pine needles.

Keep streams and lakes pristine. When brushing your teeth or washing dishes, do it well away from water sources and tentsites. Use only biodegradable soap. Carry water far enough so the wastewater will percolate through soil and break down without directly polluting the wilderness water. Scatter wastewater widely. Even biodegradable soap is a pollutant; keep it out of streams and lakes. On short backpack trips, you shouldn't need to wash clothes or yourself. If necessary, rinse your clothes or splash yourself off—without soap.

Respect the reverie of other hikers. On busy trails, don't feel it's necessary to communicate with everyone you pass. Most of us are seeking solitude, not a soiree. A simple greeting is sufficient to convey good will. Obviously, only you can judge what's appropriate at the time. But it's usually presumptuous and annoying to blurt out advice without being asked. "Boy, have you got a long way to go." "The views are much better up there." "Be careful, it gets rougher." If anyone wants to know, they'll ask. Some people are sly. They start by asking where you're going, so they can tell you all about it. Offer unsolicited information only to warn other hikers about conditions ahead that could seriously affect their trip.

Hiking With Your Dog

"Can I bring Max, my Pomeranian?"

Yes. With the stipulation that they be leashed the entire time, dogs are allowed on all the trails in this book except those in Kokanee Glacier and Valhalla provincial parks.

Bringing your dog, however, isn't simply a matter of "Can I?" Ask yourself, "Should I?"

Consider safety. Dogs infuriate bears and are thus a danger to themselves, their owners and other hikers. If a dog runs off, it might reel a bear back with it.

Consider the environment. Many dog owners blithely allow their pets to pollute streams and lakes. Every time Maxie craps on the trail, will you dispose of it properly?

Consider the rest of us. Most dog owners think their pets are angelic, but other hikers rarely agree. A curious dog, even if friendly, can be a nuisance. A barking dog is irksome. A person continually yelling unheeded

commands at a disobedient dog is infuriating, because it amounts to *two* annoying animals, not just one. An untrained dog, despite the owner's hearty reassurance that "he won't hurt you," can be frightening.

This isn't a request to leave your dog at home. We've backpacked with friends whose dogs we enjoyed immensely. This is a plea to see your dog objectively.

Moose

Wildlife

It's possible to see all kinds of animals—big and small—throughout the West Kootenay. Deer, chipmunks, squirrels, raccoons, skunks, bats and owls, you might expect. But also be on the lookout for osprey, eagles, elk, mountain goats, moose, coyotes, black bears and grizzlies. In the evening, watch for porcupines waddling out of the forest and beavers cruising ponds. On alpine trails, you're likely to see pikas and marmots. It's a rare and fortunate hiker who glimpses a wolf, wolverine, or cougar.

About those porkies. West Kootenay trailheads are infamous for car-eating porcupines. Seriously. They munch tires, hoses and fan belts. Their voracious appetite for rubber could leave you stranded. Don't want to hitchhike down the mountain to call a tow truck? Bring chicken wire to wrap around your vehicle. Secure it with rocks and pieces of wood. Mothballs, liberally scattered beneath and around a vehicle, can also deter the critters. Just remember to pick up every single mothball before you drive away. You're not backpacking? Don't worry. Porcupines are nocturnal, so dayhikers don't have to erect a fortress.

Porcupine-proof

BEARS

Bears are rarely a problem in the West Kootenay. But oblivious hikers can endanger themselves, other people, and the bears. If you're prepared for a bear encounter and know how to prevent one, you can hike confidently, secure in the understanding that bears pose little threat.

Grizzly bears and black bears can be difficult to tell apart—even for an experienced observer. Both species range in colour from nearly white to cinnamon to black. Full-grown grizzlies are much bigger, but a young grizzly can resemble an adult black bear, so size is not a good indicator.

The most obvious differences are that grizzlies have a dished face; big, muscular shoulder humps; and long, curved front claws. Blacks have a straight face; no hump; and shorter, less visible front claws. Grizzlies are potentially more dangerous than black bears, although a black bear sow with cubs can be just as aggressive. Be wary of all bears.

Any bear might attack when surprised. If you're hiking, and forest or brush limits your visibility, you can prevent surprising a bear by making noise. Bears hear about as well as humans. Most are as anxious to avoid an encounter as you are. If you warn them of your presence before they see you, they'll usually clear out. So use the most effective noisemaker: your voice. Shout loudly. Keep it up. Don't be embarrassed. Be safe. Yell louder near streams, so your voice carries over the competing noise. Sound off more frequently when hiking into the wind. That's when bears are least able to hear or smell you coming. To learn more, download the *Bears Beware!* MP3 at hikingcamping.com.

Grizzly bear

Bears' strongest sense is smell. They can detect an animal carcass several kilometers (miles) away. So keep your pack, tent and campsite odor-free. Double or triple-wrap all your food in plastic bags. Avoid smelly foods, especially meat and fish. On short backpack trips, consider eating only fresh foods that require no cooking or cleanup. If you cook, do it as far as possible from where you'll be sleeping. Never cook in or near your tent; the fabric might retain odor. Use as few pots and dishes as you can get by with. Be fastidious when you wash them.

Black Bear

At night, hang all your food, trash, and anything else that smells (cooking gear, sunscreen, bug repellent, toothpaste) out of bears' reach. Use the metal food caches provided at some provincial-park backcountry campgrounds. Elsewhere, a tree branch will suffice. Bring a sturdy stuffsack to serve as your bear bag. Hoist it at least 5 m (16 ft) off the ground and 1.5 m (5 ft) from the tree trunk or other branches. You'll need about 12 meters (40 feet) of light nylon cord. Clip the sack to the cord with an ultralight carabiner.

Backpackers who don't properly hang their food at night are inviting bears into their campsite, greatly increasing the chance of a dangerous encounter. And bears are smart. They quickly learn to associate a particular place, or people in general, with an easy meal. They become habituated

Bear tear

and lose their fear of man. A habituated bear is a menace to any hiker within its range.

If you see a bear, don't look it in the eyes; it might think you're challenging it. Never run. Initially be still. If you must move, do it in slow motion. Bears are more likely to attack if you flee, and they're fast, much faster than humans. A grizzly can outsprint a racehorse. And it's a myth that bears can't run downhill. They're also strong swimmers. Despite their ungainly appearance, they're excellent climbers too.

Climbing a tree, however, can be an option for escaping an aggressive bear. Some people have saved their lives this way. Others have been caught in the process. To be out of reach of an adult bear, you must climb at least 10 m (33 ft) very quickly, something few people are capable of. It's generally best to avoid provoking an attack by staying calm, initially standing your ground, making soothing sounds to convey a nonthreatening presence, then retreating slowly.

What should you do when a bear charges? If you're certain it's a lone black bear—not a sow with cubs, not a grizzly—fighting back might be effective. If it's a grizzly, and contact seems imminent, lie face down, with your legs apart and your hands clasped behind your neck. This is safer than the fetal position, which used to be recommended, because it makes it harder for the bear to flip you over. If you play dead, a grizzly is likely to break off the attack once it feels you're no longer a threat. Don't move until you're sure the bear has left the area, then slowly, quietly, get up and walk away. Keep moving, but don't run.

Arm yourself with pepper spray as a last line of defense. It's available at outdoor stores. Keep it in a holster—on your hip belt or shoulder strap—where you can grab it fast. Cayenne pepper, highly irritating to a bear's sensitive nose, is the active ingredient. Without causing permanent injury, it disables the bear long enough to let you escape. Many people have successfully used it to turn back charging bears.

Research presented to more than 300 bear experts at the 4th International Human-Bear Conflict Workshop, in Missoula, Montana, suggests pepper spray is more effective than firearms at stopping a bear attack. The combined results from two studies are convincing: 98% of people who used pepper spray to stop charging bears walked away from their encounters unharmed, and none of the people or bears died. 56% of people who used firearms to stop charging bears were injured, and 61% of the bears died.

Vigilance and noise making, however, should ensure you never encounter a bear at close range, thus preventing you from having to so much as unholster your pepper spray. Do so only if you really think your life is at risk, at which point the bear is at risk as well. A bear confronted by a human being is at one of the most precarious, dangerous moments of its life.

Any time bears act aggressively, they're following their natural instinct for self preservation. Often they're protecting their cubs or a food source. Yet if they maul a hiker, they're likely to be killed, or captured and moved, by wildlife management officers. So when you go hiking in the West Kootenay, you're accepting responsibility for the protection of these beautiful, magnificent creatures.

Merrily disregarding bears is foolish and unsafe. Worrying about them is miserable and unnecessary. Everyone occasionally feels afraid when venturing deep into the mountains, but knowledge and awareness can quell fear of bears. Just take the necessary precautions and remain guardedly alert. Experiencing the grandeur of mountain wilderness is certainly worth risking the remote possibility of a bear encounter.

KNOW BEFORE YOU GO

Bearanoia is pandemic, hence the detailed, at-your-fingertips, bear-safety suggestions above. The other threats to your well being in the backcountry aren't necessarily less serious, but you're probably less concerned about them. So we've addressed them on our website rather than here in the book. For helpful information about cougars, ticks, lightning, and hypothermia, visit hikingcamping.com. In the home-page menu, click on "Free." Under "Free Articles," click on "Know Before You Go."

"Okay, let's go."

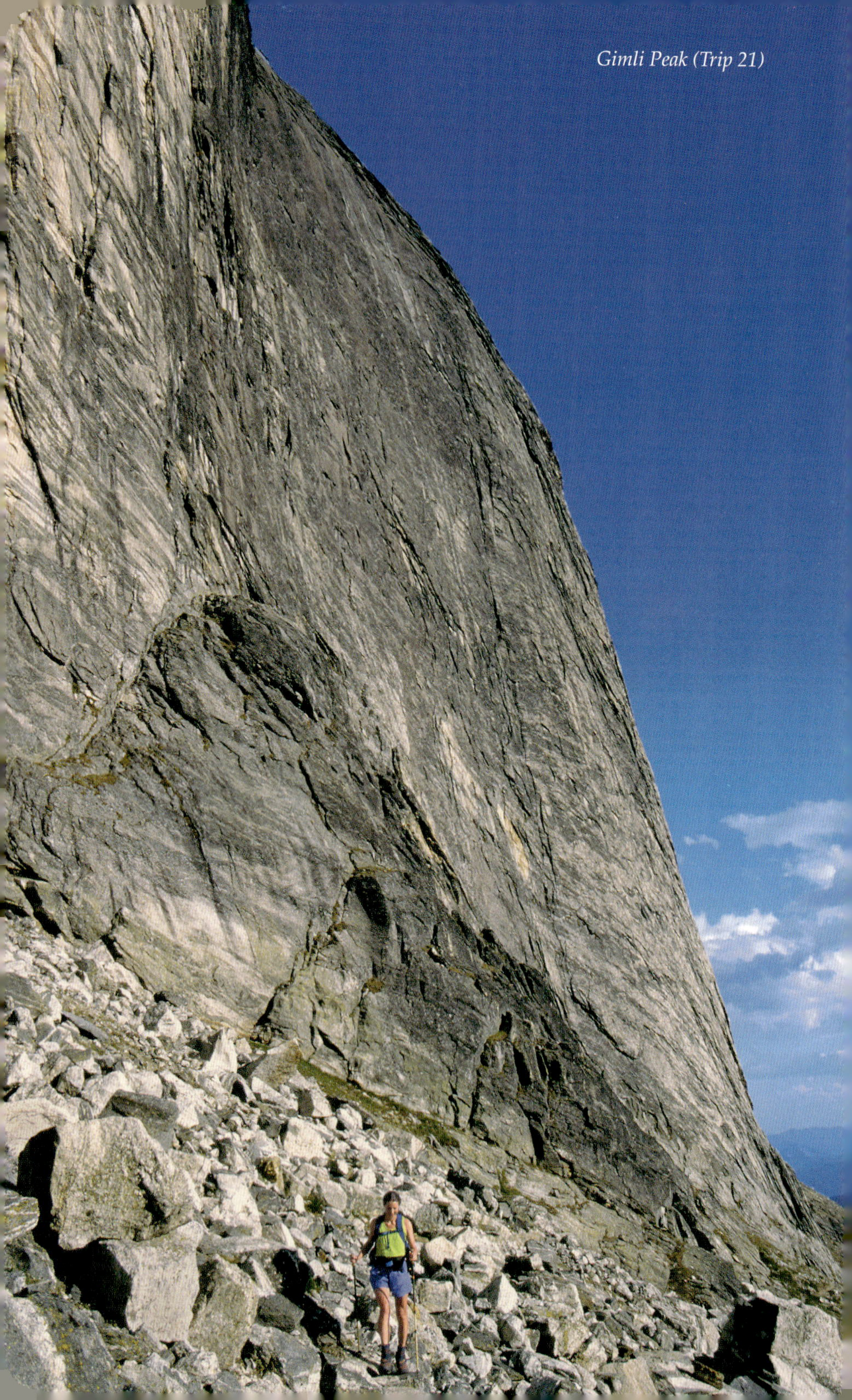
Gimli Peak (Trip 21)

Dayhikes and Backpack Trips

TRIP 1
Mt. Fosthall

LOCATION	Monashee Provincial Park, W of Upper Arrow Lake SW of Shelter Bay
ROUND TRIP	18.4 km (11.4 mi)
ELEVATION GAIN	1177 m (3861 ft)
KEY ELEVATIONS	Sol Mtn Lodge trailhead 1920 m (6298 ft) trail's end near South Cariboo Pass 2100 m (6888 ft) Mt. Fosthall 2697 m (8846 ft)
HIKING TIME	6 to 8 hours
DIFFICULTY	challenging due to cross-country travel and routefinding
TRAILHEAD ACCESS	challenging due to 4-hour round-trip drive on maintained logging roads
MAPS	*Sol Mountain Touring* (laminated topo sold at the lodge); Mt. Fosthall 82 / L08

Opinion

Its takes a massive peak to comfortably shoulder the name of a Norse god. An entire range of such peaks[1] is a fantastic sight. And that's just one, short, head swivel of the panorama you'll witness from atop 2697-m (8846-ft) Mt. Fosthall[2]—highest point in Monashee Provincial Park.

The expected route to Fosthall is long and tedious.[3] What we recommend instead is an astonishing shortcut. It begins in the subalpine zone, where most of your route to the summit is visible, and your first step is into a meadow.

This superlative dayhike poses just one obstacle: a round-trip, off-pavement drive of up to 141 km (87.4 mi). Bear in mind, these roads are less rough and steep than most in the West Kootenay. And they lead not to a desolate trailhead, but to Sol Mountain Lodge (solmountain.com).

By backcountry standards, Sol is luxurious. It has a chef's kitchen, spacious dining room, comfy lounge, private bedrooms, hot showers, even a bar and sauna. Staying at Sol isn't a requirement to hike here, but oh what you'll miss if you don't. Three of the hikes in this book—Sol Mountain / Pride Rock (Trip 2), Mission Ridge (Trip 3), as well as Mt. Fosthall—begin in the lodge's front yard: the aforementioned meadow.

Rigid-minded critics will verbally cane us for extending our West Kootenay book into the Monashees. But we've done so for solid reasons. The trailhead / lodge is just outside Monashee Park. It's within the Arrow Lake watershed (unofficial, west boundary of the West Kootenay). The lake itself is visible from Mt. Fosthall. So is Nakusp—a civic pillar of West Kootenay life.

photos: *1, 4 & 5 Approaching Mt. Fosthall summit ridge 3 En route to Mt. Fosthall*

Ever-diminishing trailhead access is the bane of West Kootenay hikers. A lodge at road's end is substantial assurance of continued access. For that reason alone, Trips 1, 2, and 3 warrant celebration, not punctilious censure. Besides, these are sensational hikes.

Mt. Fosthall affords a sweeping look at the West Kootenay. From here, even longtime Kooteneers might be startled to see how sharply and densely mountainous their homeland actually is. The Fosthall vantage also reveals Monashee Park's enticing alplands comprising Fawn Lake and Valley of the Moon. It enables you to study the Pinnacles, in the southern Monashees. And it grants a helpful overview of Trips 2 and 3.

Yet the summit panorama is but one of Fosthall's many rewards. The terrain en route affords constant views and is itself gorgeous: rolling, rocky, meadowy, peppered with tarns, etched by streamlets. The total elevation gain is significant, but the ascent is mercifully gradual throughout. After following a bootbeaten, flagged route nearly to South Cariboo Pass, you'll resume cross-country. A short, steep push will earn you the mountain's south ridge: a broad, gentle, highway of boulders leading to the top.

From Sol Mountain Lodge, you'll see Mt. Fosthall's enticing profile out the window. From the summit cairn, you can spot the lodge below—at the edge of the meadow where you began hiking. So if you're new to cross-country travel, this is a less intimidating place than most to advance your skills.

---

1   The *Norse Peaks*, as we call them, are outside Monashee Park. They're as difficult to access as their fierce appearance suggests. They include 2971-m (9745-ft) Mt. Odin. A frightfully powerful god in Norse mythology, Odin's influence spans war, battle, victory and death, as well as wisdom, magic, poetry, prophecy, and the hunt. He has many sons. The most famous is Thor, who's associated with thunder, lightning, storms, strength, oak trees, the protection of mankind, healing, and fertility. The Norse Peaks also comprise 3146-m (10,322-ft) Thor Mtn. While Mt. Odin is notably shorter than Thor Mtn, Odin's 2409-m (7900-ft) prominence (elevation between summit and lowest contour line encircling it and no higher summit) is greater. Odin's prominence exceeds that of any peak along the spine of the Canadian Rockies and distinguishes it as the ninth most prominent peak in British Columbia.

2   *Fosthall* is not a Norse god. According to *British Columbia Place Names* (Helen Akrigg, 3rd edition), Mt. Fosthall was named after a clerk in a Hudson's Bay post.

3   Monashee Provincial Park is remote, heavily forested, largely trail-less, thus lightly visited. Of the few hikers who explore it, most drive north from Cherryville, past Sugar Lake, to the Spectrum Creek trailhead. From there, they hike the park's only maintained trail. It's a steep, ten-hour trudge through trees: east past Spectrum Lake to the backcountry campground on the south shore of Big Peters Lake, at 1737 m (5697 ft). By then, most hikers have invested two days in the endeavour and will likely spend another two days hiking out. So 2697-m (8846-ft) Mt. Fosthall—even though it's a one-day round-trip from Big Peters Lake—hosts but a fraction of Monashee Park hikers. From the summit of Fosthall, you'll overlook nearly all of the Spectrum-to-Peters terrain and be very glad you opted for the laughably easier, vastly more scenic dayhike starting at Sol Mountain Lodge.

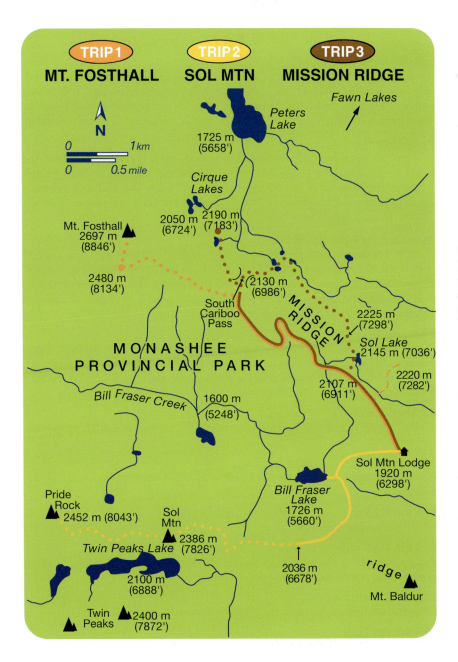

TRIP 1

MT. FOSTHALL

TRIP 2

SOL MTN

TRIP 3

MISSION RIDGE

N

0   1 km

0   0.5 mile

Fawn Lakes

Peters Lake

1725 m (5658')

Cirque Lakes

Mt. Fosthall 2697 m (8846')

2050 m (6724')

2190 m (7183')

2480 m (8134')

2130 m (6986')

South Cariboo Pass

M I S S I O N   R I D G E

2225 m (7298')

Sol Lake 2145 m (7036')

M O N A S H E E
P R O V I N C I A L   P A R K

2220 m (7282')

2107 m (6911')

Bill Fraser Creek

1600 m (5248')

Sol Mtn Lodge 1920 m (6298')

Pride Rock 2452 m (8043')

Sol Mtn 2386 m (7826')

Bill Fraser Lake 1726 m (5660')

r i d g e

Twin Peaks Lake

2100 m (6888')

2036 m (6678')

Mt. Baldur

Twin Peaks

2400 m (7872')

Fact

before your trip

It's possible to access Sol Mountain Lodge in a 2WD car. 4WD is not necessary. Ideally, however, you should have a high clearance vehicle with strong torque, good tires, and a reliable spare. The roads are not excessively rough or steep, but you'll be driving a long way—several hours round trip—off pavement.

by vehicle

You can approach Sol Mountain Lodge from the S via Nakusp, or from the N via Revelstoke. The lodge has posted directional signage on both routes. Approaching from the N has an advantage. It will spare you and your vehicle a significant amount of off-pavement driving: 19 km (11.8 mi) one way, 38 km (23.6 mi) round trip.

Approaching from the South

From **Nakusp**, drive S on Hwy 6. At 23 km (14.3 mi) turn right, onto Arrow Park Road. Continue downhill 0.4 km (0.2 mi) to the Arrow Park ferry landing. The elevation of Upper Arrow Lake is 445 m (1460 ft). The cable ferry operates daily, on demand, 5:10 a.m. to 12:15 p.m., and 2 p.m. to 9:10 pm. The lake is narrow here, so the crossing takes only a few minutes.

0 km (0 mi)

Reset your trip odometer on the ferry. After disembarking on the NW shore, proceed straight, uphill. Pavement ends here. The rest of the drive is on unpaved, logging roads. At the T-junction in 130 meters, turn right (E) following the sign for Cameron, Catherine, and Bear lakes.

0.2 km (0.1 mi)

Go right, onto signed Saddle Mountain Road. It's the higher, wider, main road. Proceed E.

9.8 km (6.1 mi)

Continue straight on the main road. Left is Saddle Lookout Road, which leads to Trip 4.

18.5 km (11.5 mi)

Nakusp is visible across the lake.

22.1 km (13.7 mi)

Proceed straight on the main road. Saddle Mtn Road ascends left. You're heading generally N, paralleling the W shore of Upper Arrow Lake.

28 km (17.4 mi)

Continue straight on the main road. Ignore the ascending left fork.

29.5 km (18.3 mi)

Proceed straight. Ignore left and right forks.

32.7 km (20.3 mi)

Proceed straight. Ignore left and right forks.

34.8 km (21.5 mi)

Turn left at this major junction. Then continue straight, ignoring the left fork to Cameron Lake.

Peters Lake and Monashee Park peaks, from Mt. Fosthall

34.9 km (21.6 mi)
You're now on Fosthall Road, signed for Revelstoke.

36.8 km (22.8 mi)
Proceed straight. Ignore the right fork.

39.3 km (24.4 mi)
Fork right (level), onto North Fosthall Road. Ignore the ascending left fork.

39.9 km (24.7 mi)
Continue straight. Ignore the left fork.

41.1 km (25.5 mi)
Proceed straight. Ignore the rough, ascending, left fork.

42 km (26 mi)
Cross a bridge spanning a creek.

42.8 km (26.5 mi)
Go right.

43.3 and 43.5 km (26.8 and 27 mi)
Proceed straight. Ignore the left forks.

44.5 km (27.6 mi)
Continue straight. Ignore the steep, ascending, left fork.

44.7 km (27.7 mi)
Proceed straight (level) on North Fosthall Road. Ignore the ascending left fork.

46 km (28.5 mi)
Cross a bridge spanning a creek.

Nearing summit ridge of Mt. Fosthall

49 km (30.4 mi)
Continue straight. Ignore the signed, right fork ascending to Catherine Lake.

50.2 km (31.1 mi)
Turn left at this major junction. Reset your trip odometer to 0. Proceed W on North Fosthall Road. Directions resume on page 39. The remaining 20 km (12.4 mi) to the lodge are rougher, narrower, and eventually steeper. Shelter Bay Road leads straight (N) toward Revelstoke, reaching Shelter Bay in 31 km (19.2 mi).

Approaching from the North

From Hwy 1, on the W edge of **Revelstoke**, drive S on Hwy 23. It's 49 km (30.4 mi) to the Shelter Bay ferry landing on Upper Arrow Lake. The elevation of the lake is 445 m (1460 ft). At 47.5 km (29.5 mi), just before the final descent to the landing, turn right onto Shelter Bay Road. Pavement ends here. The rest of the drive is on unpaved, logging roads.

0 km (0 mi)
Reset your trip odometer and proceed onto Shelter Bay Road. Follow it generally S, paralleling the W shore of Upper Arrow Lake.

2.4 km (1.5 mi)
Continue on the main (middle) road, following signs for Eagle Bay and Sol Mountain.

10.7 km (6.6 mi)
Proceed straight on the main road. The left fork descends to Eagle Bay campground.

12.4 km (7.7 mi)
Bear left on the main road.

13.1 km (8.1 mi)
Continue straight on the main road. Ignore the right fork to Pingston Hydro Facility.

16.4 km (10.2 mi)
Bear right on the main road. Ignore the left fork.

16.7 km (10.4 mi)
Proceed straight on the main road. Right is Limekiln Road, ascending to Paint Lake.

18.3 km (11.3 mi)
Continue straight on the main road. Ignore the left fork.

22.2 km (13.8 mi)
Bear left on the main road. Ignore the right fork.

25 km (15.5 mi)
Bear right and descend on the main road. Ignore the left fork.

27 km (16.7 mi)
Cross the bridge over Pingston Canyon. It's worth stopping here to peer into the abyss.

28.7 km (17.8 mi)
Proceed straight on the main road. Ignore the descending, sharp left fork.

30.6 km (19 mi)
Continue straight on the main road. Ignore the right fork.

31 km (19.2 mi)
Intersect **North Fosthall Road** at a major junction. It leads straight (S) toward the Arrow Park ferry (50.2 km / 31.1 mi distant), and right (W) toward Sol Mountain Lodge. Turn right. Reset your trip odometer to 0. Proceed W on North Fosthall Road. The remaining 20 km (12.4 mi) to the lodge are rougher, narrower, and eventually steeper.

From Either Approach

0 km (0 mi)
Proceeding W on North Fosthall Road from the major junction 50.2 km (31.1 mi) from Arrow Park ferry to the S, or 31 km (19.2 mi) from Shelter Bay to the N.

0.9 km (0.6 mi)
Cross a bridge spanning a creek.

1.5 km (0.9 mi)
Go left. Ignore the ascending right fork.

2.2 km (1.35 mi)
Fork right and ascend.

2.3 km (1.4 mi)
Pass a small, signed, parking area (right). It's for lodge guests who choose not to continue in their own vehicle.

2.8 km (1.7 mi)
A clearcut extends upslope from the road.

4.1 km (2.5 mi)
Cross a bridge spanning a creek.

4.8 km (3 mi)
Pass a lodge sign stating that cell-phone coverage is available for the next 2 km (1.2 mi).

5.5 km (3.4 mi)
Pass the signed Fosthall Creek trail (right).

6.5 km (4 mi)
Cross a bridge spanning a creek, and pass a small pullout.

7.9 km (4.9 mi)
Pass impressive, giant cedars.

12.2 km (7.6 mi)
Cross a bridge spanning a creek.

12.5 km (7.8 mi)
Bear right. Ignore the left fork.

13.6 km (8.4 mi)
The ascent steepens, and the road is rockier. Above, switchbacks temper the grade.

14.2 km (8.8 mi)
Continue through a clearcut.

16.4 km (10.2 mi)
Fork left and ascend on Bear Lake Road.

18.6 km (11.5 mi)
Proceed straight. Ignore the ascending left fork.

18.8 km (11.7 mi)
Arrive at the lodge-guest parking area. Fork right to reach the lodge.

20.2 km (12.4 mi)
Arrive at Sol Mountain Lodge. The elevation here is 1920 m (6298 ft).

on foot

From the front (N side) of Sol Mountain Lodge, follow the flagged trail N, into the **meadow**. The trail bends left (WNW).

At 10 minutes, ignore the right (NNE) fork leading to Mission Ridge, E of Sol Lake. Continue straight (NNW) on the main trail.

In about 30 minutes, reach a **cairned fork** at 2107 m (6911 ft). Right leads N, quickly passing Sol Lake at 2145 m (7036 ft) before crossing a low point on Mission Ridge (Trip 3). Go left (WNW) for Mt. Fosthall.

The trail dips into a drainage about 50 minutes from the lodge. It then rises left (NW). The trail continues crossing meadowy depressions, heading generally NW, **paralleling Mission Ridge** (right / NE). About 1 hour from the lodge, Mt. Fosthall looms ahead (NW).

Rockhop a creek near a **tarn** at 2120 m (6954 ft), about 70 minutes from the lodge. Surprisingly, the flagged trail curves left (SSW), around the W shore of the tarn. For the moment, do not proceed right (W). From the S end of the tarn, ascend left (SE).

Descending now, the trail leads you on a counter-intuitive but ultimately expedient detour. After a few minutes working your way down gentle, **rock**

outcrops to 2050 m (6724 ft), resume in the logical direction: right (WNW). You've now hiked about 80 minutes from the lodge.

After undulating through subalpine meadows, ascend right (NNW) between creeklets. The **flagged trail ends** at 5.3 km (3.3 mi), 2100 m (6888 ft), about 1¾ hours from the lodge. Pause here. Beyond, you'll be traveling cross-country, without the aid of flagging or a trail.

A few minutes above (N) is 2130-m (6986-ft) **South Cariboo Pass**. You'd proceed that way if hiking around Mission Ridge (Trip 3). But don't detour to the pass now; see if time and energy permit that option on the way back. For Mt. Fosthall, ascend left (NW).

Soon clamber through a **boulder slide**. Then follow a faint, short, contouring route bootbeaten into talus. Ahead are several **drainages** you must drop into an ascend out of. In general, hike toward Mt. Fosthall (NW). Strive for upward progress, but flow with the terrain, negotiating obstacles as necessary.

The easiest, quickest way forward is (a) below the steep scree, yet (b) above most of the trees. Keep traversing the **heathery alplands** on the S slope of Fosthall's E ridge

You might encounter a few **cairns**. We did, and they were helpful, because they corroborated our routefinding instincts. But don't follow any cairns contradicting the guidelines in the previous paragraph. And please don't build more cairns.

Looking back (SE), you can see deep into the West Kootenay. Prominent landmarks include Upper Arrow Lake, the east-shore town of Nakusp, and the canyon that Hwy 6 threads to New Denver.

Looking ahead (NW), the face of Fosthall's S ridge appears vertical. Don't be intimidated. There's a breach in its defenses, and you'll see it as you get closer: a steep but hikeable slope about midway along the face of the ridge. So as you near the mountain, aim for the **ridge midpoint**. Here's how to identify the breach.

By fall, the horizontal snow patches lingering on the E face of the ridge might offer guidance. If you see (a) several smaller patches to the right, nearer the summit, and (b) a single, larger patch left of the ridge midpoint, voilà… surmount the ridge by angling left, ascending between the smaller patches and the larger one.

The snow patches are not as described? Then take your cue from the bands of dark rock. Long, thick bands guard the upper-right and lower-left portions of the ridgecrest. Several shorter, thinner bands stairstep up the middle of the ridge face. Look between the thick, upper-right band, and the multiple, thin bands. You'll see a swath of scree. The easiest way to surmount the ridge is to angle left, up that scree, starting on the right edge of the multiple, thin bands of black rock.

Approaching the midpoint of Mt. Fosthall's S ridge, angle left (SW), ascending steep scree and/or snow. This strenuous-but-nontechnical passage soon leads to the **crest of Fosthall's S ridge**. Top out near 2480 m (8134 ft), about 3 hours from Sol Mountain Lodge. Memorize where you crested the ridge, so you'll know precisely where to descend when you return from the summit.

The S ridge of Mt. Fosthall is a **broad, boulder-strewn, gently-sloping ramp**. Turn right (N) and follow it 20 minutes to the summit. Favour the far (left / W) side of the crest, where the boulders are smaller and a bootbeaten route above 2520 m (8266 ft) makes ascending easier.

Pride Rock (Trip 2),
from Mt. Fosthall summit ridge

Arrive at the cairn atop 2697-m (8846-ft) **Mt. Fosthall** about 3 hours and 20 minutes from Sol Mountain Lodge. The panorama is vast and enthralling. It comprises countless massifs, glaciers, lakes, tarns, meadows, and forests.

Highlights include Big Peters Lake (NNE), the Cirque Lakes (NE, immediately below the summit), Fawn Lake and the Valley of the Moon (NE), 2971-m (9745-ft) Mt. Odin (whose soaring, sheer face is NE beyond Fawn Lake, and whose ice-armoured, N chest is hidden from view), Margie Lake (ESE), Sol Lake (SE), Bear Lake (farther SE, beyond the lodge), Arrow Lake (even farther SE), Bill Fraser Lake (SSE, below the lodge), Sol Mtn (just left of S), Pride Rock (just right of S), the ridge linking Sol and Pride (Trip 2), two remote tarns sequestered beneath Sol-Pride ridge, and Twin Peaks (S, just beyond Sol-Pride ridge, between Sol Mtn and Pride Rock).

TRIP 2
Sol Mountain / Pride Rock

LOCATION	Monashee Provincial Park, W of Upper Arrow Lake, SW of Shelter Bay
ROUND TRIP	12 km (7.4 mi) to Sol Mtn 17.4 km (10.8 mi) to Sol Mtn & Pride Rock
ELEVATION GAIN	959 m (3145 ft) for Sol Mtn plus 410 m (1345 ft) for Pride Rock 1369 m (4490 ft) for Sol Mtn & Pride Rock
KEY ELEVATIONS	Sol Mtn Lodge trailhead 1920 m (6298 ft), Bill Fraser Lake 1726 m (5660 ft), Sol Mtn 2386 m (7826 ft) Pride Rock 2452 m (8043 ft)
HIKING TIME	5½ to 6½ hours for Sol Mtn 7½ to 9 hours for Sol Mtn & Pride Rock
DIFFICULTY	challenging due to cross-country travel and routefinding
TRAILHEAD ACCESS	challenging due to 4-hour round-trip drive on maintained logging roads
MAPS	page 35, *Sol Mountain Touring* (laminated topo sold at the lodge); Mt. Fosthall 82/L08

Opinion

A prow-shaped boulder called *Pride Rock* plays a central role in the Disney film *The Lion King*. It's an iconic image you're probably familiar with. If so, you can accurately imagine the climactic destination of this hike.

It's one of three trips—along with Mt. Fosthall (Trip 1), and Mission Ridge (Trip 3)—that begin at Sol Mountain Lodge (solmountain.com). We describe the lodge and how to get there in Trip 1, so that's a must read. Now here's what you need to know about Sol Mountain / Pride Rock.

Like the others here, this trail soon fades to a cross-country, alpine route into world-class scenery. It's similar to Mt. Fosthall in terms of distance. It's similar to Mission Ridge because it traverses alplands so beautiful we call them "magic lands." (See page 48, paragraph 5.)

Compared to Fosthall, however, summiting both Sol and Pride entails more elevation gain, poses greater physical challenge, and requires more time. You must also be more attentive navigating to Sol than to Fosthall. And unlike either Mission or Fosthall, much of the Sol/Pride route follows an airy ridgecrest.

The navigation to Sol Mtn is not complex. The route—between trail's end above Bill Fraser Lake, and the summit of Sol—just isn't always obvious. If you have some off-trail experience, plus our directions in mind and the topo in hand, you should have no difficulty. You'll enjoy working through it.

Sol Mtn, Twin Lakes, Mt. Baldur beyond

Navigation is not a concern between the Sol Mtn and Pride Rock summits, because there you'll simply follow the ridge linking the peaks. The crest is narrow enough to be exciting but never entails scrambling or exposure. It's also long yet relatively level: no soaring, plummeting, discouraging elevation changes. And it provides a constant overview of the surrounding high country.

So start early with the intention of standing, à la Simba, on top of Pride Rock. Don't let Sol Mtn's glorious summit panorama erode your will to complete this premier ridgewalk.

Fact

by vehicle

See Mt. Fosthall (Trip 1) for driving directions from the S (via Nakusp, and the Upper Arrow Lake cable ferry at Arrow Park), or from the N (via Revelstoke, and the Upper Arrow Lake ferry landing at Shelter Bay).

on foot

From the front (N side) of Sol Mountain Lodge, follow the flagged trail left (NW). Pass the fire pit. Proceed 5 minutes through meadow, then descend left (SW) into forest.

At 1.3 km (0.8 mi), 1738 m (5700 ft), about 30 minutes from the lodge, reach a right spur. It leads 2 minutes WSW to **Bill Fraser Lake** at 1726 m (5660 ft). Mt. Fosthall is visible beyond the far shore (NNW). Resuming on the main trail, bear left (SE) for Sol Mtn and Pride Rock. A steep ascent ensues.

At 1850 m (6068 ft), after hiking about 50 minutes, the trail leads SW across a grassy, soggy **clearing**. Pass giant boulders. Continue the steep ascent.

About 1 hour from the lodge, the grade eases near 3.1 km (1.9 mi), 2050 m (6724 ft), on a **finger** extending from the **NW arm of Mt. Baldur**. The lodge is visible NE. Beyond it (N) is Mission Ridge (Trip 3).

Twin Lakes, from ridgecrest between Sol Mtn and Pride Rock

The trail diminishes on the finger. You're now following a flagged route. But before reaching Sol Mtn, even the flagging ends. So from here on, you're routefinding.

Your precise route might differ slightly from ours, so the remaining directions are waypoint suggestions, not requirements. Be attentive to landmarks, so navigation is easier on the return.

Your overall task is straightforward: attain the summit of Sol Mtn. It's directly W, though not yet visible. Then continue along the ridgecrest to the summit of Pride Rock.

Atop the **finger**, follow flagging briefly right (N), then left (NW), crossing the finger between the knuckles, as it were. Then ease W into a **broad, shallow, meadowy saddle** at 2036 m (6678 ft), about 1¼ hours from the lodge.

Note the peaklet ahead (W). It might appear to be Sol Mtn, but it's not. Sol is just beyond, hidden from view. Nor is it a peaklet. It's actually a blunt knoll, as you'll see, because you must surmount it en route to Sol Mtn.

Proceed W across the meadowy saddle. Pass a tarn. Cruise over a gentle, 2070-m (6790-ft) rise. Then negotiate a short-but-sharp descent into a distinct **notch** where narrow ravines plummet right (N) and left (S). This is at 4.1 km (2.5 mi), 2045 m (6708 ft), about 1¾ hours from the lodge.

Ascend left (SW), skirting the immediate wall. Traverse to about 2080 m (6822 ft), where the route turns right (N) and assaults the very steep, S slope. The audible (but not visible) cascading stream below issues from Twin Peaks Lake.

About 2 hours from the lodge, enter a meadow where the ascent eases. Head WNW over the 2160-m (7085-ft) **knoll** that earlier appeared to be a peaklet. Sol Mtn is now visible directly W. Reach a heathery **bench**. Descend to a **gully**.

Ascend boulder slabs left of two, white, mineral veins. Gain the E end of Sol Mtn's **summit block**. Above, various routes are possible. Freelance the final ascent however you feel most comfortable. We traversed right, to the NE face, then clambered left (SW) up the boulders.

Tag the summit cairn atop 2386-m (7826-ft) **Sol Mtn** at about 6 km (3.7 mi), having hiked about 2¾ hours from the lodge. Twin Peaks Lake is directly below Sol Mtn's broad, S face. Sitkum Lake is slightly farther WSW. The Twin Peaks (SSW and SW) are above Twin Peak Lake's S shore. Pride Rock is WNW. Mt. Fosthall (Trip 1) is N. Mission Ridge (Trip 3) is NE.

Pride Rock is about 1 hour distant. The ridgecrest linking it with Sol Mtn is the route, so detailed directions are unnecessary. Simply keep to the crest. In general, hike W along the top of Sol Mtn. Descend to a 2329-m (7639-ft) saddle. Ascend W to 2350 m (7708 ft). Descend WSW to a 2268-m (7439-ft) saddle. Ascend WNW to 2378 m (7800 ft). Descend W to 2345 m (7692 ft). Continue W, ascending to 2380 m (7806 ft). Then angle right (NW) and work your way up the gentle, rocky slope to the summit cairn atop 2452-m (8043-ft) **Pride Rock**. Arrive there at about 8.7 km (5.4 mi), having hiked about 3¾ hours from the lodge.

photos: *1 Bill Fraser Lake, Mt. Fosthall (Trip 1) beyond 2 View from Sol Mtn Lodge guest room 3 Mt. Fosthall (Trip 1), from near Pride Rock summit 4 Ascending Sol Mtn 5 Summitting Pride Rock*

TRIP 3
Mission Ridge

LOCATION	Monashee Provincial Park, W of Upper Arrow Lake SW of Shelter Bay
CIRCUIT	10.4 km (6.5 mi), plus 2-km (1.2-mi) round trip to Cirque Lakes overlook
ELEVATION GAIN	515 m (1689 ft), plus 140 m (459 ft) for Cirque Lakes
KEY ELEVATIONS	Sol Mtn Lodge trailhead 1920 m (6298 ft)
	South Cariboo Pass 2130 m (6986 ft)
	bench NE of Mission Ridge 2200 m (7216 ft)
	Mission Ridge low point 2225 m (7298 ft)
	Sol Lake 2145 m (7036 ft)
HIKING TIME	3½ to 4 hours, plus ¾ hour for Cirque Lakes
DIFFICULTY	challenging due to cross-country travel and routefinding
TRAILHEAD ACCESS	challenging due to 4-hour round-trip drive on maintained logging roads
MAPS	page 35; *Sol Mountain Touring* (laminated topo sold at the lodge); Mt. Fosthall 82/L08

Opinion

The trip numbers in this book are based strictly on geographic location. So it's a noteworthy coincidence that trips 1, 2 and 3—Mt. Fosthall, Sol Mountain / Pride Rock, and Mission Ridge—are our favourite hikes in the book.

All are initially trails that soon fade to cross-country, alpine routes. All are scenically world class. All begin at Sol Mountain Lodge (solmountain.com). We describe the lodge and how to get there in Trip 1, so that's a must read. Now here's what you need to know about Mission Ridge.

First, a quick summary of the circuit. Mission Ridge is north of Sol Mountain Lodge, just beyond the front yard/meadow. The ridge runs northwest-southeast. You'll hike northwest, paralleling the southeast side of the ridge. You'll cross the ridge at South Cariboo Pass. You'll hike southeast, paralleling the northeast side of the ridge. Then you'll cross a low point on the ridge, returning to the lodge via Sol Lake.

Even if you include the optional detour to the Cirque Lakes overlook, this is a relatively short, easy hike involving little elevation gain. Contemplating the same stats on a viewless, forested, valley trail, you'd expect to clock in at three hours or less. But the Mission Ridge circuit is no place to burn Vibram.

Much of the way, you'll be freelancing. The navigation is not puzzling, but it will slow your pace. Moreover, you'll always be near or above treeline, in tarn-splashed, stream-laced, grassy, flowery alplands, or what we call "magic lands." This is the paradisean high-country most of us spend far more time imagining

Peters Lake, from above South Cariboo Pass

than actually hiking. The pervasive beauty here has a frictional quality that keeps you meandering slowly and observing intently instead of striding robotically.

If you spend as much time relaxing and appreciating en route as you do hiking, it's possible to devote most of a day to the Mission Ridge circuit. Do it, and you too will likely rank it among your favourite West Kootenay hikes.

Fact

by vehicle

See Mt. Fosthall (Trip 1) for driving directions from the S (via Nakusp, and the Upper Arrow Lake cable ferry at Arrow Park), or from the N (via Revelstoke, and the Upper Arrow Lake ferry landing at Shelter Bay). Reach Sol Mountain Lodge, at 1920 m (6298 ft).

on foot

From the front (N side) of Sol Mountain Lodge, follow the flagged trail N, into the **meadow**. The trail bends left (WNW).

At 10 minutes, ignore the right (NNE) fork leading to Mission Ridge, E of Sol Lake. Continue straight (NNW) on the main trail.

In about 30 minutes, reach a **cairned fork** at 2107 m (6911 ft). Right leads to Sol Lake and a low point on Mission Ridge. To complete the circuit, you'll return via that trail. For now, go left (WNW) to South Cariboo Pass.

The trail dips into a drainage about 50 minutes from the lodge. It then rises left (NW). The trail continues crossing meadowy depressions, heading generally NW, **paralleling Mission Ridge** (right / NE). About 1 hour from the lodge, Mt. Fosthall looms ahead (NW).

Rockhop a creek near a **tarn** at 2120 m (6954 ft), about 70 minutes from the lodge. Surprisingly, the flagged trail curves left (SSW), around the W shore of the tarn. For the moment, do not proceed right (W). From the S end of the tarn, ascend left (SE).

Descending now, the trail leads you on a counter-intuitive but ultimately expedient detour. After a few minutes working your way down gentle, **rock outcrops** to 2050 m (6724 ft), resume in the logical direction: right (WNW). You've now hiked about 80 minutes from the lodge.

After undulating through subalpine meadows, ascend right (NNW) between creeklets. The **flagged trail ends** at 2100 m (6888 ft), about 1¾ hours from the lodge. Pause here. Beyond, you'll be traveling cross-country, without the aid of flagging or a trail.

Left (NW) leads to a boulder slide en route to Mt. Fosthall (Trip 1). Resume ascending N. In a few minutes, arrive at 2130-m (6986-ft) **South Cariboo Pass**, 5.6 km (3.5 mi) from the lodge.

Peters Lake, below at 1725 m (5658 ft), dominates the view N from Cariboo Pass. Glimpse the trail arriving at Peters Lake from Spectrum Creek trailhead, which is how most hikers enter Monashee Park. Slate Mtn (left) and Caribou Mtn (right) are beyond the lake. Fawn Lake and Valley of the Moon are NNE.

Cirque Lakes Overlook

A 2.2-km (1.4-mi) round-trip detour from the pass will enable you to overlook the Cirque Lakes—a pair of icy tarns on the NE face of Mt. Fosthall. Depart the pass heading left (W). Round the knob flanking the pass. Curve right and ascend NW to about 2210 m (7249 ft). Proceed NNW, contouring briefly, then dropping to a tarn on a shelf at 2170 m (7118 ft). Pass the tarn, and ascend N to about 2190 m (7183 ft), where the Cirque Lakes are visible below (left / NW) at 2050 m (6724 ft).

Resuming from **South Cariboo Pass**, descend NE to cross a steep **talus slope**. Drop no more than about 40 m (131 ft), then ascend right (ENE).

About 15 minutes beyond the pass, enter **heather meadows** on a bench at 2165 m (7101 ft). Hike generally ENE. Rockhop a very short creek between the **"joined at the hip" tarns**. Proceed NE to another nearby tarn. Then curve right (SE), passing three **more tarns**.

Continue freelancing SE at about 2200 m (7216 ft) on the long, gently undulating **bench parallel to Mission Ridge** (right / SW). The hinterland of Monashee Park fills the NE horizon (left). About 1 hour from the pass, Margie Lake is visible below (ENE).

Shortly beyond, watch right (S) for an easy opportunity to cross a **low point on Mission Ridge**. Crest the ridge at 2225 m (7298 ft), about 2.7 km (1.7 mi) from South Cariboo Pass. You've now hiked about 8.3 km (5.1 mi) total. Sol Lake—a critical landmark that ensures you're en route—should be visible below (SSE).

Quickly drop to the shore of **Sol Lake** at 2145 m (7036 ft). Round the right (W) shore. Follow a gully SSW. About 1½ hours from South Cariboo Pass, or about 3½ hours total, the lodge is visible left (SSE).

A couple minutes farther, intersect the **trail** you originally followed to the pass. There's a **cairn** here, at 2107 m (6911 ft). You're now on familiar ground. Turn left and follow the trail SE to arrive at the **lodge** in another 25 minutes.

photos: *1 The Norse Peaks, from Mission Ridge circuit 2 En route to South Cariboo Pass 3 "Joined at the hip" tarns*

TRIP 4
Saddle Mountain

LOCATION	Monashees, W of Arrow Lake
ROUND TRIP	10.6 km (6.6 mi)
ELEVATION GAIN	864 m (2834 ft)
KEY ELEVATIONS	trailhead 1440 m (4723 ft), summit 2304 m (7557 ft)
HIKING TIME	3½ to 5 hours
DIFFICULTY	moderate
TRAILHEAD ACCESS	moderate
MAP	Nakusp 82 K/4

Opinion

Your field of vision spans 200 degrees. You can distinguish 500 shades of even the dullest colour: grey. You can detect a mere candle flame at a distance of 16 km (9.9 mi). Celebrate the miracle of sight by gorging on visual stimuli. Hike to the former fire lookout atop Saddle Mountain and gaze upon the lakes and mountains comprising the western reaches of the West Kootenay.

On a clear day, you'll see much of the 23-km (14.3-mi) long Arrow Lakes reservoir and get an aerial perspective of Nakusp. On the east horizon is the serrated Selkirk Range. On the west horizon are the softer Monashees. Though distant, even the distinctive Bugaboo Spires are visible in the Purcell Range.

The trail doesn't transcend treeline until 45 minutes below Saddle Mtn's rocky apex. But it grants views before then, while traversing lush meadows. Overall, the ascent is only moderately steep, so you'll get a healthy workout without extreme risk of cardiac arrest.

Though the access road is steep, you can probably vanquish it in a high-clearance 2WD car. 4WD is preferable, however, and could be necessary after heavy rain. Avoid two sections of bedrock and some scratchy brush, by parking at 15.6 km (9.7 mi)—1.3 km (0.8 mi) shy of the trailhead.

Fact

by vehicle

From **Nakusp**, drive S on Hwy 6. At 9.4 km (5.8 mi) a pullout on the right allows a view across Upper Arrow Lake to Saddle Mtn. It's the small, chunky peak atop forested slopes. At 23 km (14.3 mi) turn right, onto Arrow Park Road.

From **Fauquier**, drive 35.4 km (22 mi) N on Hwy 6. Turn left, onto Arrow Park Road.

From either approach, continue downhill 0.4 km (0.2 mi) to the Arrow Park ferry landing. The elevation of Upper Arrow Lake is 445 m (1460 ft). The cable ferry operates daily, on demand, 5:10 a.m. to 12:15 p.m., and 2 p.m. to 9:10 pm. The lake is narrow here, so the crossing takes only a few minutes.

Saddle Mtn trail above Upper Arrow Lake. Beyond are Nakusp and the Goat Range.

0 km (0 mi)

Reset your trip odometer on the ferry. After disembarking on the NW shore, proceed straight, uphill. Pavement ends here. At the T-junction in 130 meters, turn right (E) following the sign for Cameron, Catherine, and Bear lakes.

0.2 km (0.1 mi)

Go right, onto signed Saddle Mountain Road. It's the higher, wider, main road. Proceed E.

9.8 km (6.1 mi)

Turn left onto Saddle Lookout Road. It's increasingly rough and steep as it switchbacks up the mountain.

15.6 km (9.7 mi)

At 1226 m (4020 ft) parking is available for two vehicles at a wide curve.

16.5 km (10.2 mi)

At 1335 m (4380 ft) negotiate a section of bedrock.

16.8 km (10.4 mi)

Brush is overgrowing the road, and another section of bedrock poses further challenge. Near where a left fork descends, there's room for a couple vehicles to park.

16.9 km (10.5 mi)

The trailhead—flagged and signed—departs the right (SW) side of the road, at 1440 m (4723 ft). About 15 m/yd farther is a creek culvert. Continuing S, the road levels.

17.2 km (10.7 mi)

The road is wide enough that you can turn around without danger. It's possible for several vehicles to park here, if the drivers are creative and careful.

on foot

Ascend W, quickly entering an impressive stand of beautiful cedars. This initial stretch of trail is well constructed. Small bridges span seasonal runoff gullies.

About 15 minutes from the road, the trail exits the cedars and proceeds among spruce and balsam trees. Huckleberry and blueberry bushes are profuse.

The grade steepens at 1635 m (5363 ft). A rooty, rocky stretch ensues near 1712 m (5615 ft). Once the grade eases again, the trail is steep for only brief pitches.

About 45 minutes from the road, near 1900 m (6232 ft), turn sharply right onto a white bedrock rib and ascend NNW. Watch for orange blazes on trees.

About 40 m / yd farther, the summit of Saddle Mtn is visible left (NW), but a crude stone barricade indicates you should not turn in that direction. Proceed straight, onto a short stretch of dirt trail, then back onto bedrock with green lichen. Dirt trail soon resumes through forest and across intermittent bedrock.

At 1995 m (6545 ft), just below the summit, about 1½ hours from the road, pass an old, metal-roofed **cabin**. Berry bushes are rife here. The peaks of Valhalla Provincial Park are visible SSE.

A couple minutes farther, the lookout cabin atop the summit is visible. You've been ascending the E face of the mountain. Continue doing so by staying on the trail. Don't be drawn around the mountain's far side.

A long switchback traverses NW through a meadow where lavender fleabane grows thigh high. You might also see lousewort and yellow aster. The Goat Range is visible ENE.

Continue switchbacking upward. Traverse rocky slopes beneath the sheer E face of the main summit block. At 2260 m (7413 ft), about 2 hours from the road, reach the mountain's namesake **saddle**, between the S and main summits.

Tiger lily

The increasingly rough trail now turns right (N) for the final approach. About 15 minutes above, attain the 2304-m (7557-ft) summit of **Saddle Mountain** at 5.3 km (3.3 mi).

Upper Arrow Lake (N) and Lower Arrow Lake (S) are visible 1862 m (6107 ft) below. The village of Nakusp is 13 km (8 mi) NE. Farther NE are the Bugaboo Spires. Mt. Brennan (Trip 12) is E. Kokanee Park is S of Brennan. The spiky Valhallas—including Gimli Peak (Trip 21) and 2695-m (8840-ft) Mt. Woden—are SSE. Whatshan Lake (19 km / 12 mi long) is SW.

More interesting than the dilapidated fire-lookout cabin are the signatures carved into the bedrock by fire scouts who occupied the lookout starting in 1923. Joe Stanley, for example, manned this post between 1964 and 1973, then again in 1985.

Fast hikers will need only about 1¼ hours to descend to the trailhead.

Aster

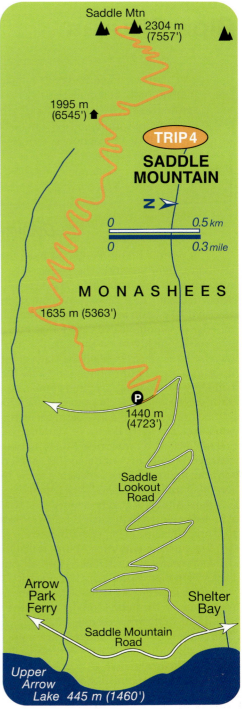

Saddle Mtn
2304 m (7557')

1995 m (6545')

TRIP 4
SADDLE MOUNTAIN

N

0   0.5 km
0   0.3 mile

M O N A S H E E S

1635 m (5363')

P
1440 m (4723')

Saddle Lookout Road

Arrow Park Ferry

Shelter Bay

Saddle Mountain Road

Upper Arrow Lake 445 m (1460')

TRIP 5
Alps Alturas

LOCATION	Goat Range Provincial Park, NE of New Denver
ROUND TRIP	10 km (6.2 mi)
ELEVATION GAIN	579 m (1900 ft)
KEY ELEVATIONS	trailhead 1762 m (5780 ft), trail's end 2332 m (7650 ft)
HIKING TIME	3 to 4 hours
DIFFICULTY	moderate
TRAILHEAD ACCESS	moderate
MAP	Rosebery 82 K/3

Opinion

The perfect hiking boots are hard to find, because they fuse contrary attributes: light but stiff. The perfect hike is equally rare, because it too is a contradiction: easy but scenic. The Alps Alturas trail, however, comes close to achieving that tricky balance. Without taxing your stamina, it lofts you into a glaciated lake basin beneath Marten Mtn, high in the realm of rock and ice, on the edge of seldom-visited Goat Range Provincial Park.

You'll quickly burst through the forest into subalpine meadows, then traverse scree slopes beneath the crags of Mt. Dolly Varden. The scenery opens up after a mere hour of hiking, because the trailhead is just outside the park boundary. The logging road that grants you this convenience is itself part of the day's entertainment. It clings to mountainsides and affords spectacular vistas.

Before reaching the lake basin beneath grand 2747-m (9010-ft) Marten Mtn, you'll look across the depths of Marten Creek canyon and see cascades hurtling 550 m (1800 ft) off Inverness Mtn. The trail is comfortably level in the alpine zone, yet is quite airy—the slope beneath it dropping steeply into the void. This too is an unusual hiking experience in the West Kootenay, duplicated on only a few other trails, like Idaho Peak (Trip 6).

Alps Alturas is grizzly country, so stay alert. Watch for mountain goats, too. Also listen for the high-pitched beeps of pikas (little rodents with big ears), and the shrill whistling of larger marmots.

The problem with Alps Alturas is that there's too little of it. The access road demands nearly as much time as the trail. Strong hikers will just be relaxing into the joy of motion on this grin-inducing trip when… whoa!… suddenly they're at trail's end. Experienced scramblers, however, can enjoy a full day's adventure by continuing up the south shoulder of Marten Mtn.

If you start early, you might have enough time left over to explore Dennis Basin. You'll pass the trailhead access (identified in the *by vehicle* directions below) while driving to Alps Alturas trailhead. The 5-km (3.1-mi) round-trip hike leads to an alpine ridge overlooking Dennis Creek. Mid-July through mid-August the alpine floral display is explosive. The area is also known for grizzlies. Be vigilant and make noise.

Fact

by vehicle

From the junction of Hwys 6 and 31A in **New Denver**, drive 5.6 km (3.5 mi) NW on Hwy 6. Turn right (NE) onto East Wilson Creek Road. It's immediately before the bridge over Wilson Creek, just before Rosebery Provincial Park.

From the junction of Hwys 6 and 23 in **Nakusp**, drive 41.4 km (25.7 mi) SE on Hwy 6. Turn left (NE) onto East Wilson Creek Road. It's just past Rosebery Provincial Park, immediately after the bridge over Wilson Creek.

0 km (0 mi)
Starting NE on East Wilson Creek Road from Hwy 6.

2.75 km (1.7 mi)
Proceed on the main road. Ignore Dennis Creek Road (right).

2.8 km (1.7 mi)
Turn right onto Hicks Creek Road, signed for Alps Alturas.

5.5 km (3.4 mi)
Go left and ascend.

9.2 km (5.7 mi)
Bear right at the junction.

11.6 km (7.2 mi)
Bear left at the junction.

12.8 km (7.9 mi)
Reach a junction. Continue on the main road, which narrows ahead. Right leads to Dennis Basin trailhead.

Lake beneath Marten Mtn

24.7 km (15.3 mi)
Reach a junction at 1625 m (5330 ft). Turn left, descend, and cross a culvert. Ascend briefly, curving right, then descend beside a cutblock.

25.8 km (16 mi)
Fork left and ascend.

27.6 km (17.1 mi)
Reach the trailhead parking area, at 1762 m (5780 ft).

on foot

The trail, initially an old mining road, heads N through a cutblock. It soon curves SE and ascends into forest. Pass a Goat Range Provincial Park boundary sign at 1814 m (5950 ft).

Follow the road / trail NE into a shallow drainage. At 2006 m (6580 ft) pass a sign indicating you've hiked 1.5 km (0.9 mi). Just beyond, where the road / trail is severely steep, go right onto a new switchbacking trail. It quickly rejoins the road / trail—now grassed over.

A few minutes beyond, where the road / trail continues right, go left on trail and cross a **bridged creeklet**. Ascend beside the right (E) bank. Proceed through a small meadow rife with Indian hellebore (corn lilies).

At 2091 m (6860 ft) pass a sign indicating you've hiked 2 km (1.2 mi). Mt. Dolly Varden is visible ahead. The trail leads NE through a **grassy saddle** between the mountain (left) and a knob (right). Skirt the left side of a rockslide. About 50 m / yd farther, veer sharply left.

About 1 hour from the trailhead, at 2195 m (7200 ft), the view W extends beyond the Selkirks to the Monashees. Follow cairns where the trail deteriorates in a draw. Continue straight (SE) through a tiny col, left of a black peaklet. The trail then wraps around the right (SE) end of Mt. Dolly Varden.

From a 2226-m (7300-ft) **notch**, descend E to another notch. Shortly beyond 3 km (1.9 mi), the trail vanishes for 70 m (230 ft). Proceed along the right side of a creeklet. A faint trail will reappear. In a shallow depression, go left. Continue heading E toward the gap just beyond the meadow.

At 2171 m (7120 ft) reach a sign indicating you've hiked 3.5 km (2.2 mi). Soon after, the airy trail traverses high above the W side of **Marten Creek canyon**. Cascades are now visible on the sheer walls of Inverness Mtn. They plummet 550 m (1800 ft) to indigo ponds. Visible S are peaks in Kokanee Glacier Provincial Park. SW are the peaks of Valhalla Provincial Park. Marten Mtn is ahead (NE).

Marmots

The trail, now well-defined and comfortable, traverses scree slopes and curves N. It ascends moderately to 2305 m (7560 ft). At a steady pace, most hikers will arrive here within 2 hours of leaving the trailhead. An old mining road is visible deep in Marten Creek canyon. The NW side of London Ridge is visible SE, near where Marten Creek canyon joins Kane Creek Valley.

Reach **trail's end** at 5 km (3.1 mi), 2332 m (7650 ft), just above the **lake basin** at the foot of 2747-m (9010-ft) Marten Mtn.

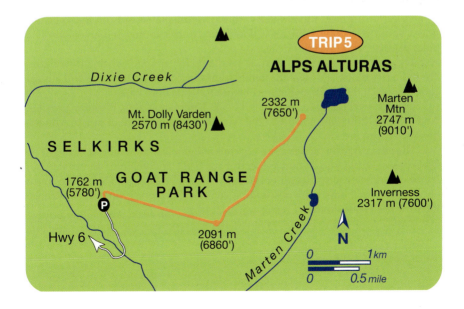

TRIP 5

ALPS ALTURAS

Dixie Creek

2332 m (7650')

Marten Mtn 2747 m (9010')

Mt. Dolly Varden 2570 m (8430')

SELKIRKS

1762 m (5780')

GOAT RANGE PARK

P

Hwy 6

2091 m (6860')

Marten Creek

Inverness 2317 m (7600')

N

0   1 km

0   0.5 mile

TRIP 6
Idaho Peak

LOCATION	Selkirks, SE of New Denver, W of Sandon
ROUND TRIP	2.8 km (1.7 mi)
ELEVATION GAIN	146 m (479 ft)
KEY ELEVATIONS	trailhead 2134 m (7000 ft), summit 2280 m (7479 ft)
HIKING TIME	1 to 1½ hours
DIFFICULTY	easy
TRAILHEAD ACCESS	challenging
MAP	Slocan 82 F/14

Opinion

Kooteneers who want to wow visiting friends cart them up Idaho Peak, where a brief walk leads to a walloping view of wilderness. Cart yourself up here if you don't have a local guide. Do it even if you're a non-hiker. This is an essential, West Kootenay experience.

The price of alpine admission is usually a long, steep trudge through forest. Here, your vehicle does the work, climbing all the way to the summit ridge. Your legs won't get much exercise, but your eyes will.

A fire lookout—occasionally manned, usually locked—crowns Idaho Peak. That tells you how comprehensive the panorama is. You'll see the Slocan, Goat, Kokanee, and Valhalla ranges. Most of Slocan Lake is also visible. So are the lakeshore towns of Silverton and New Denver.

By early summer, a world-class wildflower display erupts on Idaho Peak's grassy southwest slope. Look for yellow asters, purple lupine, Indian paintbrush, Sitka valerian, and lavender fleabane.

The trail is so short and easy, it's suitable for anyone capable of walking around a city block. It's ideal for families with tots, because the tribe will almost certainly reach the trail's end climax before the little ones balk.

Don't expect solitude atop Idaho Peak. Understandably, it's very popular. And with so little room to spread out, you'll be keenly aware of others who are here when you are.

The steep, narrow access road requires a high-clearance vehicle. It might be 2WD passable, but you'll want the security of 4WD, and you might need it. Also, try to ascend to the trailhead early in the day. The later you start, the more encounters you'll have with descending vehicles. Each one is an ordeal, because the road has few pullouts.

Fact

by vehicle

In downtown **Kaslo**, drive NW on "A" Avenue. As it begins climbing, ignore North Marine Drive (Hwy 31N) on the right. Proceed uphill. Soon reach the intersection of "A" Avenue and Washington Street. Reset your trip odometer to 0 here. Turn left onto Washington, which becomes Hwy 31A. Follow it generally NW. At 37.9 km (23.5 mi) reach Three Forks and turn left (SE) onto Sandon Road. Again reset your trip odometer to 0.

In **New Denver**, reset your trip odometer to 0 at the junction of Hwys 6 and 31A (Union Street and 6th Avenue). Drive E on Hwy 31A (6th Avenue). Follow it generally NE. At 8.3 km (5.2 mi) reach Three Forks and turn right (SE) onto Sandon Road. Again reset your trip odometer to 0.

0 km (0 mi)
Starting SE on unpaved Sandon Road from Hwy 31A.

At 5.2 km (3.2 mi)
The Klondyke Silver Corporation is visible (right).

photos: *1 Indian paintbrush 2 Globeflower 3 Arnica 4 Alpine forget-me-not*

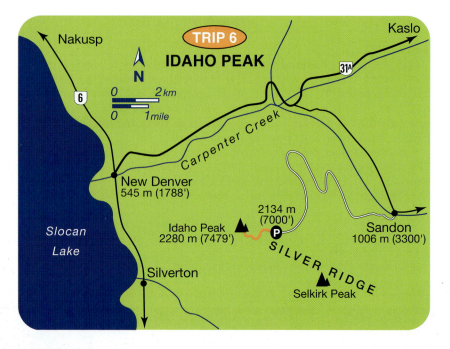

5.6 km (3.5 mi)
Arrive in Sandon. Straight (E) on Reco Road leads to the Mt. Carlyle trailhead (Trips 7, 8 and 9). Turn right (S) onto Galena Road and cross the bridge over Carpenter Creek. Then bear left (ESE) and pass the town's few remaining buildings.

5.9 km (3.7 mi)
Turn right, pass the kiosk (right), and begin ascending WNW. For about 2 km (1.2 mi) the road is comfortably wide, and the grade moderate. Then the road narrows and begins a steep, switchbacking ascent.

8.3 km (5.2 mi)
Proceed straight (bear right).

10 km (6.2 mi)
Stay left.

14 km (8.7 mi)
The ascent steepens.

15 km (9.3 mi)
Enter Wildgoose Basin. Glacier lilies are profuse here in early summer. The final switchbacks to the trailhead are visible ahead.

17.4 km (10.8 mi)
Reach road's end and the trailhead parking area. It's at 2134 m (7000 ft), on the ridge between Idaho and Selkirk peaks.

on foot

Follow the trail W. Reach the 2280-m (7479-ft) summit of **Idaho Peak** at 1.4 km (0.9 mi). Kokanee Glacier is visible SE. Mt. Brennan (Trip 12) and Whitewater Mtn (Trip 11) are NE. Mt. Cooper is also NE, beyond Whitewater. Valhalla Provincial Park is SW, across Slocan Lake. Prominent Valhalla peaks, from left to right, are Mt. Dag, Wolfs Ears, Gimli, Gladsheim, and Asgard. New Denver Glacier is directly W. Big Sister Mtn is NW of New Denver.

photos: *1 Silverton and Slocan Lake, from Idaho Peak 2 near Idaho Peak summit 3 Glacier lilies in Wildgoose Basin*

TRIPS 7 - 9

Prospector Peak / Mt. Carlyle / Misty Peak

LOCATION	Selkirks, Goat Range, between New Denver and Kaslo, S of Hwy 31A
ROUND TRIP	10.2 km (6.3 mi) to Carlyle Lodge, 2.2 km (1.4 mi) lodge to Prospector Peak, 3 km (1.9 mi) lodge to Mt. Carlyle S ridge, 2 km (1.2 mi) lodge to Misty Peak
ELEVATION GAIN	616 m (2020 ft) to Carlyle Lodge, 350 m (1148 ft) to Prospector Peak, 305 m (1000 ft) to Mt. Carlyle S ridge, 259 m (850 ft) to Misty Peak
KEY ELEVATIONS	trailhead 1686 m (5530 ft) road's end clearing 1860 m (6100 ft) Carpenter Pass 2302 m (7550 ft) Carlyle Lodge 2195 m (7200 ft) Prospector Peak 2545 m (8350 ft) Mt. Carlyle S ridge 2450 m (8036 ft) Mt. Carlyle 2648 m (8688 ft) Misty Peak 2454 m (8050 ft) Sweet Lake 2057 m (6750 ft)
HIKING TIME	4 to 5 hours for Carlyle Lodge 2 hours for Prospector Peak, 2½ hours for Mt. Carlyle 1½ hours for Misty Peak
DIFFICULTY	easy to Carlyle Lodge; moderate to Prospector Peak, Mt. Carlyle S Ridge, and Misty Peak; challenging to Mt. Carlyle
TRAILHEAD ACCESS	moderate due to water bars
MAP	Slocan 82 F/14

Opinion

Like a tsunami, civilization crashed into Carpenter Creek Valley, rearranged everything, then washed away.

For a brief span—the last ten years of the 1800s—the valley was cosmopolitan beyond our imagining, because today we see only woebegone shreds of the former, mining-mania cities: Sandon and Cody.

Once again this is just a lonely sliver of the wild West Kootenay. But there is a glint of civilization here: an alpine lodge that hosts skiers and hikers from all over North America.

Mt. Carlyle Lodge (skihikebc.com) is a classic, backcountry refuge: small, humble, respectful of its surroundings, yet a haven of comfort and conviviality.

photos: *1 Carlyle Basin 2 1894 claim post on Prospector Peak 3 Talus slope en route to Prospector Peak 4 Kokanee Glacier, from lodge 5 Carlyle Lodge*

Approaching Mt. Carlyle's S ridge, Kokanee Park beyond

It clings to steep terrain, just below the south side of Carpenter Pass, beneath Mt. Carlyle, Prospector Peak, and Misty Peak.

It's possible to clamber up and down any of these mountains in a single day via Carpenter Creek Valley. The optimal plan, however, and the one we describe here, is to base yourself at Carlyle Lodge. All three dayhikes emanate from the front door.

The first, to Prospector Peak, you can do the same day you hike into the lodge. The second, to Mt. Carlyle, is the longest, so do it once you're already at the lodge and intend to stay there that night. The third, to Misty Peak, you can do the same day you hike from the lodge back to the trailhead. So that's a three-day trip comprising three, separate dayhikes, made possible by spending two nights at Carlyle Lodge.

Think of it as hyperlight backpacking. No need for a tent or sleeping pad, because you'll bed down on a comfy mattress in the lodge. No need for your warmest layers, because the lodge is always cozy, heated by a wood-burning stove and propane heaters. No need for a stove or cooking gear, because the lodge kitchen is fully equipped. Just bring food and your sleeping bag. And a pack towel, because the lodge has a sauna and hot shower.

Our *on foot* directions lead you to Carlyle Lodge via an overgrown road, a bootbeaten route, and finally an historic mining trail. That's the most efficient way to get there on day one. But we suggest you not retrace your steps when returning to the trailhead. Instead, vary your return by descending most of the way down-valley on the historic mining trail. En route, you can make a scenic stop at Sweet Lake.

Bear in mind, once you're at Carlyle, you'll be hiking cross-country. No trails lead to the three summits ringing the lodge. But the distances are short. And you'll always be near or above treeline, where staying oriented is easy because landmarks remain visible.

Actually, Carlyle is well suited to intermediate hikers seeking to advance their routefinding and scrambling skills. The lodge is always nearby. The navigation is not challenging and does not require precision. The basin beneath Mt. Carlyle is big and the terrain varied, allowing you to find and stay within your comfort zone.

Carlyle is also ideal for families or groups comprising a range of skills and interests. Some will be happy just roaming the basin beneath Mt. Carlyle. Most will want to summit the peaks. A few will probe the sharp ridges beyond. All will be reluctant to leave the lodge deck, because Kokanee Glacier dominates the horizon.

This is the best, hiker-accessible view of Kokanee Glacier you'll find. Every morning and evening, delicate light plays across the ice. Watching this spectacle is yet another benefit of staying at Carlyle lodge.

TRIP 7 PROSPECTOR PEAK

Prospector Peak is the slightly shorter, Siamese twin of Mt. Carlyle. Both are huge, boulder piles. They look as if they were turned inside out by the miners that once swarmed the region. You'll frequently look up at Prospector while hiking to Carlyle Lodge, because its shoulder drops to Carpenter Pass.

Our day-one recommendation is to proceed over the pass, quickly settle in at Carlyle Lodge, then hoist a lighter pack, return to Carpenter Pass, and devote the afternoon to surmounting Prospector Peak.

The summit panorama is rewarding, but you'll earn it. The steep, bouldery ascent and descent qualifiy as *scrambling*. It demands an athletic combination of strength, balance, and endurance.

TRIP 8 MT. CARLYLE

Goal-oriented peak baggers will be keen to summit Mt. Carlyle. We suggest you do it on your second day at the lodge. You'll see most of the West Kootenay from there, including Kootenay Lake. You'll even glimpse Kaslo.

Be aware, however, that Mt. Carlyle is a step up in difficulty from Prospector Peak. Beyond where you crest Carlyle's south ridge, it's a challenging scramble. You must negotiate boulders nonstop. All are big. Some are loose. Your safety depends on spidering lightly over them.

We find the basin beneath Mt. Carlyle's southwest face more compelling than the summit. The West Kootenay has peaks like porcupines have quills, but alplands like this are rare here. Allow yourself plenty of time to wander among the granite, meadows, tarns, and streams.

Set as your goal the south ridge of Mt. Carlyle. You'll cross the basin en route. From the ridgecrest, you can assess the summit. Should you decide not to grapple with the malevolent boulders, you can linger longer in the basin on your return.

TRIP 9 MISTY PEAK

Viewed from Carlyle Lodge, Misty Peak does not loom so prominently as Prospector Peak or Mt. Carlyle, so it doesn't beckon quite so fervently. But Misty's summit panorama is comparable. And you'll attain it faster and easier, because the distance is shorter, the ascent is less steep, and the peak doesn't spit boulders at you.

This is a steep, off-trail hike, not a scramble. So do it on day three, after you've expended more energy on Prospector and Misty. You can zip up and down Misty and still trek back to the trailhead at a leisurely pace.

Leaving Misty for your last day is also fitting because it's the optimal vantage for surveying Carpenter Creek Valley, through which you arrived and will soon depart. Might your Carlyle experience inspire a flash of insight? This would be the time and place.

Fact

by vehicle

Low-clearance cars will struggle on the final, unpaved approach to this trailhead, due to numerous water bars (trenches dug across the road to prevent erosion). Moderate clearance is necessary. High clearance is preferable. 4WD is ideal.

In downtown **Kaslo**, drive NW on "A" Avenue. As it begins climbing, ignore North Marine Drive (Hwy 31N) on the right. Proceed uphill. Soon reach the intersection of "A" Avenue and Washington Street. Reset your trip odometer to 0 here. Turn left onto Washington, which becomes Hwy 31A. Follow it generally NW. At 37.9 km (23.5 mi) reach Three Forks and turn left (SE) onto Sandon Road. Again reset your trip odometer to 0.

In **New Denver**, reset your trip odometer to 0 at the junction of Hwys 6 and 31A (Union Street and 6th Avenue). Drive E on Hwy 31A (6th Avenue). Follow it generally NE. At 8.3 km (5.2 mi) reach Three Forks and turn right (SE) onto Sandon Road. Again reset your trip odometer to 0.

0 km (0 mi)
Starting SE on unpaved Sandon Road from Hwy 31A. It's about a 1-hour drive to the trailhead.

At 5.2 km (3.2 mi)
The Klondyke Silver Corporation is visible (right).

5.6 km (3.5 mi)
Arrive in Sandon. Proceed straight (E) on Reco Road, staying on the left (N) side of Carpenter Creek. Right (S) is Galena Road, which crosses the bridged creek and leads to Idaho Peak (Trip 6).

6 km (3.7 mi)
Pass the trailhead parking area (left) for the Galena Trail (Trip 43). It's near the Historic Railway Trail kiosk.

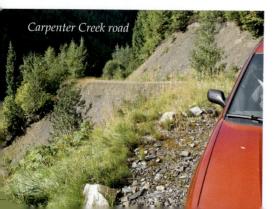

Carpenter Creek road

6.9 km (4.3 mi)
Cross a bridge to the S bank of Carpenter Creek.

7.3 km (4.5 mi)
Ascend straight, ignoring the right fork.

7.6 km (4.7 mi)
Bear right, ignoring the "road deactivated" sign.

8.2 km (5.1 mi)
Pass a cabin. Cross a bridge to the E bank of Cody Creek. Proceed through Cody.

8.4 km (5.2 mi)
Fork left and cross a wooden bridge over Carpenter Creek.

8.6 km (5.3 mi)
The road curves right, ascends, and gets rougher.

10.4 km (6.4 mi)
Negotiate water bars (trenches dug across the road to prevent erosion).

12.7 km (7.9 mi)
Reach a fork at 1686 m (5530 ft). This is the trailhead. The overgrown road left (ESE) is the trail. The wider road descending right (SSE) to Carpenter Creek offers more room to turn around. Park wherever you can pull your vehicle off the road.

on foot

Pause before departing the trailhead. Orient yourself by surveying the far (S) end of Carpenter Creek Valley. Two of the mountains comprising your destination are visible: Prospector Peak (left), and Misty Peak (right). Carpenter Pass is between Prospector and Misty. Carlyle Lodge is near the pass but on the far (S) side, hidden from view.

Follow the overgrown road left (ESE). About 15 minutes along, expect to encounter **avalanche deadfall** for the next 15 minutes.

After hiking about 1 hour, reach **road's end** in a **clearing** at 2.5 km (1.6 mi), 1860 m (6100 ft). Proceed onto the flagged, **bootbeaten route** angling right (SW) into the trees. It drops briefly, then climbs steeply.

Ascend the left (E) side of a **boulder field**. The route generally bears left: SSE, SE, then ENE. Be alert for helpful flagging. At about 1½ hours, intersect an **historic trail** at 3.4 km (2.1 mi), 2115 m (6937 ft). Miners built this trail in the 1890s.

Pause here. Note your surroundings. Remember this junction. From here, the historic trail ascends right (SE) to Carpenter Pass, and it descends left (NNW) toward the trailhead. For now, ascend right. Later, you can vary the return by descending the historic trail (as described below), rather than retracing your steps on the bootbeaten route and the overgrown road.

Resuming from the junction, ascend the historic trail right (SE). It switchbacks through a **boulder field** littered with rusty, mining relics and the remains of a cabin. Ignore the left (NE) spur to the nearby **Mountain Con Mine** shaft; visit it on the return, if you have time and inclination. For now, bear right (S) and proceed to the pass: the low point on the ridge ahead. The final switchbacks are visible in the scree above.

Crest **Carpenter Pass** at 4.7 km (2.9 mi), 2302 m (7550 ft), about 2¼ hours from the trailhead. It's between 2545-m (8350-ft) Prospector Peak (left / NE), and 2454-m (8050-ft) Misty Peak (right / W). Ahead (S) is Long Creek Valley, a tributary of Keen Creek Valley.

Descend the S side of the pass. As the trail fades, shift left (E) where it's distinct. Proceed S, down the fall line. Reach **Carlyle Lodge** at 5.1 km (3.2 mi), 2195 m (7200 ft), 15 minutes below the pass, or 2½ hours from the trailhead.

Skip below for *on foot* descriptions of the three dayhikes emanating from Carlyle Lodge. Here are directions for returning to the trailhead via the historic trail:

Return via Historic Mining Trail

When departing the lodge, you can, of course, retrace your steps N by following the trail over Carpenter Pass, the bootbeaten route down to the road's end clearing, and finally the overgrown road back to the trailhead. Instead, we recommend varying the return by descending most of the way down-valley on the historic trail. It's the same distance, but consider the pros and cons.

The advantages of the historic trail include a more gradual descent most of the way on a constructed, wilderness path through a beautiful forest; a scenic stop at Sweet Lake; and a new perspective of Carpenter Creek Valley from high on its E wall. The disadvantage is that the historic trail passes well above the trailhead. So, near the end, you must descend a steep, untracked, debris-ridden avalanche slope for about 15 minutes. You'll then be back on the overgrown road for the final 20 minutes to the trailhead.

Opting for the historic trail? Hike over **Carpenter Pass**, perhaps stopping to inspect the **Mountain Con Mine**, then switchback down through the **boulder field**. At 1.7 km (1.1 mi) reach the 2115-m (6937-ft) **junction** with the bootbeaten route (left) that you originally ascended from the road's end clearing. Proceed straight (NNW) on the historic trail.

The trail descends gradually, traversing generally N across the **E wall of Carpenter Creek Valley**. Watch right (E) for Sweet Lake at 2057 m (6750 ft). (See main photo, back cover.) Probe the lake's right (S) shore to see the remains of a cabin.

Resuming N on the historic trail, pass a standing, derelict **cabin** (left). At 1912 m (6271 ft), enter an **avalanche path**. Shortly beyond, a rockslide obliterated the trail. So this avalanche path is where you must abandon the trail and descend 135 m (443 ft) to the road directly below.

The slope is steep. Negotiating the chaotic debris requires careful foot placement. But it poses no serious difficulty to experienced hikers. Within 15 minutes of departing the historic trail, reach the **overgrown road** at 1777 m (5830 ft).

You're now on familiar ground. Turn right (N) and follow the road down-valley about 20 minutes to the **trailhead**. Distance from Carlyle Lodge: 5.1 km (3.2 mi).

TRIP 7 PROSPECTOR PEAK

ROUND TRIP	2.2 km (1.4 mi)
ELEVATION GAIN	350 m (1148 ft)
HIKING TIME	2 hours
DIFFICULTY	moderate

on foot

From **Carlyle Lodge** at 2195 m (7200 ft), follow the trail N. In 15 minutes reach 2302-m (7550-ft) **Carpenter Pass**. Turn right (E) and begin the off-trail ascent of Prospector Peak's bouldery, **SW ridge**.

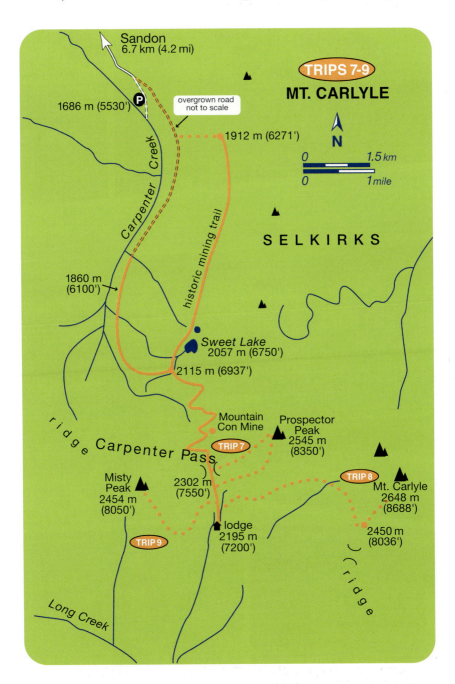

Sandon
6.7 km (4.2 mi)

1686 m (5530')

overgrown road
not to scale

Carpenter Creek

1912 m (6271')

TRIPS 7-9
MT. CARLYLE

N

0   1.5 km
0   1 mile

S E L K I R K S

historic mining trail

1860 m
(6100')

Sweet Lake
2057 m (6750')

2115 m (6937')

Mountain
Con Mine

Prospector
Peak
2545 m
(8350')

r i d g e Carpenter Pass

TRIP 7

TRIP 8

Mt. Carlyle
2648 m
(8688')

Misty
Peak
2454 m
(8050')

2302 m
(7550')

lodge
2195 m
(7200')

2450 m
(8036')

TRIP 9

r i d g e

Long Creek

Your general direction of travel will remain NE. But freelance as necessary to stay on the most stable boulders. Avoid loose boulders that might shift. Overhanging boulders are especially dangerous.

After hiking about 35 minutes, angle right: away from the ridgecrest, onto more secure boulders. At about 45 minutes, angle left: back to the **ridgecrest**.

If, at any point, the remaining ascent intimidates you, stop: enjoy the view you've achieved, then turn back.

At 2560 m (8397 ft), about 1 hour from the lodge, pass a weathered, wood, mining-claim stake dated 1894. Just beyond, top out on 2545-m (8350-ft) **Prospector Peak** at 1.1 km (0.7 mi).

Prospector is a satellite of 2648-m (8688-ft) Mt. Carlyle, which is very near (ESE). An arête links the two peaks, but don't continue in that direction. To summit Mt. Carlyle, start at the lodge and traverse the mountain's SW basin, as described below.

Here are a few highlights of the Prospector Peak panorama. Idaho Peak (Trip 6) is nearby WNW. The *Norse Peaks* in Monashee Park (Trips 1-3) are NW. Whitewater Mtn (Trip 11) is just left of N. Mt. Brennan (Trip 12), whose summit is split by a vertical couloir, is directly N. Mt. Jardine (Trip 13) is NNE; beyond is the Four Squatters Glacier. MacBeth Icefield (Trip 15) is NE. Kokanee Glacier is S. The Valhallas (Trips 20-21) are WSW.

On the return, don't retrace your steps to Carpenter Pass. For an easier descent, and to create a circuit, drop SW, then angle left (SSW) seeking smaller, more stable boulders. Soon reach a more gradual slope. Continue onto dirt and heather. Then bear right (W). Intersect the trail midway between Carpenter Pass and Carlyle Lodge. You're now on familiar ground. Turn left (S) to quickly reach the lodge.

TRIP 8 MT. CARLYLE

ROUND TRIP	3 km (1.9 mi) to S ridge	
ELEVATION GAIN	305 m (1000 ft) to S ridge	
HIKING TIME	2½ hours for S ridge	
DIFFICULTY	moderate to S ridge, challenging to summit	

on foot

Mt. Carlyle is ENE of Carlyle Lodge. Between the lodge and its namesake peak is an alpine basin beneath the peak's SW face. Overall, the basin is very gentle. But it's trail-less, and the terrain underfoot is complex. Attempting to lead you through the basin via detailed directions would be difficult. And the more exacting the directions, the more confused and frustrated you'd likely become if you tried to follow them assiduously.

The basin is an alpine playground comprising slabby boulders, pocket meadows, and creeklets. So, go play. We won't shackle you with an *on foot* description that restricts creativity and quashes the joy of discovery. We'll simply offer these general guidelines:

From Carlyle Lodge at 2195 m (7200 ft), briefly follow the trail N toward Carpenter Pass. Study the terrain to your right (E). When you see an inviting, prospective passage, abandon the trail, hop the creeklets, and ascend.

photos: *1 Prospector Peak above Carlyle Basin 2 Sweet Lake 3 Ascending to Carpenter Pass 4 Mt. Carlyle*

As always when hiking cross country, avoid trampling fragile vegetation; step on rock whenever possible. And note your surroundings, so you can later reverse your route.

From the top of the first **ridge**, drop to a **shelf** where a **grassy gully** (boulders left, slab right) leads left (ENE). If you see it, follow it. If not, you'll find another way forward.

Beyond that gully, head generally E. Work your way across the basin. Aim for the low point on Mt. Carlyle's S ridge. You want to surmount the ridge just left (N) of and above the larch trees.

A **natural ramp**, ascending left to right, affords easy access to the ridge. White rock distinguishes the ramp from the surrounding charcoal-hued stone.

Crest **Mt. Carlyle's S ridge** at 2450 m (8036 ft), about 1.5 km (0.9 mi) from the lodge. Left (NNE), 200 m (653 ft) above, is the 2648-m (8688-ft) **SE summit of Mt. Carlyle**. The 30-minute scramble to the top is demanding, because the ridge is composed entirely of huge boulders, some of which are easily dislodged. But the route is straightforward: up the crest.

The Mt. Carlyle panorama is grand. In addition to what you witnessed from Prospector Peak, you'll see Kaslo, Kootenay Lake, and the Purcells across the E horizon. Directly below (NE) are the Flint Lakes, the source of Carlyle Creek, which flows into Keen Creek.

TRIP 9 MISTY PEAK

ROUND TRIP	2 km (1.2 mi)
ELEVATION GAIN	259 m (850 ft)
HIKING TIME	1½ to 2 hours
DIFFICULTY	moderate

on foot

From **Carlyle Lodge** at 2195 m (7200 ft), follow the trail N toward Carpenter Pass. In about 7 minutes, at 2265 m (7430 ft), abandon the trail. Turn left, cross the **gully**, and continue SW.

Soon pass a **tarn** on a bench. A couple minutes beyond (about as far S as the lodge), turn right (W) and ascend the heathery slope.

The steep grade eases about 5 minutes above, at 2300 m (7544 ft), on the SE ridge of Misty Peak. Turn right and follow the **ridgecrest** upward (NNW), freelancing around obstacles as necessary.

Reach the 2454-m (8050-ft) summit of **Misty Peak** at 1 km (0.6 mi), about 50 minutes from Carlyle Lodge.

Misty Peak is an excellent vantage from which to survey West Kootenay hiking destinations. The Valhallas (Trips 20-21) are visible WSW. New Denver Glacier is W. Idaho Peak (Trip 6) is WNW. The *Norse Peaks* in Monashee Park (Trips 1-3) are NW. Reco Mtn is left of N. Beyond Reco is Marten Mtn near Alps Alturas (Trip 5). Whitewater Mtn (Trip 11) is N. Mt. Brennan (Trip 12), whose summit is split by a vertical couloir, is right of N. Texas Peak (Trip 10) is in front of and below Brennan. Four Squatters Glacier is NNE. MacBeth Icefield (Trip 15) is left of E. Prospector Peak is just beyond Carpenter Pass. Mt. Carlyle is E. Mt. Loki (Trip 30) is ESE. Snowcrest Mtn is distant SE. Cariboo Glacier is SSE. Woodbury Glacier (Trips 27 and 28) is S. Mt. Heyland (the black, snaggletooth peak also visible from the lodge) is nearby SSW.

Carpenter Creek Valley, from Misty Peak

TRIP 10
Texas Peak

LOCATION	Selkirks, Goat Range, between New Denver and Kaslo, S of Hwy 31A
ROUND TRIP	9.6 km (6 mi) to West Texas Peak 10.8 km (6.7 mi) to Texas Peak
ELEVATION GAIN	838 m (2749 ft) to West Texas Peak 1067 m (3500 ft) for Texas Peak
KEY ELEVATIONS	trailhead 1686 m (5530 ft), Reco-Texas Ridge 2135 m (7006 ft), West Texas Peak 2454 m (8050 ft) Texas Peak 2485 m (8150 ft)
HIKING TIME	4 to 5 hours for West Texas Peak 5 to 6 hours for Texas Peak
DIFFICULTY	moderate
TRAILHEAD ACCESS	easy
MAPS	Roseberry 82 K/3, Slocan 82 F/14

Opinion

In a mountain range where alpine terrain sometimes seems as elusive as Bigfoot, "quick access to alpine" is a meaningful badge of distinction. And that's but one of Texas Peak's enticements.

Driving to the trailhead is relatively easy. The trailhead access road is unpaved, of course, but it's neither rough nor steep and the distance is relatively short. From there, you'll continue hiking the road for about 45 minutes. It's steep, unaesthetic. But it's a speedy approach. Plus it allows you to see and appreciate the high country you're here to explore.

You'll be on a trail only briefly: along the crest of Reco-Texas Ridge. Beyond, you'll surge above treeline, hiking cross-country.

You're new to trail-less navigation? Here's a reasonable place to cultivate skill. The way forward remains apparent. Landmarks are distinct. Disorientation is unlikely.[1]

The hike climaxes as you ascend a broad, alpine slope. With grass underfoot, and rapidly swelling 360° views, the freedom to meander is exhilarating.

Shortly after greenery gives way to rock, you'll surmount an unnamed summit. We call it "West Texas Peak," because slightly-higher Texas Peak is very near.

A saddle separates the Texans. To cross it, you must scramble down, then up. It's an invitation, not a requirement. Attaining Texas Peak does add an athletic finale to the hike. But if you're short on will or daylight, relax on West Texas Peak. The Texas Peak panorama is little different.

---

1   Disorientation is always possible in the mountains. Never take cross-country navigation lightly. Always hike with keen, directional awareness, knowing your safety is your responsibility.

Whitewater Mtn (left), Mt. Brennan (right), from West Texas Peak

Texas Peak (left), West Texas Peak (right)

From either vantage, you'll see as many peaks as there are mining-claims in the region. In particular, you can survey Whitewater Mtn (Trip 11), Mt. Brennan (Trip 12), Mt. Jardine (Trip 13), and Mt. Carlyle (Trip 8), then decide which dayhike to do next.

Fact

by vehicle

In downtown **Kaslo**, drive NW on "A" Avenue. As it begins climbing, ignore North Marine Drive (Hwy 31N) on the right. Proceed uphill. Soon reach the intersection of "A" Avenue and Washington Street. Reset your trip odometer to 0 here. Turn left onto Washington, which becomes Hwy 31A. Follow it generally NW. At 27.3 km (17 mi) turn left (S) at the sign for Retallack Lodge. Again reset your trip odometer to 0.

In **New Denver**, reset your trip odometer to 0 at the junction of Hwys 6 and 31A (Union Street and 6th Avenue). Drive E on Hwy 31A (6th Avenue). Follow it generally NE. At 8.3 km (5.2 mi) proceed through Three Forks and pass Sandon Road (right). At 18.9 km (11.7 mi) turn right (S) at the sign for Retallack Lodge. Again reset your trip odometer to 0.

0 km (0 mi)
Turning S off Hwy 31A onto the unpaved road accessing Retallack Lodge. Cross the bridge. In 100 m (110 yd), fork right and ascend.

0.9 km (0.5 mi)
Bear right, ascending on Stenson Creek Road.

3.9 km (2.4 mi)
Fork right.

5.5 km (3.4 mi)
Bear left, ignoring the descending right fork.

6.9 km (4.3 mi)
Bear right and cross the bridge.

7.9 km (4.9 mi)
A creek is visible nearby left. The road switchbacks right.

8.7 km (5.4 mi)
Bear right, ignoring the descending left fork.

8.8 km (5.5 mi)
Pass a cabin (below, left).

9 km (5.6 mi)
Ignore the left spur leading to the creek. Proceed straight, then park on the left immediately before the road switchbacks right. Elevation: 1686 m (5530 ft).

At a conservative speed, you'll arrive here about 40 minutes after leaving the highway. Though the road beyond this pullout looks easy to drive, it soon steepens sharply and becomes rough. Better to walk.

on foot

Ascend the road, which immediately switchbacks right (N). In a couple minutes, arrive at a fork. Right continues N. Go left (WSW). The road soon steepens markedly and becomes much rougher.

In 15 minutes, ignore the right (NNW) fork. Proceed left (SW), ascending toward a low point on the ridge ahead (S). But keep this right fork in mind for another dayhike. It climbs the E face of Reco Mtn, granting access to Reco's long, N ridge, which—as you'll later see—is very inviting.

About 40 minutes from your vehicle, the **road briefly levels and curves right** (NW). Cairns on both sides, however, alert you not to continue in that direction. **Abandon the road**, which soon ends above among mine tailings. Forge left (SSW) onto a **narrow, bootbeaten, flagged route**. It leads in 3 minutes to the crest of **Reco-Texas Ridge** at 2.6 km (1.6 mi), 2135 m (7006 ft). Total hiking time: about 45 minutes from your vehicle.

Already the view is impressive. Across the Kaslo River Valley (N) is Whitewater Canyon (Trip 11), flanked by Whitewater Mtn (left) and Mt. Brennan (right, Trip 12). Brennan is recognizable by its split top and vertical couloir. Farther right (SE of Brennan) is Mt. Jardine (Trip 13). Farther left (NW of Whitewater) is Mt. Dolly Varden, which is near Alps Alturas (Trip 5).

Intersect a **trail atop the ridgecrest**. Right leads to Mt. Reco. Left leads to Texas Peak. Go left (E). The trail undulates along the slender crest. It's easy to follow for about 30 minutes, to where a **drainage** plummets left (NW) and the terrain immediately ahead (E) steepens sharply.

Go left (N) here. Dip into the **top of the drainage**, then ascend a path scuffed between tall trees. This path skirts the sharp terrain, quickly leading behind it, where the grade is slightly more laid back. Note this passage, so you'll recognize it on the return. Bear right (E), surging into the alpine zone on a **broad, grassy, flowery, steep, trail-less slope**.

Bear diggings, known as "bear tear," are prolific here—a reminder to be alert for bruins. Several of the excavations we saw resembled mini, mining shafts, suggesting the four-legged miners were enormous.

The panorama now expands rapidly. The Valhallas, punctuated by New Denver Glacier, are visible W. Inverness and Marten mountains are NNW.

The slope culminates at 4.4 km (2.7 mi), 2355 m (7725 ft), on a **crest above the Robb Creek drainage**. Total hiking time: about 1¾ hours from your vehicle. The E horizon is now visible, pulling your gaze beyond Kootenay Lake (hidden from view), into the Purcell Range. Four Squatters Glacier is NE. Glacier Creek Valley and Macbeth Icefield (Trip 15) are ENE. St. Mary's Alpine Provincial Park is E. Mt. Loki (Trip 30) is ESE.

Resume right (SE). Tenacious, alpine vegetation soon gives way to **scree and boulders**. Freelance upward to the (2454 m) 8050 ft summit we call **"West Texas Peak."** Total distance: 4.8 km (3 mi). Total hiking time: 2¼ hours. Here, Mt. Carlyle (Trip 8) is visible just left of S. Beyond it, directly S, is Kokanee Glacier.

Texas Peak is nearby (ENE). At 2485 m (8150 ft), it's the taller of the two Texans, but only slightly, so it's not scenically superior. It simply adds a note of finality to the day and grants an aerial view of a lake in the Utica Creek basin (SE). Most hikers will linger longer on West Texas Peak instead of undertaking the down-up scramble to the true summit.

Here are the approximate statistics for the scramble. Round-trip distance between the peaks: 1.2 km (0.7 mi). Descent from West Texas Peak: 99 m (325 ft). Low point between the peaks: 2355 m (7725 ft). Ascent to Texas Peak: 130 m (425 ft). Round-trip elevation gain between the peaks: 229 m (750 ft).

Returning from West Texas Peak, it's possible to reach the road below Reco-Texas Ridge in 1 hour, then descend the road to your vehicle in less than 30 minutes.

TRIP 11
Whitewater Canyon

LOCATION	Selkirks, Goat Range, between New Denver and Kaslo, N of Hwy 31A
ROUND TRIP	12.2 km (7.6 mi) to bench highpoint 14.2 km (8.8 mi) to Whitewater Tarn 15.8 km (9.8 mi) to Whitewater Col
ELEVATION GAIN	690 m (2263 ft) for bench highpoint 817 m (2680 ft) for Whitewater Tarn 988 m (3241 ft) for Whitewater Col
KEY ELEVATIONS	trailhead 1540 m (5051 ft), subalpine pocket 1950 m (6396 ft), Easter Island Rock 2040 m (6691 ft) bench highpoint 2200 m (7216 ft), Whitewater Pass 2160 m (7085 ft), Whitewater Tarn 2287 m (7500 ft) Whitewater Col 2458 m (8062 ft)
HIKING TIME	4 hours for bench highpoint, 5 hours for Whitewater Tarn, 6 hours for Whitewater Col
DIFFICULTY	moderate
TRAILHEAD ACCESS	moderate
MAP	Rosebery 82 K / 3

Opinion

A friend joined us for a hike up Whitewater Canyon. He's calm, cool headed, no more given to emotional outbursts than his totem animal, the stoic mountain goat. But here, he startled us. Nearing Whitewater Col, he bounded ahead, surveyed the wilderness in all directions and bellowed in excitement: "Ahhhhooooooooooooghaaaa!" It was a spontaneous, creative expression of joy, and an articulate description of the emotional effect this trip can have on a sensitive soul.

Trails in mountain canyons usually start at the canyon mouth and tediously ascend through forest. It can be a Roto-Rooter experience: an unscenic tour of the earth's plumbing. The Whitewater trail, however, leaps onto the canyon wall and soon breaks out of the trees. Frequent views allow you to appreciate this beautiful, untamed gash in the Selkirk Range and see where it's leading you. Midway up-canyon, as if to keep you entertained, the trail hops to the opposite wall. So hiking here is instantly enjoyable and remains intriguing and motivating all day.

Whitewater Pass, at the head of the canyon, is an excellent vantage point. From there, you can overlook your ascent route and peer down South Cooper Creek Valley, deep into the Goat Range, and beyond Duncan Lake to Macbeth Icefield (Trip 15). The pass is wedged between Whitewater Mtn and Mt. Brennan (Trip 12), so the view upward is equally impressive.

1

2

Meltwater from the modest glacier on Whitewater Mtn pools up in a teal tarn—a lakelet left behind by retreating ice. A few minutes of upward, cross-country effort will convey you from the pass to the shore of Whitewater Tarn. From the tarn—snow conditions permitting—it's an easy scramble to Whitewater Col, an exhilarating perch on the slender ridge that soars to the summit of 2768-m (9080-ft) Whitewater Mtn.

Fact

by vehicle

Low-clearance cars will struggle on the unpaved approach to this trailhead, due to water bars (trenches dug across the road to prevent erosion). Moderate clearance is necessary. High clearance is preferable. 4WD is ideal.

In downtown **Kaslo**, drive NW on "A" Avenue. As it begins climbing, ignore North Marine Drive (Hwy 31N) on the right. Proceed uphill. Soon reach the intersection of "A" Avenue and Washington Street. Reset your trip odometer to 0 here. Turn left onto Washington, which becomes Hwy 31A. Follow it generally NW. At 25.7 km (16 mi) cross Whitewater Creek. At 26.5 km (16.5 mi), just past the historic buildings, turn right (N) at the brown, *Whitewater Trail* sign.

In **New Denver**, reset your trip odometer to 0 at the junction of Hwys 6 and 31A (Union Street and 6th Avenue). Drive E on Hwy 31A (6th Avenue). Follow it generally NE. At 8.3 km (5.2 mi) proceed through Three Forks and pass Sandon Road (right). At 19.5 km (12.1 mi), just before the historic buildings, turn left (N) at the brown, *Whitewater Trail* sign.

0 km (0 mi)
Starting N. Pavement ends. Reset your trip odometer to 0. Proceed across the clearing. Begin ascending the rutted road.

200 m (200 yd)
Ascend right on the main road. Ignore the overgrown, level spur, sharp right. Proceed straight through the junction. Go left, following the sign. Ignore the left, descending, overgrown fork.

1.4 km (0.9 mi)
Fork left. Just beyond, ignore the overgrown left spur. Then continue ascending straight on the main road, ignoring the right fork.

2 km (1.2 mi)
New Denver Glacier, in the Valhallas, is visible WSW.

2.2 km (1.4 mi)
Negotiate a deep waterbar.

2.5 km (1.6 mi)
Ignore the left fork. Switchback right.

3.2 km (2 mi)
More water bars. Switchback left, following the sign.

3.5 km (2.2 mi)
Proceed straight on the main road. Ignore the right fork. Just beyond, ignore the left fork.

3.7 km (2.3 mi)
More water bars. The ascent briefly steepens.

4.3 km (2.7 mi)
About 200 m (220 yd) past mine tailings, enter the spacious, trailhead parking area, at 1540 m (5051 ft).

on foot

The trail departs the far (E) end of the parking area. Pass mine tailings (left). Briefly descend ESE. Soon pass a map / sign.

After jogging left (NNW), the trail curves right, heading generally NNE. It ascends to 1640 m (5379 ft), then contours. The lower slopes of Mt. Brennan (Trip 12) form the far wall of Whitewater Canyon, visible ahead. Whitewater Creek is audible.

At about 30 minutes, the creek is loud. Pass a signless post (right) and begin ascending left (N). At about 40 minutes, the trail angles left (NNW).

Look right (ENE), across the canyon. You can see the original Whitewater trail on the far canyon wall. It was closed, and the trail moved to where you are now, because those grassy slopes are prime habitat for grizzly bears.

Traverse three **boulder fields** above 1800 m (5906 ft). Here the trail is in the open: high on the steep, canyon wall, with rugged cliffs above (left). Distinctly pyramidal Mt. Loki (Trip 30) is visible SSE.

At 4.5 km (2.8 mi), 1950 m (6396 ft), about 1½ hours along, the trail drops into a grassy, creek fed, **subalpine pocket**. Pass a level campsite and the remains of an outhouse (right). Pause here, with a clear view up-canyon (NW).

Ahead is a massive rockslide. Above and slightly right (NNW) is a bench on the skirt hem of Mt. Brennan. Atop the bench is the rectangular,

Mt. Brennan, above Whitewater Canyon

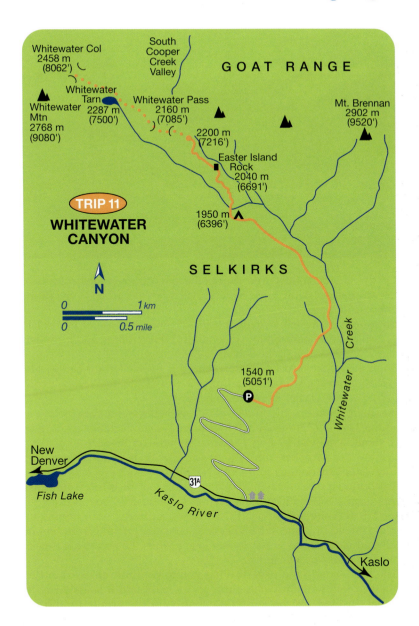

skyward-jutting boulder we call *Easter Island Rock*. That's your immediate goal. The trail passes behind the boulder and continues up the bench.

From near the campsite in the subalpine pocket, the trail proceeds straight (N) into the rockslide. But don't keep following it. Instead, descend right (NE) on a bootbeaten spur. Drop into the shallow **gorge** and work your way across the boulders covering **Whitewater Creek**.

Bench en route to highpoint. Whitewater Mtn beyond.

On the far side of the gorge, the bootbeaten route resumes, now ascending toward Easter Island Rock. Several paths fan out. Keep to the primary, switchbacking route.

Surmount the bench at 2040 m (6691 ft), near the base of Easter Island Rock. Trail resumes here. Follow it generally NNW, rolling and meandering upward along the crest of the bench.

Soon the massive rockslide you skirted is visible left (S) below. Ahead (NW) is an imposing wall culminating at 2768-m (9080-ft) Whitewater Mtn, with Whitewater Glacier frozen to its belly.

At about 2¼ hours, the trail levels above Whitewater Pass (below, left). This is the 2200-m (7216-ft) **bench highpoint**—a comfortable, scenic grandstand, should you wish to stop. Distance from the trailhead: 6.1 km (3.8 mi). But Whitewater Tarn, beneath Whitewater Glacier, is within easy reach. So is Whitewater Col, on the mountain's NE ridge.

To continue, descend left (WNW). Bottom-out in **Whitewater Pass** at 6.4 km (4 mi), 2160 m (7085 ft). It divides Whitewater Canyon from South Cooper Creek Valley (right / NE). The pass is littered with mining junk, including an old pipeline. If backpacking, consider pitching your tent here. The ground is level and grassy, water is available, the scenery is excellent, and the trip climaxes just above.

The trail ends in the pass, leaving you to continue cross-country. It's tempting to follow the pipeline through the pass, but it leads away from your goal. Instead, ascend left (NW). Find your own route up the steep, trackless terrain.

Whitewater Tarn is at 7.1 km (4.4 mi), 2287 m (7500 ft), about 2¾ hours from the trailhead. Visible SSE are the peaks of Kokanee Glacier Park. Round the tarn's right (NE) shore to examine car-size chunks of shiny, green serpentine. Then proceed left (NW), up the talus to 2458-m (8062-ft) **Whitewater Col**, at 7.9 km (4.9 mi), about 3¼ hours from the trailhead. There you can gaze across Kane Creek Canyon at Marten Mtn and peer more than 1067 m (3500 ft) into the canyon depths.

TRIP 12
Mt. Brennan

LOCATION	Selkirks, Goat Range, between New Denver and Kaslo, N of Hwy 31A
ROUND TRIP	14.6 km (9 mi)
ELEVATION GAIN	1525 m (5001 ft)
KEY ELEVATIONS	trailhead 1378 m (4520 ft), basin 2012 m (6600 ft) summit 2902 m (9521 ft)
HIKING TIME	8 to 10 hours
DIFFICULTY	challenging
TRAILHEAD ACCESS	challenging
MAP	Rosebery 82 K/3

Opinion

Though Kootenay Lake is girded by the peaky Selkirks and Purcells, the lake valley is so deep and narrow that views from the water's edge are generally limited to rounded, forested slopes. One exception is just north of Riondel. Standing on the rocky shore, facing northwest up the lake, much of the year you'll see a white crack in the otherwise green panorama. That crack is the snow-laden immensity of Mt. Brennan, 35 km (22 mi) distant, looming above Kaslo River Valley. Late summer through fall, the white fades to steel gray. It's an invitation. The mountain is saying to adventurous hikers: "Come on up!"

Do it. Brennan is a friendly giant. You can walk up his shoulder and dance on his head. No climbing skills required. Once the snow is gone, it's just a steep hike. A good trail leads 3.1 km (1.9 mi) into the upper cirque of Lyle Creek basin. This upper cirque is so ravishing you could be seduced into abandoning the ascent. Resist the temptation to stop and plop. Though the cascade, lakelets, meadows and steep walls make this an exceptionally beautiful enclave, it's not the scenic climax of the trip. You're less than half way. Proceed up the trail, then continue following the cairned route. An astonishing sight awaits you on the mountaintop.

Brennan affords one of the grandest views of any hiker-accessible perch in the West Kootenay. The summit panorama is studded with significant landmarks, including Four Squatters Glacier, the Bugaboo Spires, Kootenay Lake, MacBeth Icefield, glaciers near Jumbo Pass, even the Rocky Mountains. On subsequent West Kootenay hikes, Brennan will be one of the landmarks you seek on the horizon. Spotting it will be gratifying, like meeting an old friend in a crowd.

If the cairns between the upper cirque and the summit are no longer in place, don't worry. The route is easy, with lots of leeway and no technical difficulties. Experienced off-trail hikers won't need directions; they'll find the ascent logical, straightforward. Everyone else can rely on our *on foot* description. It's sufficiently detailed so you don't have to bounce off every cairn like a human pinball. Just don't attempt to surmount Brennan before late July. Wait until most

Upper Lyle Creek basin

of the snowpack has melted. The route we suggest will be recognizable then. And a slip-and-slide injury will be less likely.

Grizzly-bear sightings are common between the trailhead and the upper cirque. Be alert and make noise. The rocky environs above that provide little or no bear food, so you can relax your guard somewhat on the rest of the ascent.

Fact

by vehicle

The entire area, just S of Goat Range Provincial Park, is riddled with mining claims that have made access problematic for hikers. The Forest Service negotiated easements for this passage. You'll need a strong, high-clearance vehicle, preferably 4WD, to vanquish more than 50 waterbars en route.

In downtown **Kaslo**, drive NW on "A" Avenue. As it begins climbing, ignore North Marine Drive (Hwy 31N) on the right. Proceed uphill. Soon reach the intersection of "A" Avenue and Washington Street. Reset your trip odometer to 0 here. Turn left onto Washington, which becomes Hwy 31A. Follow it generally NW. At 23.5 km (14.6 mi) turn right (NE) onto Rossiter Road. It's just before Rossiter Creek bridge.

In **New Denver**, reset your trip odometer to 0 at the junction of Hwys 6 and 31A (Union Street and 6th Avenue). Drive E on Hwy 31A (6th Avenue). Follow it generally NE. At 8.3 km (5.2 mi) proceed through Three Forks and pass Sandon Road (right). At 22.7 km (14.1 mi) turn left (NE) onto Rossiter Road. It's just after Rossiter Creek bridge.

Reset your trip odometer to 0 starting on unpaved Rossiter Road. At 1 km (0.6 mi) bear left and ascend. At 2.4 km (1.5 mi) go left, staying on the main road. At 3.8 km (2.4 mi) cross a bridged creek. At 5.9 km (3.7 mi) bear left. At 7 km (4.3 mi) park at a switchback curve. Elevation: 1378 m (4520 ft).

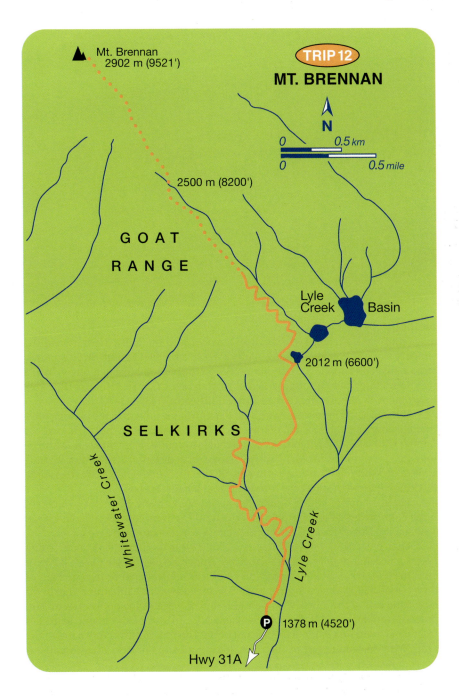

Mt. Brennan
2902 m (9521')

TRIP 12

MT. BRENNAN

N

0   0.5 km

0   0.5 mile

2500 m (8200')

G O A T

R A N G E

Lyle
Creek   Basin

2012 m (6600')

S E L K I R K S

Whitewater Creek

Lyle Creek

1378 m (4520')

Hwy 31A

Ascending Mt. Brennan

on foot

From the switchback curve, drop 2 m/yd into the gully. Then ascend the slippery slope, following flagging. Quickly reach a **road** and go left. In 10 minutes, cross a creek on a footlog. Continue WNW on the old road through forest. In just over 15 minutes, join the original access road signed LYLE TRAIL. Turn right (N). In a total of 40 minutes, reach the **former trailhead** at 1433 m (4700 ft).

The trail starts immediately right of the sign at the far end of the parking area. Initially your general direction of travel is NW. Don't set out on the barricaded old mining road. Despite switchbacks, the ascent is instantly steep. Brush, however, is minimal. Soon rejoin the old mining road for a short distance, then resume on trail. Cross a rockslide and traverse the **headwall** directly N of the trailhead. Then curve N, climbing through subalpine forest and huckleberry bushes.

About 1 hour of hiking grants you an expanded view. SW is the prominent ridge culminating at Idaho Lookout. Beyond it (right) is New Denver Glacier in Valhalla Provincial Park. The Kokanee Range is S, across Kaslo Creek Valley.

After gaining 579 m (1900 ft) in 3.1 km (1.9 mi)—a task that takes strong hikers a little more than 1 hour—enter the **upper cirque of Lyle Creek Basin** at 2012 m (6600 ft). A dramatic cascade leaps off the headwall to feed a chain of three small lakes. Surrounding them are meadows and subalpine forest. To assess the rest of the journey, angle right, rockhop across the outlet stream, and proceed until more of Mt. Brennan is visible NW. To resume the ascent, angle left from where you first entered the upper cirque. The trail climbs across a rockslide. From here on, you're out of the trees, hiking mostly on rock, occasionally on grass or heather.

Switchbacking up the SW side of a creek gorge, you can soon see Mt. Loki (Trip 30) and Kootenay Lake, both SE. Near the head of the gorge, turn left (S) onto rockier terrain. The trail is cairned, still discernible here, but disappears just above, near the abandoned **mining shafts along a mineral seam**.

Go left (SW) along the mineral seam for a couple minutes, then ascend NW toward a narrow, shallow gap in the chunky, white rocks. That gap leads to a **tarn** clutched in a rocky declivity. Following cairns, ascend the small ridge right of the tarn. At 2271 m (7450 ft), about 30 minutes from the upper cirque, the ice-splattered peaks of Kokanee Provincial Park are visible S. Your goal, the summit of Mt. Brennan, reveals most of its bulk NW.

From the small ridge above the tarn, ascend N. Cross a creeklet, angle right (NE), and attain the next ridge. Go left (NW) for a few minutes, then proceed through a cleft in the ridge and follow that draw N. The ascent eases now.

Whitewater Mtn and glacier, from summit of Mt. Brennan

Head toward the first big, **year-round snowfield**. Ascend steeply right of it. The ascent eases again just above. A wide, vertical **vein of white and brown rocks** provides a natural pathway toward the summit. Follow it. Go left around the next, even **bigger snowfield**. The top of Mt. Brennan is obvious now. Take aim and work your way up the bouldery slope to the **summit** cairn: 2902 m (9521 ft). Strong hikers will be high-fiving each other 1¾ hours from the upper cirque, or 3¾ hours after departing their vehicle. Total elevation gain: 1525 m (5001 ft).

Given a clear day, the 360° horizon is crowded with prominent, recognizable features. These are a few of the highlights. NNE is Four Squatters Glacier; beyond are the Bugaboo Spires. NE is Kootenay Lake; beyond is MacBeth Icefield (Trip 15); farther yet are glaciers in the upper Glacier Creek valley N of Jumbo Pass (Trip 17); and way beyond are the Rocky Mountain peaks of Kootenay National Park. ESE are domino-like spires in the Purcell Wilderness Conservancy. S are glaciers in Kokanee Glacier Provincial Park. Below (SW) is Whitewater Creek Canyon (Trip 11). Directly W is Whitewater Mtn, with a small glacier on its face and a tarn below. Distant NNW are the Monashees. Cascades at the headwaters of South Cooper Creek Canyon are below (N).

TRIP 13
Mt. Jardine

LOCATION	Selkirks, Goat Range, between New Denver and Kaslo, S of Hwy 31A
ROUND TRIP	14.4 km (8.9 mi) to W ridge highpoint 15 km (9.3 mi) to summit
ELEVATION GAIN	1113 m (3651 ft) to W ridge highpoint 1205 m (3952 ft) for summit
KEY ELEVATIONS	trailhead parking 1295 m (4248 ft), trailhead 1280 m (4198 ft), W ridge highpoint 2378 m (7800 ft) summit 2442 m (8012 ft)
HIKING TIME	5 to 6 hours for W ridge highpoint 6 to 7 hours for summit
DIFFICULTY	challenging due to brief route-finding plus significant elevation gain
TRAILHEAD ACCESS	moderate due to water bars
MAP	Rosebery 82 K/3

Opinion

In 1891, "Lardo" McDonald, Jack Allen and Andy Jardine discovered silver in the Kaslo River Valley, between Kootenay and Slocan lakes. Their claim, called *the Beaver*, sparked other prospectors' interest. The valley was soon generating enormous wealth.

The Beaver claim never became a producing mine. Yet it was pivotal in the flash-transformation of the West Kootenay. Subsequent successful mines attracted legions of fortune seekers who turned a tranquil wilderness into a beehive of industry: the source of more than 60% of Canada's silver production.

So when a friend told us, "The trail to the Beaver claim is still there," we were rapt. "It's in surprisingly good condition," he said. "Easy to follow, even though almost nobody's walked it for more than a century. And it launches you above treeline, because that's where the claim was: on an alpine ridge." The next day, we were following him up the trail.

He was right. It's a premier hike leading to the west ridge of Mt. Jardine, where you can cruise the ridgecrest past the Beaver claim stake (yes, the original one), or press on to the summit. Either way, you'll admire a peaky panorama.

Approaching the west ridge, the trail does eventually fizzle. About 30 minutes of routefinding ensue. But our detailed directions should make that a simple, connect-the-dots exercise if you have some confidence born of cross-country hiking experience.

Until the final approach, the trail is always discernible, usually distinct, only occasionally faint. And it switchbacks frequently, so the ascent is comfortable. Only during the final approach, however, is the hike notably scenic. On the forested ascent below, it's the trail itself that intrigues.

The miners navigated a vast, trackless forest, pinpointed the silver atop Mt. Jardine's west ridge, forged the trail, then trudged up and down countless times?

Whitewater Mtn (left), Mt. Brennan (right), from Mt. Jardine's west ridge

Astonishing. Of all the trails in the West Kootenay, this one—nearly forgotten—is of legendary significance? Fascinating. And it remains hikeable after 100 years of disuse? Miraculous.

Help maintain a national monument. Hike to Mt. Jardine and keep this venerable trail pounded into the mountainside.

Fact

by vehicle

Low-clearance cars will struggle on the final, unpaved approach to this trailhead, due to numerous water bars (trenches dug across the road to prevent erosion). Moderate clearance is necessary. High clearance is preferable. 4WD is ideal.

In downtown **Kaslo**, drive NW on "A" Avenue. As it begins climbing, ignore North Marine Drive (Hwy 31N) on the right. Proceed uphill. Soon reach the intersection of "A" Avenue and Washington Street. Reset your trip odometer to 0 here. Turn left onto Washington, which becomes Hwy 31A. Follow it generally NW. At 23.5 km (14.6 mi) turn right (NE) onto Rossiter Road. It's just before Rossiter Creek bridge.

In **New Denver**, reset your trip odometer to 0 at the junction of Hwys 6 and 31A (Union Street and 6th Avenue). Drive E on Hwy 31A (6th Avenue). Follow it generally NE. At 8.3 km (5.2 mi) proceed through Three Forks and pass Sandon Road (right). At 22.7 km (14.1 mi) turn left (NE) onto Rossiter Road. It's just after Rossiter Creek bridge.

0 km (0 mi)
Starting on unpaved Rossiter Road.

1 km (0.6 mi)
Bear left on the main road and ascend steeply. Ignore the Wagon Road right (E).

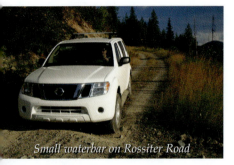

Small waterbar on Rossiter Road

2.4 km (1.5 mi)
Ascend right. Ignore the descending left spur.

2.5 km (1.6 mi)
Follow the main road right.

4.1 km (2.5 mi)
Note the cairned trail departing the left (NW) side of the road, but drive slightly farther to the narrow pullout on the right. Park here, at 1295 m (4248 ft).

on foot

Descend the road to the **cairned** trail on the right, at 1280 m (4198 ft). Follow the trail NNW into forest. A switchbacking ascent ensues. Your general direction of travel will be NE.

About 1 hour up, Mt. Jardine's S flank is visible right (E). The reddish trees were beetle infested and are now dead; they're known as *beetle kill*. Above this viewpoint, huckleberry bushes are prolific.

The trail soon follows a **ridge**, ascending the left (W) slope below the crest. About 1⅓ hours from the trailhead, Whitewater Mtn (Trip 11) is visible left (WNW).

For about 10 minutes, the trail is narrow, traversing in the open. It then returns to forest. Cross an unbridged creeklet (possibly dry) at 2020 m (6626 ft). About 5 minutes farther, at 2042 m (6698 ft), nearly 1¾ hours along, pass the remains of a cabin (left). About 46 m (50 yd) farther, in the gully (right), is a spring where you can refill waterbottles.

About 10 minutes past the former cabin, or nearly 2 hours from the trailhead, the way forward (N) has been intentionally blocked with tree branches by previous hikers. **Pause here**, at 2127 m (6977 ft).

The ridge you'll ultimately surmount is visible ahead (N). There are many ways to get there. Any direct route you choose will be trail-less and steep. The most gradual ascent, which we outline below, is indirect. It, too, is largely cross-country but comprises a few, helpful scraps of bootbeaten path.

For the gradual, indirect ascent, turn right (E) at 2127 m (6977 ft). Follow a passage through **avalanche deadfall**.

In a couple minutes, exit the avalanche deadfall and enter a N-S swath of **meadow** edged by trees. Turn left (N). See route photo 1.

Follow the meadowy swath for about 70 m (77 yd). Just shy of the hip-high, broken trees at the top of the meadow, turn right (E) into a **clearing**.

Quickly approach mature trees. Turn left (N), ascending between a rock outcrop (left / W) and the wall of trees (right / E).

Follow this **channel** for about 20 m/yd. Then turn right (E) into a depression edged with embedded boulders.

After ascending about 15 m (49 ft), angle left (NNE) on a distinct, **bootbeaten path**. Your immediate goal is the crest of the low, N-S ridge just ahead.

Atop the **ridgecrest**, go left (N) following scraps of bootbeaten path. A short detour right (E) will grant you an aerial view of a tarn in a basin beneath Mt. Jardine.

Resuming N on the ridgecrest, soon reach a **big cairn** at 2160 m (7085 ft). See route photo 2.

Just past the big cairn, angle left (NNW), descending briefly, then ascending on grass, among exposed rock and a few trees. See route photo 3.

Soon surpass most of the trees. The slope eases and is more meadowy. Just beneath a **band of scree**, curve right (NNE). See route photo 4.

About 15 minutes beyond the big cairn, top out on **Mt. Jardine's W ridge** at 6.7 km (4.2 mi), 2270 m (7448 ft). See route photo 5.

Total hiking time: about 2¾ hours. You're just above and W of the ridge lowpoint.

Mt. Jardine towers nearby (ENE). The route to the 2442-m (8012-ft) summit is obvious: descend E to the 2256-m (7400-ft) W ridge lowpoint, then ascend the open slope NE. Distance from the trailhead: 7.5 km (4.7 mi).

The scenery is vast in all directions. Left (NW) is 2902-m (9521-ft) Mt Brennan (Trip 12). Farther left (WNW) is 2768-m (9081-ft) Whitewater Mtn (Trip 11). Immediately below you (NW) is the headwaters basin of Rossiter Creek. In the opposite direction (SW), beyond the Kaslo River Valley (*Silver Avenue*, Trip 44), is Texas Peak (Trip 10). And that's but a sliver of the panorama.

Upon arriving atop Mt. Jardine's W ridge, Kootenay Lake is also visible far below (SSE). And you'll see more of it if you hike W along the ridgecrest. Continuing briefly in that direction is essential if you don't pursue the summit.

Proceeding W along the crest of the W ridge, pass a mining claim (marked by a weathered, wood post), then reach the 2378-m (7800-ft) **W ridge highpoint** in about 15 minutes. Distance from the trailhead: 7.2 km (4.5 mi). Whitewater Mtn now appears impressively close. Having declined the summit of Mt. Jardine, you'll earn a satisfying sense of completion here.

At a determined pace, it's possible to return to the trailhead in 1¾ hours.

TRIP 14
Silvercup Ridge

LOCATION	Selkirks, NE of Trout Lake
ROUND TRIP	39.5 km (24.5 mi) from NW trailhead to Ottawa Creek overlook
ELEVATION GAIN	1190 m (3900 ft) plus
KEY ELEVATIONS	NW trailhead 1230 m (4035 ft), Rue du Beau trailhead 1524 m (5000 ft), Ottawa Creek overlook 2305 m (7560 ft) Silvercup Ridge 2150 m (7050 ft)
HIKING TIME	2 to 4 days
DIFFICULTY	moderate
TRAILHEAD ACCESS	moderate
MAPS	Trout Lake 82 K/11, Lardeau 82 K

Opinion

The average North American walks less than 121 km (75 mi) per year. That's about 2.3 km (1.4 mi) per week. Or just two city blocks per day. As a result, 85% of us are essentially sedentary. And 35% of us are totally sedentary. We have bodies capable of marching with Caesar, yet we use them only to shuffle across the room, or waddle across the street. Any farther than that, we drive.

But you're obviously way above average. You're reading about the longest sustained ridgewalk in the West Kootenay. Congratulations. You've picked an exhilarating adventure worthy of your marvelous physicality.

Hiking in the mountains is usually up, up, up, then down, down, down. Not on Silvercup Ridge. Here, once you're up, you stay up. You keep cruising near treeline, happily devoting your energy to striding rather than grinding. It feels less like an ordeal, more like a celebration.

Comfortable, scenic campsites are abundant. Tarns and trickles are frequent, so water is plentiful. Meadows are extensive, because you're always in the zone: upper subalpine to alpine. Wildflowers are usually profuse by late July. Best of all, views are nearly constant, with enough voltage to hot-wire your emotions.

The trail—alternating between a well-defined path, an abandoned mining road, and a cairned route—runs the length of Silvercup Ridge. It stays just west of and below the crest. The snowcapped Lardeau Range (part of the Selkirk Mountains) and 24.5-km (15-mi) long, turquoise Trout Lake are visible so frequently you might take them for granted.

Heading SE, as recommended, the scenery intensifies. The peaks and glaciers SW are increasingly prominent and arresting. Near 20 km (12.5 mi), the Ottawa Creek drainage breaks the ridge, allowing you a long-distance view in a new direction: north to the stirring Badshot Range.

About that mining road. It's a scar. A long one. And you'll be walking it a big chunk of the way. Purists will find it rudely interrupts their reverie. And what hiker wouldn't feel a flash of resentment if one of those average North

Americans statistically described above came putt-putting along on an ATV? Accept it: the road is there, and an ATV encounter is possible. But if it weren't for this road and the connecting network built by miners and loggers, few if any hikers would bust their nut through 1220 vertical meters (4000 ft) of forest to attain Silvercup Ridge.

You've got to wonder: Is hiking in a road-accessible backcountry area, like this one, safe during hunting season? Maybe—if you wear blaze-orange clothing and stay on the trail/road/route—but not necessarily. So plan to hike Silvercup Ridge before hunting season. It starts the second week of September.

The cairned-route section of the ridge, beyond Ottawa Creek overlook, is several kilometers long. Though the cairns are infrequent and not always obvious, experienced off-trail backpackers should be unfazed and will probably enjoy a heightened sense of exploration. Heading southeast, you'll follow a natural, logical course, easily recognizable to the trained eye. Our explicit directions should clarify any uncertainties.

You're an off-trail newbie? Choose another trip, or at least don't go beyond Laughton Creek basin, because the navigation challenge could overwhelm you, especially in the limited-visibility weather that's common at this elevation.

A compass is essential equipment for any hiker, anywhere. On this trip, bring a topo map if you might want to scramble up Fays Peak, where a dayhike circuit is possible.

Now, consider your options: (1) Start at the northwest trailhead, backpack southeast along the ridge, set up a basecamp, then dayhike to the Ottawa Creek overlook or beyond. (2) Drive Rue du Beau to within 3 km (1.9 mi) of the mining road atop Silvercup Ridge, then dayhike or backpack southeast to the Ottawa Creek overlook or beyond.

Backpacking from the northwest trailhead begins with a demanding ascent. The access road is overgrown. At the time of publication, there was no promise it might be cleared, so expect to hike the whole 3.5 km (2.2 mi). Your reward? Communing with a beautiful, mature forest, and enjoying the wildest section of the trip, where the heavy hand of man is least evident. Starting here, you'll gain a more complete appreciation for Silvercup Ridge, and you'll feel a greater sense of accomplishment. Driving Rue de Beau, however, will save you 1½ to 2 hours of hard labour on the ascent. You'll start hiking near where the views begin to expand. Both options have merit.

Scenic campsites are abundant on Silvercup Ridge.

Fact

trailhead access

(1) A nameless logging road accesses the NW trailhead. It's initially steep but does not climb high. At the time of publication, however, it was overgrown—impassable beyond 2 km (1.2 mi)—and there was no promise it might be cleared. If you park at the bottom (near Hwy 31, at 965 m / 3165 ft), the round trip lengthens by 7 km (4.3 mi) and the elevation gain increases by 265 m (870 ft).

(2) Rue du Beau accesses the mining road atop Silvercup Ridge. After a long, steep climb, it tops out near the NW end of the ridge. Two-thirds of it is in good condition and passable in a strong 2WD car to within 3 km (1.9 mi) of the mining road. To go farther, high-clearance is necessary. 4WD is preferable. There's confusion regarding the name. It's signed Rue du Beau, derived from Le Beau Creek, which the road's first switchback grazes. The Forest Service, however, calls it Copper Queen Road, because it ascends to the headwaters of Copper Queen Creek.

by vehicle

To reach the above access roads, **from the junction of Hwys 23 and 31** (just uphill from Galena Bay ferry terminal on Upper Arrow Lake), drive E on Hwy 31. Proceed 28.2 km (17.5 mi) to a signed intersection with John Street, which leads W into the **village of Trout Lake**. This intersection is 100 meters N of a bridge over Lardeau River. Reset your trip odometer to 0 at the intersection before continuing SE on Hwy 31. Pavement soon ends.

To reach the above access roads, **from the village of Lardeau** (at the N end of Kootenay Lake), drive NW on Hwy 31. Proceed 82.5 km (51.2 mi) to **Gerrard**, at the SE end of Trout Lake, where a bridge crosses Lardeau River. Reset your trip odometer to 0.

(1) For the nameless logging road, either (A) continue SE 8.3 km (5.1 mi) on Hwy 31 from the Trout Lake village intersection, then turn sharply left (N); or (B) continue NW 19 km (11.8 mi) on Hwy 31 from the Lardeau River bridge at Gerrard, then fork right (N). The nameless road is 1 km (0.6 mi) NW of Rue du Beau, and just beyond a creek culvert. It's also 200 m SE of the KM 28 sign. Reset your trip odometer to 0.

The nameless road is steep for 2.2 km (1.3 mi), until crossing a creek at 1130 m (3705 ft). Most vehicles should make it that far. About 100 m (110 yd) before the creek, the road is wide enough for one vehicle to park. Proceed only in a 4WD vehicle you're unconcerned about scratching.

Beyond the creek, enter a brushy clearcut. Where the road levels, proceed straight. Ignore a smaller road forking right (S). You might notice mining-claim signs on trees. Proceed through a clearcut. Alder and brush are swallowing the road. Where a rocky outcrop is visible on the slope above (right / E), look for a brown signpost nearby, right. It indicates the beginning of the Silvercup Ridge trail. Just beyond—at 3.5 km (2.2 mi), 1230 m (4035 ft)—a pullout on the left might still accommodate a couple vehicles.

Fays Peak, near south end of Silvercup Ridge

(2) For Rue du Beau, either (A) continue SE 9.3 km (5.8 mi) on Hwy 31 from the Trout Lake village intersection; or (B) continue NW 18 km (11.2 mi) on Hwy 31 from the Lardeau River bridge at Gerrard. From either approach, turn E onto the broad, graded road signed Rue du Beau. The elevation here is 965 m (3165 ft). Reset your trip odometer to 0.

Switchback upward through regrowing clearcuts. Park in the cutblock at 6.2 km (3.8 mi), 1524 m (5000 ft). The road beyond was long ago deactivated and left unmaintained. At the time of publication, mining-claim signs, surveillance cameras, and a gate were in place near 8 km (5 mi). Don't tamper with any equipment, but keep hiking.

Continuing from the 6.2-km (3.8-mi) fork, go right, and climb an older, narrower road. Ascend through a pretty hemlock forest. At 8.1 km (5 mi), 1777 m (5830 ft), reach another fork. Go left and ascend.

Crest timberline at 8.6 km (5.3 mi). The remaining, very steep 0.7 km (0.4 mi) is badly eroded, with lots of loose rock. Intersect the **Silvercup Ridge mining road** at 9.3 km (5.8 mi), 2070 m (6790 ft). Go right (SE). Follow our *On Foot* directions on page 103, starting at 7.7 km (4.8 mi). You'll be on the mining road for about the next 2 km (1.2 mi).

on foot

The following directions will lead you along the entire length of Silvercup Ridge, from NW to SE. Overall, your general direction of travel will be SE. You'll be W of and well below the ridgecrest most of the way.

At the **NW trailhead** (1230 m / 4035 ft), a small white sign depicts a horse and hikers. You'll see more of these signs, as well as orange or white-and-orange blazes, along the trail. The road sections of the route, however, are neither blazed nor signed.

Initially follow the trail through a brushy, regrowing **clearcut** for about 0.5 km (0.3 mi). In 10 minutes, at 1280 m (4200 ft), enter a **mature forest** of mostly

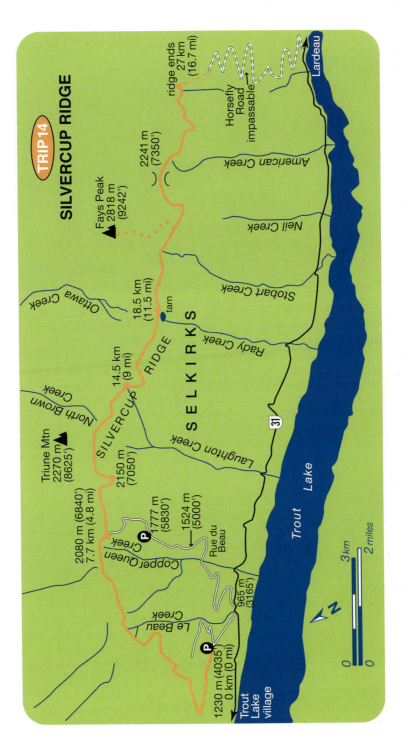

TRIP 14

SILVERCUP RIDGE

ridge ends
27 km
(16.7 mi)

Lardeau

Fays Peak
2818 m
(9242')

2241 m
(7350')

Horsefly
Road
impassable

American Creek

Neil Creek

Stobart Creek

Ottawa Creek

18.5 km
(11.5 mi)

tarn

SELKIRKS

Rady Creek

North Brown Creek

14.5 km
(9 mi)

SILVERCUP RIDGE

31

Triune Mtn
2270 m
(8625')

2150 m
(7050')

Laughton Creek

Trout Lake

2080 m (6840')
7.7 km (4.8 mi)

1777 m
(5830')

1524 m
(5000')

Copper Queen Creek

Rue du
Beau

965 m
(3165')

Le Beau Creek

1230 m (4035')
0 km (0 mi)

Trout
Lake
village

N

3 km

2 miles

0

0

Silvercup Ridge

western hemlocks. The path is clearly defined and easy to follow as it heads generally E, ascending moderately through cool forest with lush undergrowth.

About 20 minutes along, at the top edge of a clearcut, Trout Lake is visible below. A few minutes farther, re-enter forest and continue just within its margin. Expect deadfall to impede your progress. The deeper you penetrate the forest and the farther you are from the clearcut, the less deadfall. The trees on the edge have no protection from wind and are thus more prone to topple.

Passing several noble, giant Douglas firs, enter the drainage of an **unnamed creek**. Even after an exceptionally dry summer, this creek was still burbling in September. About 1 hour from the trailhead, at 1433 m (4700 ft), cross the second branch of this reliable creek. Nearing 1524 m (5000 ft), you'll leave the big trees behind. Negotiate more troublesome deadfall, then begin a long, steeply ascending traverse.

After about 1¾ hours, strong hikers will reach 1600 m (5250 ft), where glacier-draped Tenderfoot Mtn is visible SSE, 25 km (15.5 mi) beyond Trout Lake. From here, the trail curves noticeably NE, then heads N, away from Trout Lake views.

At 1860 m (6100 ft)—about 2 hours of determined hiking from the trailhead—the **path levels**. Rejoice. You've vanquished most of the climb. Total elevation gain so far: 630 m (2065 ft). The rest of the gain to Ottawa Creek overlook is in small segments scattered over a long distance.

The forest is now predominantly Engelmann spruce and subalpine fir. The trail bends W briefly before meandering N, then gets back on course E. Huckleberry bushes abound. About 20 minutes of this easy striding will bring you to a small meadow in a depression—the **first viable campsite**, and a comfortable place to drop packs and rest. Beyond, the forest is broken by more of these fragrant **heather meadows**.

Looking NW from an open area, you can see several big peaks including icy Mt. Pool. Proceed SE. Upon reaching 2000 m (6560 ft), a more extensive view NW includes solitary Mt. Begbie, near Revelstoke.

A bit farther, at 6.4 km (4 mi), 2040 m (6690 ft), having hiked about 3 hours from the trailhead, attain a **revelatory view** SE over most of Silvercup Ridge. You're now 1325 m (4345 ft) above Trout Lake. See the road dropping from the ridge crest, down through a clearcut, toward the lake? That's Rue du Beau. By granting vehicle access to Silvercup Ridge, it makes dayhiking more feasible. It also offers backpackers an escape route down to Hwy 31.

From where most of the ridge is visible, the trail ushers you onto the **old mining road** that will be your path for roughly the next 3.6 km (2.2 mi). In 0.8 km (0.5 mi), the road curves through a meadow where flat ground and a fine view might tempt you to camp despite the lack of water.

At 7.7 km (4.8 mi), 2070 m (6790 ft), having hiked about 4 hours from the trailhead, reach a junction with **Rue du Beau**. It forks right, descending from the road you've been following. Stay on the main road, ascending left to gain 60 m (197 ft). Continue enjoying expansive views of the Lardeau Range, W and SW, beyond Trout Lake.

About 7 minutes past Rue du Beau junction, a smaller, rougher road forks left. It quickly ascends to an open, grassy bench—another attractive but waterless campsite. Stay on the main road as it curves left (E), gradually descending into the **headwater basin of Burg Creek**. You'll be facing Triune Mtn.

About 35 minutes past Rue du Beau junction, at 10.1 km (6.3 mi), 2105 m (6900 ft), pass a **lakelet** with a meadowy shoreline. It's easily reached, just below the road, and offers comfortable, reasonably sheltered camping. At lake level, however, trees block views W. And the ridgecrest E blocks early-morning sunlight. So try to push on. A superior campsite awaits you about 1 hour and 20 minutes SE.

Soon pass another **tarn**, below on the right. The **mining road ends** shortly beyond. Bear left into a **trough** between two hills, then descend. The trail is now very faint. Drop another 7 m (23 ft) to where the trail is again distinct though still narrow, little more than a game path. Disuse and lack of maintenance are taking a toll. Erosion and brush are slowly diminishing the tread, but it's still hikeable. Contour left, rounding a forested shoulder. Look back and take note of where you exited the trough, so on the return trip you'll recognize this easily-overlooked but important landmark.

About 10 minutes beyond the trough, cross a **rockslide** where Trout Lake and the mountainous, W horizon are visible. As on most of this hike, the ridge crest is above you, preventing views E, but the scenery is nevertheless vast and impressive. You're now contouring at about 2150 m (7050 ft), entering **Laughton Creek drainage**, gradually turning E.

This is an exciting leg of the journey, because the narrow, airy trail is in open, subalpine forest, on the edge of a steep slope. Profuse berry bushes here turn deep purple and brilliant scarlet by September.

After the rockslide, enter a little bowl where the **trail splits**. The right fork, marked with a cairn atop a big boulder, descends deeper into forest. It's possible to go that way, but don't; it's more complicated and taxing. Take the left fork. It stays higher, provides better views, and leads directly to the next tarn.

Forking left, climb to the top of a grassy defile. Just beyond is the **tarn, in a broad, meadowy, E-W pass**, at 2256 m (7400 ft). Here you'll find one of the two most desirable campsites along the entire ridge (the other is at the headwater

basin of Rady Creek), and the most stirring scenery since departing the N trailhead. Above (N) is 2270-m (8625-ft) Triune Mtn. The **North Brown Creek drainage** descends NE into the depths of upper Lardeau Creek valley.

Resuming your Silvercup trek, aim for the talusy ridge to the S and pick up the old mining road. A short ascent over a shoulder leads to a long descent into the **headwater basin of Laughton Creek** at 14.5 km (9 mi). Fast hikers can reach the basin in 2 hours from Rue du Beau junction.

The road carves a semi-circle around the upper basin. A rugged, unnamed mountain towers to your left (E) and the verdant, tarn-dotted basin is in full view below to your right. Good campsites abound. Ignore the road that forks left and rockets up a talus slope. Stay on the main road and hop across the outlet stream just beneath the first big tarn.

The road contours briefly at about 2180 m (7150 ft), then descends. About 30 minutes after crossing the first tarn's outlet, round the W-jutting shoulder that forms the basin's S wall. Pay attention here. Where the road turns S and descends, the trail resumes left (SE). Look for **blazes and a horse/hiker sign**. Do not continue on the road. Follow the trail as it ascends the shoulder through subalpine forest. Soon cross another road and keep ascending. See a small lake well below the trail. Tenderfoot and Spyglass mountains and the Goat Range are visible S.

The **trail fades** in the open grassy expanses at the head of the next small basin. But staying precisely on the trail is unnecessary. Simply continue the pattern you've been following all along the ridge: cross a shoulder, traverse the head of the basin, cross the next shoulder, traverse the head of the next basin, etc. And in this basin, your goal will become obvious as you proceed. Look for a large barren patch of dark, rusty-brown soil—a mining scar. Just above it is where you'll cross the shoulder that forms the basin's S wall.

Proceeding across the grass, the trail follows barely visible remnants of an old, two-track road. Watch for blazes and white horse/hiker signs on small trees. After a short rise, a blaze indicates where the trail drops to the headwaters of the basin's unnamed stream. Rockhop across then ascend directly S through the **barren patch of dark soil**. (When returning NW through this basin, look for an orange blaze indicating where the trail ascends from the stream.)

Beyond this shoulder, you'll once more be traversing the head of a basin and climbing another shoulder. Though the trail again fades in the grass, the way is clear: ESE, grazing a lovely, **long tarn**. It feeds the **Rady Creek drainage** below (right / W). At 18.5 km (11.5 mi), 2238 m (7340 ft), this tarn's meadowy shore is one of the two most desirable campsites along the ridge. (The other is in the pass above the North Brown Creek drainage.) Views here are across Trout Lake to the myriad peaks of the Goat Range. Early morning sunlight reaches the tarn sooner than most other potential campsites along the Silvercup route.

Atop the next shoulder, SE of the Rady Creek headwaters tarn, a grand view unfolds. This is the **Ottawa Creek overlook**, at 19.7 km (12.2 mi), 2305 m (7560 ft). Looking NE, 3050-m (10,000-ft) Mt. Templeman, and 2744-m (9000-ft) Razors Edge are visible through the plunging Ottawa Creek drainage. Bearing a glacier on its N face is 2818-m (9242-ft) Fays Peak (E). Ahead, the route meanders SE through open terrain before ascending the S shoulder of Fays Peak.

You can turn around at this scenic climax knowing you've fully appreciated the ridge. The pleasurable high-country trekking you've experienced so far, however, continues. So if you're dayhiking, either from a basecamp along the ridge or from your vehicle parked at Rue du Beau junction, continue as far as your energy and the daylight will allow.

Topo map in hand, capable route-finders are not limited to dayhiking out and back on the Silvercup Ridge route. From Ottawa Creek overlook, you can opt for a **scramble/circuit**. See the lowpoint midway up the **S shoulder of Fays Peak**? Aim for that, then descend SE to intersect the mining road near the pass between the American and Butte creek drainages. From there, return on the Silvercup Ridge route by turning right (W), skirting the shoulder, then hiking NW back to Ottawa Creek overlook.

To continue the Silvercup Ridge route from Ottawa Creek overlook, traverse the slope to your right, staying on the E side of a small bump. Then descend SE into the **pass** formed by Ottawa Creek drainage (left / NE) and Stobart Creek drainage (right / SW). Watch for a wooden post in the open and a blaze on a tree.

The next leg of the journey continues the familiar pattern: traverse the head of **Stobart Creek basin**, then cross the basin's S wall. In this case, the basin's S wall is the **S shoulder of Fays peak**. Scan ahead to familiarize yourself with the terrain, because you'll be routefinding without the help of trail or road.

As you proceed, sporadic cairns and flagging will also help guide you. After passing a tarn and viable campsite in the Stobart Creek headwaters, gradually ascend 186 m (610 ft) and curve S. Round the outlier at about 2363 m (7750 ft), then contour generally E. Discernible **trail now resumes** and descends. Within about 20 minutes, the trail leads you onto the **mining road**. It continues all the way to Horsefly Creek Road (impassable) at Silvercup's SE end.

If you're pushing on to the SE end, simply stay on the road. The going is straightforward; ups and downs are minor. Hike SE through the 2241-m (7350-ft) pass formed by Butte Creek drainage (left / NE) and American Creek drainage (right / SW). You'll find water and campsites there. Views are NE to Mt. Templeman and Razors Edge, and down into Healy Creek.

Beyond, the road traverses the head of **American Creek basin**, curving S to cross the shoulder forming the basin's S wall. Then it turns E to traverse the head of **Horsefly Creek basin**. After gradually curving S again, reach the **SE end of the ridge** at 27 km (16.7 mi), 2120 m (6955 ft). Return the way you came.

Lupine

TRIP 15
MacBeth Icefield

LOCATION	Purcells, Glacier Creek Valley, NE of Duncan Lake
ROUND TRIP	15.6 km (9.7 mi) from Glacier Creek Road
	12 km (7.4 mi) from 4WD trailhead
ELEVATION GAIN	1198 m (3929 ft) from Glacier Creek Road
	990 m (3247 ft) from 4WD trailhead
KEY ELEVATIONS	Glacier Creek Road 1052 m (3450 ft)
	4WD trailhead 1260 m (4133 ft)
	high viewpoint 2250 m (7380 ft)
HIKING TIME	7 to 9 hours
DIFFICULTY	challenging
TRAILHEAD ACCESS	easy, until final 1.8 km (1.1 mi)
MAP	Duncan Lake 82 K/7

Opinion

Isn't this an amazing planet? That's the sentiment behind all the enthusiastic exclamations of wonder that hikers blurt out when they emerge above treeline and see the double waterfall pouring off MacBeth Icefield. (See photo on inside back cover.) The entire setting is powerfully wild; so recently glaciated that it bears the still-fresh fingerprints of creation.

The hike begins beside a creek whose thundering roar hints at the magnitude of the marvels you've come to witness. Then, like a hypnotist regressing you to a past life, the trail guides you into a quiet, dark, moist, leafy-green middle world—a hanging basin, above the valley floor, beneath the icefield. At times of peak runoff, hiking here can be a soggy ordeal.

The ascent out of the basin is arduous. It climbs a wickedly steep slope, through the chaos of a forest choking on its own deadfall. A network of staircases—some built out of milled lumber, others chopped into fallen trees—assists your upward progress.

After wringing a water bottle's worth of sweat out of you, the trail finally boots you into the alpine zone. And there it is: the vaunted, double waterfall, dramatic evidence that MacBeth Icefield is melting furiously. From here on, you'll follow a moderately ascending route. You'll work your way around and over several rock ribs, then follow the crest of a moraine, all the while admiring spectacles near and far.

The most impactful sight of all asks a bit more effort of you. A quick descent into a shallow gorge, then a few minutes of light scrambling will place you atop the ledge that the falls leap off. Here, you can survey the icefield from a commanding, inspiring perspective.

MacBeth Icefield

Ascending out of Glacier Creek Valley, to MacBeth Icefield

Fact

before your trip

Most hikers would be stopped about 1½ hours from the trailhead, were it not for extensive, cliff-side, wooden staircases. They're now decrepit. Ascend them only if you determine they're safe, and then only with vigilance. If not repaired, they'll continue deteriorating and become unusable. Phone the Kootenay Lake Forest Service office for current conditions: (250) 825-1100.

by vehicle

Until the final 1.8 km (1.1 mi) to the trailhead, this unpaved road is 2WD friendly. Even low-clearance cars can manage it. But that could change before you arrive. Phone the Kootenay Lake Forest Service office for current conditions: (250) 825-1100.

In **Kaslo**, reset your trip odometer to 0 at the junction of Hwys 31A and 31N. That's the intersection of "A" Avenue and North Marine Drive, just NW of and uphill from downtown.

0 km (0 mi)
Starting N on Hwy 31N, from the junction with Hwy 31A in Kaslo. Head toward Lardeau and Duncan Lake.

28.4 km (17.6 mi)
Pass the village of Lardeau.

34.5 km (21.4 mi)
Turn right (E) onto Argenta Road and reset your trip odometer to 0.

0 km (0 mi)
Starting E on Argenta Road from Hwy 31N.

0.5 km (0.3 mi)
Cross a bridge over the Duncan River. Pavement ends.

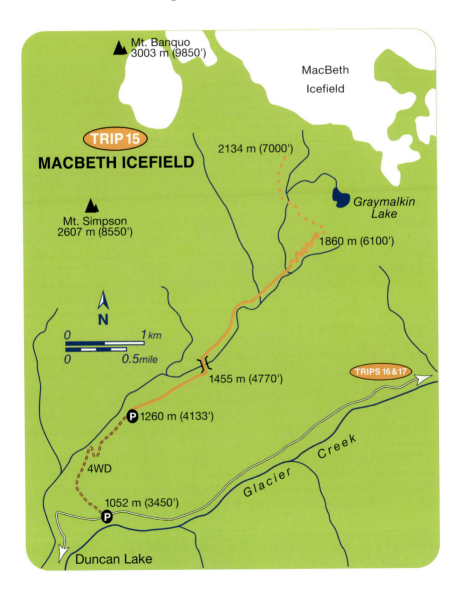

1.2 km (0.7 mi)
Proceed straight through the 4-way intersection. Left is unsigned. Right is Argenta Road, which leads to Argenta, Johnson's Landing, and the trailheads for Fry Creek Canyon (Trip 48) and Earl Grey Pass (Trip 18).

1.4 km (0.9 mi)
Cross a bridge over Hamill Creek.

10.5 km (6.5 mi)
Pass Duncan-Lavina Road (right).

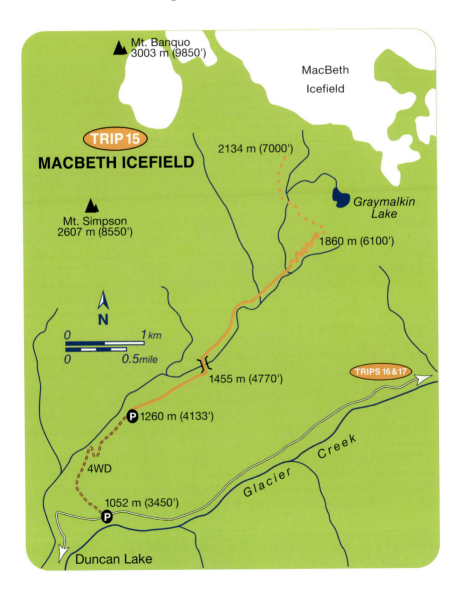

11.3 km (7 mi)
Proceed straight. Left descends to Glacier Creek campground in 0.4 km (0.25 mi).

11.9 km (7.4 mi)
Cross a bridged creek and arrive at a signed, 3-way junction. Ascend right on Glacier Creek Road. Left descends to Glacier Creek North campground.

15 km (9.3 mi)
A torrent cascading off MacBeth Icefield is visible ahead.

15.6 km (9.7 mi)
Slow down. Watch for horses grazing beside the road.

16 km (10 mi)
Pass Rainbow's End Ranch.

22.5 km (14 mi)
Reach a fork. Left is the steep, rough spur to MacBeth Icefield trailhead. Glacier Creek Road proceeds straight (E), crossing a bridge over Glacier Creek at 23.8 km (14.8 mi), en route to Monica Meadows (Trip 16) and Jumbo Pass (Trip 17).

Turning left onto the spur, it's only 1.8 km (1.1 mi) farther to MacBeth Icefield trailhead. Attempt it only in a 4WD vehicle. Otherwise park on Glacier Creek Road at 1052 m (3450 ft) and hoof it. Keep right at the fork about 10 minutes up. Strong hikers can dispatch the 208-m (682-ft) ascent to the trailhead in 20 minutes. It's signed on the right, at 1260 m (4133 ft), just before the final descent to the small parking area at road's end.

on foot

Begin a long, ascending traverse NE, on a slumping, brushy slope. In about 15 minutes, pass a **trail register** at 1345 m (4410 ft) and enter a stand of timber. The trail steepens but is now better defined.

Beyond the trees, sidle through more brush above convulsing, glacier-fed Birnam Creek. Proceed into forest. At 1455 m (4770 ft), about 40 minutes along, the trail turns left and drops to a bridge. Cross to the far bank of **Birnam Creek**, then follow the trail right (NE).

For the next 1.6 km (1 mi) you'll be on a level, **basin floor** that can be inundated in summer. Snowmelt from above sometimes courses down the trail. It's not an obstacle, just annoying. Footlogs help in places but are too few to ensure dry boots.

Soon attain your first view NNE of waterfalls spilling off MacBeth Icefield. The trail then ascends moderately through an exquisite, mossy, **virgin forest**. At 1494 m (4900 ft), about 1¼ hours from the trailhead, cross a **bridged tributary stream**. Giant cedars are numerous here.

Steel yourself for a long, steep climb through snarly terrain. Tight switchbacks dodge through chaotic **deadfall** on a forbidding 45° slope. The once marvelous, extensive, cliff-side, **staircases** are deteriorating. Ascend them only if you determine they're safe, and then only with vigilance.

About 2 hours from the trailhead, cross a **bridged creek** at 1860 m (6100 ft). The worst of the ascent is behind you. Refill waterbottles and rest in this cool, shady nook, because you'll soon be at treeline, where stunted, subalpine fir and spruce provide no shade.

From the creek crossing, ascend a steep rock rib. The trail now dwindles to a winding, rolling route. Head generally NE, following cairns and short paths between **rock ribs**. About 15 minutes beyond the creek crossing, crest an **escarpment**. Graymalkin Lake, a silty tarn at 1890 m (6200 ft), is visible below. It's fed by dramatic Birnam Falls pouring off a huge cliff. Above and beyond the cliff is MacBeth Icefield, which you can fully appreciate only by resuming the ascent.

Angle left (NNW). Following a few cairns, ramp your way up bands of rock. Icy-shouldered Mt. Brennan (Trip 12) and Duncan Lake are visible SW. The massive Horseshoe Glacier is SE, way across Glacier Creek Valley. Pass a wall of krummholz and look for flagging that will guide you up a very steep pitch to the **crest of a moraine**.

Ascend N at a moderate grade along the trail-width crest. About 15 minutes of this easy, very scenic hiking will bring you to 2134 m (7000 ft), across the gorge from and just past the waterfalls. Total hiking time: about 3 hours.

If you ascend another 15 minutes, you'll see a glacier tongue squeezed between two pyramidal, talusy peaks: Mt. Banquo (NNW) and Mt. Fleance (N). You'll also see a larger tarn in a barren, talus bowl above and SE of Graymalkin Lake.

But you'll see much more by dropping into the gorge and scrambling NE onto the escarpment over which the waterfalls pour. There, at about 2150 m (7052 ft), you'll witness a great expanse of **MacBeth Icefield**. Descend SE on glacier-scoured rock slabs to peer down at the meltwater stream splitting into two waterfalls. Mountain goats roam the slopes beyond the falls.

Monica Meadows (Trip 16)

TRIP 16
Monica Meadows

LOCATION	Purcells, Glacier Creek Valley, NE of Duncan Lake
CIRCUIT	8.5 km (5.3 mi)
ELEVATION GAIN	580 m (1902 ft)
KEY ELEVATIONS	trailhead 1810 m (5900 ft), meadows 2256 m (7400 ft) N end of ridgecrest 2390 m (7840 ft)
HIKING TIME	3 hours
DIFFICULTY	easy
TRAILHEAD ACCESS	challenging due only to distance
MAP	Duncan Lake 82 K/7

Opinion

Mountains are vertical. They stand—defiant and forbidding. Meadows are horizontal. They lounge—relaxed and welcoming.

Mountains are severe, harsh, rocky. Meadows are serene, soft, carpeted.

Mountains, above treeline, are mostly lifeless shades of black, brown and gray, or sterile white. Meadows are vibrantly alive, brilliant green, annually dappled with psychedelic wildflowers.

Mountains sternly demand effort and risk. Meadows kindly invite ease and comfort.

That's why a meadow clutched among mountains is a sublime anomaly. And why meadows enthrall hikers.

Monica Meadows is the Enthraller in Chief of the West Kootenay. It's the region's best known meadow, thus a popular hiking destination. You've no guarantee of solitude here. But if sharing these meadows with a few other hikers is the price of admission, it's inconsequential. Monica is majestic.

The climax wildflower display, mid-July through early August, is riotous. The surrounding, glacier-clad mountains are always fantastic. To the west, across the upper reaches of Glacier Creek Valley, glaciers ooze off the crags between Mt. Lady MacBeth and Mt. Macduff. To the south is Horseshoe Glacier, a massive complex of ice. It's studded with peaks, including Tranquility Mtn, which separates Quibble Peak from Squabble Peak.

The Monica Meadows trail ends on a low, alpine ridge. If you keep to the path—out and back—your hiking time will be a mere three hours. But it's a long drive to the trailhead. Make the most of it. Devote at least another hour to rambling among the tarns to the west, beneath Mt. Amon Ra. Also allow time to recline, and let your eyes—not your legs—do the wandering.

All meadows are sensitive, easily damaged. The longer your stay, the greater your impact. So please don't camp at Monica. Even fastidious backpackers leave evidence behind. Each trace is compounded by those who follow, many of whom are less than conscientious. Besides, you can easily, fully appreciate Monica on a dayhike. By not camping, you'll help preserve the area for others, and for when you come back.

Horseshoe Glacier, from Monica Meadows ridgecrest

Fact

by vehicle

Though long, the unpaved road to the trailhead is 2WD friendly. Even low-clearance cars can manage it, because the water bars (trenches dug across the road to prevent erosion) are few and shallow. But that could change before you arrive. Phone the Kootenay Lake Forest Service office for current conditions: (250) 825-1100. Even if the road's in good shape, it takes about 1¼ hours to drive from pavement's end to road's end.

In **Kaslo**, reset your trip odometer to 0 at the junction of Hwys 31A and 31N. That's the intersection of "A" Avenue and North Marine Drive, just NW of and uphill from downtown.

0 km (0 mi)
Starting N on Hwy 31N, from the junction with Hwy 31A in Kaslo. Head toward Lardeau and Duncan Lake.

28.4 km (17.6 mi)
Pass the village of Lardeau.

34.5 km (21.4 mi)
Turn right (E) onto Argenta Road and reset your trip odometer to 0.

0 km (0 mi)
Starting E on Argenta Road from Hwy 31N.

0.5 km (0.3 mi)
Cross a bridge over the Duncan River. Pavement ends.

1.2 km (0.7 mi)
Proceed straight through the 4-way intersection. Left is unsigned. Right is Argenta Road, which leads to Argenta, Johnson's Landing, and the trailheads for Fry Creek Canyon (Trip 48) and Earl Grey Pass (Trip 18).

1.4 km (0.9 mi)
Cross a bridge over Hamill Creek.

Alpine larch beneath Mt. Amon Ra

10.5 km (6.5 mi)
Pass Duncan-Lavina Road (right).

11.3 km (7 mi)
Proceed straight. Left descends to Glacier Creek campground in 0.4 km (0.25 mi).

11.9 km (7.4 mi)
Cross a bridged creek and arrive at a signed, 3-way junction. Ascend right on Glacier Creek Road. Left descends to Glacier Creek North campground.

15 km (9.3 mi)
A torrent cascading off MacBeth Icefield is visible ahead.

15.6 km (9.7 mi)
Slow down. Watch for horses grazing beside the road.

16 km (10 mi)
Pass Rainbow's End Ranch.

22.5 km (14 mi)
Reach a fork. Proceed straight (E) for Monica Meadows and Jumbo Pass (Trip 17). Left is the steep, rough spur to MacBeth Icefield trailhead (Trip 15).

23.8 km (14.8 mi)
Cross a bridge over Glacier Creek.

25.3 km (15.7 mi)
Cross a bridged tributary.

29.8 km (18.5 mi)
Cross a bridged tributary, and two more in the next 6 km (3.7 mi). The forest here is mature, mountain hemlock.

36 km (22.3 mi)
Immediately after another bridged tributary, arrive at a signed junction. Reset your trip odometer to 0. For Monica Meadows, bear left (NW). For Jumbo Pass (Trip 17), turn right (E).

0 km (0 mi)
Starting left (NW) for Monica Meadows, from the signed junction at 36 km (22.3 mi).

0.8 km (0.5 mi)
Horseshoe Glacier is visible N.

1.1 km (0.8 mi)
Bear right and ascend. Ignore the descending left fork.

1.7 km (1.1 mi)
Fork right (NE) and ascend. Ignore the level, left spur.

4.9 km (3 mi)
Cross a culvert and pass a cascade. The road is now rougher.

5.4 km (3.3 mi)
Reach the signed trailhead at 1810 m (5900 ft). Do not continue beyond (SE). Already the scenery is impressive. Many, small glaciers are visible W, on the far wall of Glacier Creek's N fork valley. They're bracketed by 2880-m (9450-ft) Mt. Lady MacBeth (left / SW), 3030-m (9950-ft) Mt. MacBeth (left / WSW), and 2990-m (9810-ft) Mt. Macduff (right / NW). Hidden behind that wall is the mammoth, MacBeth Icefield (Trip 15). Left (SSW) is Horseshoe Glacier and numerous cascades.

on foot

The well-engineered trail departs the N end of the parking lot, near where you arrive. It starts behind the sign, initially ascending N.

The nearby glaciers are more visible just 2 minutes up. Switchbacks—long, sweeping ones at first, shortening as you ascend—gradually lead NE.

At 50 minutes, 2150 m (7052 ft), while contouring ENE, Horseshoe Glacier dominates the horizon (right / S and SSE). Looking SE, it's possible to identify the "V" of Jumbo Pass, about 6 km (3.7 mi) distant.

The trail sidles around a **shoulder** above an unnamed drainage. Ahead is the prominent S ridge of 2912-m (9550-ft) Mt. Amon Ra.

Reach a **basin** at 2.3 km (1.4 mi), 2165 m (7100 ft), within 1 hour of the trailhead. Larch trees are prolific here. Soon pass a signed right (S) spur to a toilet. Bear left, descending E.

Just 1 minute farther, the main trail veers left (N). Ignore another right (S) spur. Extensive, milled footlogs keep your boots dry while conveying you through wet, fragile, creekside, **subalpine meadows**.

After hiking about 1¼ hours, reach the alpine zone and enter **Monica Meadows** at 2256 m (7400 ft). About 5 minutes farther, pass a **trailside tarn** (below, left) at 3.2 km (2 mi), 2280 m (7480 ft).

Pause here and observe. Following our circuit directions, you'll later descend E, cross country, off the low ridge (left / W). You'll skirt the S shore of the trailside tarn, rejoining the trail just below your present location.

MACBETH ICEFIELDS 10.5 KM

JUMBO PASS 27.0 KM

MONICA MEADOWS 29.4 KM

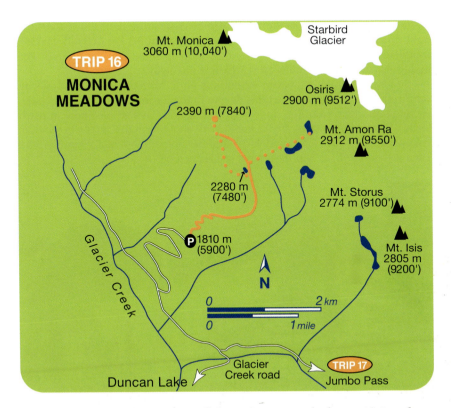

TRIP 16

MONICA MEADOWS

Mt. Monica
3060 m (10,040')

Starbird
Glacier

Osiris
2900 m (9512')

2390 m (7840')

Mt. Amon Ra
2912 m (9550')

2280 m
(7480')

Mt. Storus
2774 m (9100')

1810 m
(5900')

Mt. Isis
2805 m
(9200')

Glacier Creek

N

0   2 km

0   1 mile

Duncan Lake

Glacier
Creek road

TRIP 17

Jumbo Pass

For now, proceed N on the trail. It continues a gradual ascent into a **draw**. Left (W) is the low ridge. Right (E) is a higher ridge. The trail narrows and fades but remains evident, bending left (NW).

Crest the **low ridge** at 4 km (2.5 mi), 2353 m (7720 ft), within 1½ hours. You can again see W, across the deep, N fork of Glacier Creek Valley. Sprawling MacBeth Icefield (Trip 15) remains hidden, but its Ice Age children—smaller, peripheral glaciers—are visible on the far, valley wall.

Bear right (N). Quickly reach the **N end of the ridgecrest** at 4.2 km (2.6 mi), 2390 m (7840 ft). From this rocky perch you can overlook tarns below and survey 3060-m (10,040-ft) Mt. Monica ahead (N).

Ready to resume? Turn around, retrace your steps along the crest, but don't drop into the draw. Continue S for about 0.8 km (0.5 mi) atop the ridge.

At 5 km (3.1 mi), 2360 m (7740 ft), approach the **S end of the ridgecrest**, where it begins descending. From here, the view S—to Horseshoe Glacier and the peaks holding it aloft as if on a sedan chair—ranks among the West Kootenay's premier sights.

Once again, the trailside tarn is visible: left (ESE), in the grassy bowl beneath you. Beyond it, farther E, you can now see three other tarns deeper in the basin, closer to the W wall of Mt. Amon Ra.

photos: **1** *Monica Meadows trailside tarn* **3** *Alpine larch*

Ready to resume? Abandon the ridge by descending left (ESE). Skirt the right (S) shore of the **trailside** tarn. Rejoin the **trail** at 5.3 km (3.3 mi). Having completed the Monica Meadows circuit, you're again on familiar ground. The trail leads right (S). The trailhead is 3.2 km (2 mi) away.

It's worthwhile, however, extending your Monica Meadows hike by venturing cross-country to the **tarns deeper in the basin**, closer to Mt. Amon Ra. Having seen them from the ridgecrest, you should have an idea how to reach them. The two larger tarns are 0.8 km (0.5 mi) and 1.3 km (0.8 mi) from the trail. Follow your compass ENE, and you'll find the first of those at 2278 m (7475 ft). Then veer left (NE) to find the second at 2342 m (7685 ft).

Returning to trailhead

TRIP 17
Jumbo Pass

LOCATION	Purcells, Glacier Creek Valley, NE of Duncan Lake
ROUND TRIP	8.4 km (5.2 mi)
ELEVATION GAIN	715 m (2345 ft)
KEY ELEVATIONS	trailhead 1585 m (5200 ft), pass 2270 m (7446 ft)
HIKING TIME	3½ to 4 hours
DIFFICULTY	moderate
TRAILHEAD ACCESS	challenging due only to distance
MAP	Duncan Lake 82 K/7

Opinion

Pluck the Jumbo Pass trail from the West Kootenay, drop it into Banff National Park, and it would still be a premier destination. The scenery's that good.

The Jumbo Pass environs offer an exciting look at the peaks and glaciers comprising the northern Purcell Range. If you must decide between hiking here or to nearby Monica Meadows (Trip 16), consider that the views from Jumbo are more panoramic. Mount Monica blocks the eastern horizon at Monica Meadows. Besides, from the ridge extending north from Jumbo Pass, you can see the same, ice-clad massif (Mounts MacDuff, MacBeth and Lady MacBeth) that commands attention at Monica Meadows. Only if you prefer meadow wandering to optimal mountain views should you opt for Monica, because the meadows at Jumbo are comparatively small.

The joy of a Jumbo trip begins well before arrival at the trailhead. By vehicle, you'll travel the entire Glacier Creek Valley, occasionally glimpsing the namesake glaciers and passing through a grand, mountain-hemlock forest. Hemlocks possess heart-rending grace. You'll recognize them by their colossal height (40 m / 120 ft), drooping leaders (tops), long, swooping branches, and deeply furrowed bark. It's worth driving here just to see these regal trees.

The trail to Jumbo is in forest. Views are limited. You'll glimpse just enough of the massif clutching Horseshoe Glacier to inspire upward progress. Not until the final approach to the pass, where the trail emerges into the subalpine zone, does the scenery begin to explode. To see all you can see, turn north at the pass and continue ascending the ridge behind the hut. If spending a night in this small, cozy alpine refuge appeals to you, read the *before your trip* section for details.

Fact

before your trip

If you want to stay in the Jumbo Pass hut, reserve in advance by phoning the booking agent for Columbia Valley Hut Society. Visit www.cvhsinfo.org for the current agent's phone number. The recently-built hut is clean and comfortable but small, with room for about eight people. It's equipped with foamies, a couple

Horseshoe Glacier, from near Jumbo Pass

propane stoves, propane tanks, cooking pots, dishes and utensils. When making reservations, ask what extra supplies or equipment you might need.

by vehicle

Though long, the unpaved road to the trailhead is 2WD friendly. Even low-clearance cars can manage it, because the water bars (trenches dug across the road to prevent erosion) are few and shallow. But backroads evolve. Phone the Kootenay Lake Forest Service office for current conditions: (250) 825-1100. Even if the road's in good shape, it takes about 1¼ hours to drive from pavement's end to road's end.

In Kaslo, reset your trip odometer to 0 at the junction of Hwys 31A and 31N. That's the intersection of "A" Avenue and North Marine Drive, just NW of and uphill from downtown.

0 km (0 mi)
Starting N on Hwy 31N, from the junction with Hwy 31A in Kaslo. Head toward Lardeau and Duncan Lake.

28.4 km (17.6 mi)
Pass the village of Lardeau.

34.5 km (21.4 mi)
Turn right (E) onto Argenta Road and reset your trip odometer to 0.

0 km (0 mi)
Starting E Argenta Road from Hwy 31N.

0.5 km (0.3 mi)
Cross a bridge over the Duncan River. Pavement ends.

1.2 km (0.7 mi)
Proceed straight through the 4-way intersection. Pass an unsigned road (left),

and Argenta Road (right) leading to Argenta, Johnston Landing, Fry Creek Canyon (Trip 48), and the Earl Grey Pass trailhead (Trip 18).

1.4 km (0.9 mi)
Cross a bridge over Hamill Creek.

10.5 km (6.5 mi)
Pass Duncan-Lavina Road (right).

11.3 km (7 mi)
Proceed straight. Left descends to Glacier Creek campground in 0.4 km (0.25 mi).

11.9 km (7.4 mi)
Cross a bridged creek and arrive at a signed, 3-way junction. Ascend right on Glacier Creek Road. Left descends to Glacier Creek North campground.

15 km (9.3 mi)
A torrent cascading off MacBeth Icefield is visible ahead.

15.6 km (9.7 mi)
Slow down. Watch for horses grazing beside the road.

16 km (10 mi)
Pass Rainbow's End Ranch.

22.5 km (14 mi)
Reach a fork. Proceed straight (E) for Jumbo Pass and Monica Meadows (Trip 16). Left is the steep, rough spur to MacBeth Icefield trailhead (Trip 15).

23.8 km (14.8 mi)
Cross a bridge over Glacier Creek.

25.3 km (15.7 mi)
Cross a bridged tributary.

29.8 km (18.5 mi)
Cross a bridged tributary here, and two more in the next 6 km (3.7 mi). Pass through mature, mountain hemlock forest.

36 km (22.3 mi)
Immediately after another bridged tributary, arrive at a signed junction. Reset your trip odometer to 0. For Jumbo Pass, turn right (E). For Monica Meadows (Trip 16), bear left (NW).

0 km (0 mi)
Starting right (E) for Jumbo Pass, from the signed junction at 36 km (22.3 mi).

0.4 km (0.2 mi)
Bear right, following a small sign depicting a hiker. The road is level and not too brushy.

3 km (1.9 mi)
Reach Jumbo Pass trailhead and the end of passable road, at 1585 m (5200 ft). The parking area is small. Park efficiently to leave room for others.

on foot

The trail is in good condition. Switchbacks ease the steep ascent. Expect to be in forest until approaching the pass.

Karnak and Jumbo mountains, from Jumbo Pass

The trailhead sign is at a fork in the road. The overgrown right branch continues toward a moraine of Horseshoe Glacier. Ascend left. In a few minutes this road narrows to trail. Soon cross a creeklet and begin ascending steeply. In about 15 minutes, enter standing timber near 1677 m (5500 ft).

Visible SW is the sprawling Horseshoe Glacier, pierced by various summits including several with an amusing name theme: Quibble and Squabble peaks, Truce, Covenant and Tranquillity mountains. Occasionally glimpse glacier-adorned Mt. Lady MacBeth back NW.

After gaining 305 m (1000 ft)—a 45-minute task for swift hikers—the grade relents. At 2045 m (6700 ft), about 1 hour along, huckleberry bushes are profuse. The trail then curves E for the final approach to the pass. Moderately steep pitches are broken by short, level respites.

About 1½ hours from the trailhead, ascend a gentle, meadowy draw followed by steep switchbacks. Soon enter subalpine meadows laced with larch trees at 2195 m (7200 ft).

Attain 2270-m (7446-ft) **Jumbo Pass** at 4.2 km (2.6 mi), after a 1¾-hour ascent. Clearcuts mar the view NE, but there's abundant beauty to distract your gaze. Soaring above the scalped slopes are twin peaks. The jagged one on the right is Jumbo Mtn. Left is Karnak Mtn. A glacier oozes between them on the S side. The dull, talusy peak S of Jumbo is unnamed.

The trail splits at Jumbo Pass. Right ascends briefly SE toward the grey talus slopes of Bastille Mtn before dropping past a tarn and continuing down to the Jumbo Creek logging road E of the pass. The road provides access to Jumbo Pass from Panorama Ski Area and, farther down valley, Invermere.

The signed left fork at Jumbo Pass leads to the **Jumbo Hut**, at 2320 m (7610 ft). You'll be there in 10 minutes. Just below and E of the hut is a tarn. From the hut,

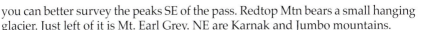

you can better survey the peaks SE of the pass. Redtop Mtn bears a small hanging glacier. Just left of it is Mt. Earl Grey. NE are Karnak and Jumbo mountains.

To ascend the **ridge N of the hut**, start behind the outhouse and proceed directly N. This 0.8-km (0.5-mi) one-way extension takes only about 20 minutes but will greatly enhance your appreciation of the Jumbo Pass environs.

As you climb, waterfalls crashing off Horseshoe Glacier at the S end of Glacier Creek Valley become more audible. A bootbeaten path leads most of the way up the first 2470-m (8100-ft) bump. From there, Glacier Dome is visible N. The Lieutenants are NE. Obscured behind them is Lake of the Hanging Glacier, a premier hiking destination accessed from Radium Hot Springs via Horsethief Creek Road.

NW, across upper Glacier Creek Valley, is the massif comprising Mounts MacDuff, MacBeth and Lady MacBeth. Obscured behind them is the sprawling MacBeth Icefield. The tarn beneath Horseshoe Glacier is now visible SW, as is the overgrown road leading to the moraine. Glacier-trussed Blockhead Mtn is partially visible S of Bastille Mtn.

The next couple bumps on the ridgecrest are easily attainable, but the scenery doesn't improve sufficiently to justify the elevation loss and gain. Go only for the going's sake. Experienced scramblers can forge N along the ridgecrest about 3 km (1.9 mi) before it gets seriously narrow and rugged.

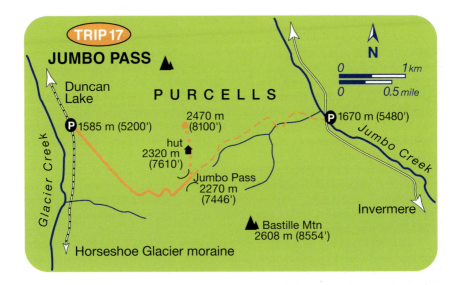

TRIP 18
Hamill Creek / Earl Grey Pass

LOCATION	Purcells, NE of Kootenay Lake's N end
DISTANCE	61 km (37.8 mi) one way
	plus 3.4-km (2.1-mi) round trip to Slate Peak
ELEVATION GAIN	1615 m (5297 ft) to Earl Grey Pass
	plus 458 m (1502 ft) to Slate Peak
KEY ELEVATIONS	W trailhead 875 m (2870 ft)
	upper Hamill Creek Valley 1433 m (4700 ft)
	Earl Grey Pass 2280 m (7480 ft)
	Slate Peak 2695 m (8841 ft)
	E trailhead 1174 m (3850 ft)
HIKING TIME	3 to 5 days
DIFFICULTY	challenging
TRAILHEAD ACCESS	easy
MAPS	Lardeau 82 K/2, Duncan Lake 82 K/7
	Toby Creek 82 K/8

Opinion

Trekking across the Purcells, you'll experience the West Kootenay's greatest gift to the outdoor adventurer: solitude. It's possible you'll encounter no other hikers in the three to five days it takes to complete the west-to-east journey up Hamill Creek, over Earl Grey Pass, then down Toby Creek. But if you surmount Slate Peak (a no-worries, one-hour scramble north of the pass), the summit-cairn register will give you a glimpse of your predecessors. They've included a 5-year-old kid, a 12-year-old dog, and mountaineering clubs from across the continent. The register was established in August, 1968. Many of the scribbled entries are revealing.

"I will never be the same," effusively declared one hiker. Another, from Nelson, B.C., marveled that "Heaven is so close to home." "England will never be the same," said a Brit. "May the loggers drool," wrote a BC Parks employee, rejoicing that Hamill Creek's giant-cedar forest was saved when the Purcell Wilderness was granted Class A status.

Climbers penned many of these comments, because Slate Peak's easily-attained 360° view comprises numerous 3050-m (10,000-ft) summits (including Quibble, Squabble, Tranquility, Ochre, Toby, Hamill, and Red Top) and is therefore invaluable for reconnaissance. But even if your goal is simply to cross the pass, you'll be inexorably drawn off trail to Slate Peak. That's because your initial delight and physical relief upon attaining the pass will fade rapidly when you realize you're still below treeline, straddling the ridge in what is just a tiny notch with severely restricted views.

Your effort was not wasted. Invest a little more. Bag Slate Peak. You'll be enraptured by a panorama of Purcell-range grandeur: gnarly summits, ornery ridges, sprawling glaciers, alpine bowls, and 750-m (2460-ft) cascades. Both the

Hamill Creek cedar grove

Hamill and Toby valleys are visible from Slate Peak, as are the glacial headwaters of the two creeks. This vista rivals premier scenery in the southern B.C. Coast Mountains, the Canadian Rockies, and the North Cascades. The difference is that backpacking to Earl Grey Pass and nipping up to Slate Peak takes longer than hiking to comparable vantage points in other ranges.

Want to shorten the trip? Swift, tireless dayhikers can tag Earl Grey Pass via the shorter, eastern approach along Toby Creek. But they risk not having sufficient time to attain the journey's scenic climax atop Slate Peak. Another reason to make this a multi-day backpack trip via the western approach along Hamill Creek is to revel in a vast, ancient forest of mammoth cedars. You'll spend at least an entire day hiking through it—a mystical experience. The Toby Creek trail offers enticing, up-valley views earlier and more frequently, but the predominantly spruce forest on this drier, eastern side is underwhelming, and too often the path itself is a muddy, horse-tromped morass. The Hamill Creek route swings back and forth across roaring whitewater, so equestrians are precluded and the trail is better preserved. Yet if all the Hamill Creek cable cars and footlogs are intact, hikers are spared any dangerous fords.

Starting at the west trailhead—near the village of Argenta, above the north end of Kootenay Lake—the trail drops 210 m (689 ft) to Hamill Creek. It then gains 610 m (2000 ft) in the next 14 km (8.7 mi)—an ascent so gentle it's rarely noticeable. You'll be constantly awed by glorious cedars and often entertained by the rambunctious creek. Wrestling with your pack at all the cable-car crossings is a hassle, but pulling yourself to the opposite bank is fun, and not having to ford is a luxury.

Near the upper end of Hamill Creek Valley, at about 17 km (10.5 mi), the challenge begins. The trail diminishes in more rugged terrain. Expect to thrash through brush and bogs. At about 32.5 km (20.2 mi), you face a taxing 823-m (2700-ft) ascent in the final 8.5 km (5.3 mi) to the pass. The trail then descends

Upper Hamill Creek Valley, en route to Earl Grey Pass

Toby Creek valley to the east trailhead. Though downhill, it's no cakewalk. Unbridged tributary crossings (not threatening, just a nuisance), overgrown avalanche paths, and the aforementioned horse-churned mud demand fortitude. But if you occasionally look backward, you'll enjoy grand views of the high country you just traversed.

Now, bear with us for two more minutes. We admit the following warnings are elaborate enough to rival those of the most nervous, lecture-prone parent. But we offer them knowing they'll increase your safety and enjoyment and help you maintain the pristine quality of this wilderness stronghold.

The Earl Grey Pass trail is always distinct, so navigation shouldn't be a concern. Still, this is an arduous trip, not for wimps or novices. At the midpoint, help will be at least a long day's travel away, perhaps more. A well-stocked first-aid kit is essential. Be alert for bears; you'll be in grizzly habitat the entire way.

Much of the way is rooty, rocky, muddy, or brushy. Avalanche paths are frequent; if they haven't been recently cleared, you'll often wade through dense, scratchy greenery. Most of the trail is forested; if the deadfall hasn't been recently removed, you'll encounter obstacles that might be gymnastically challenging.

Though you'll find a cable car or footlog at all major creek crossings, a couple of the logs can be unnerving, especially when wet. Several minor stream crossings in Toby Creek valley necessitate wading, unless low water-levels allow you to rockhop.

From Rock Creek (a tributary of Hamill), all the way over the pass and down Toby Creek, campsites are few and far between. That means you must be a strong, disciplined hiker. Except at the campsites listed in the route description below, you'll find almost no bare ground level enough for a comfortable night in a tent. Plan on reaching one of the established sites every evening. And hope the one you've chosen isn't occupied, because all are tiny. Each has space for only a couple tents. So your group should comprise no more than about four people.

There are no outhouses at any of the campsites. Even the smallest groups must be fastidious while cooking and cleaning, and especially diligent about disposing human waste. Leave no trace of your stay. And if you camp at the pass, be sure to haul up plenty of water. You'll find none there, except perhaps in a seasonal creeklet about 100 m (328 ft) below the west side.

Have all those admonishments doused the flame of adventure flickering in your soul? Don't want to backpack the entire distance? Consider dayhiking up Hamill Creek to enjoy the walloping whitewater and see the mother of West Kootenay cedar groves. From the west trailhead, round-trip distance to Big Bar is 24 km (15 mi), but you can turn around earlier and feel satisfied. Even a short dayhike, however, will require you to ascend 210 m (689 ft) on the way out. In shoulder season, when alpine destinations are inaccessible, Hamill Creek is arguably the best dayhike in this book. It's also a cool choice on a scorching hot summer day, because the deep canyon is shady.

Fact

before your trip

Check current trail conditions at www.bcparks.ca (click on Purcell Wilderness). Bring cash in case you need to pay the BC Parks backcountry camping fee. Bring 10 m/yd of small-gauge rope, in case you need it at the sixth crossing of Hamill Creek.

by vehicle

If you follow the *on foot* directions below, you'll be hiking W to E. To reach the **W trailhead**, set your trip odometer to 0 at the junction of Hwys 31A and 31N. That's the intersection of "A" Avenue and North Marine Drive, just W of and uphill from downtown **Kaslo**.

0 km (0 mi)
Starting N on Hwy 31N, from the junction with Hwy 31A in Kaslo. Head toward Lardeau and Duncan Lake.

28.4 km (17.6 mi)
Pass the village of Lardeau. A BC Parks sign warns of the turn you'll be taking toward the Purcell Mountains and Fry Canyon.

34.5 km (21.4 mi)
Turn right (E) onto Argenta Road and reset your trip odometer to 0.

0 km (0 mi)
Starting E on Argenta Road from Hwy 31N.

0.5 km (0.3 mi)
Cross a bridge over the Duncan River. Pavement ends.

1.2 km (0.7 mi)
Reach a 4-way intersection. Turn right (S) onto Argenta Road. It leads to Argenta, Johnsons Landing, Fry Creek Canyon trailhead (Trip 48), and the Earl Grey Pass trailhead. Left is unsigned. Straight leads to the trailheads for MacBeth Icefield (Trip 15), Monica Meadows (Trip 16), and Jumbo Pass (Trip 17).

5.8 km (3.6 mi)
The road ascends and narrows.

6.5 km (4 mi)
Reach a signed junction. Turn sharp left (N) for the Earl Grey Pass trailhead. Right (S) leads to Johnsons Landing and the Fry Creek Canyon trailhead (Trip 48).

7.1 km (4.4 mi)
Proceed straight. Ignore the right fork.

7.5 km (4.7 mi)
Pass the community hall and post office.

8.4 km (5.2 mi)
Continue straight where Press Road forks right.

11.5 km (7.1 mi)
Arrive at the **Earl Grey Pass trailhead** (left), at 875 m (2870 ft).
   If you're picking up hikers at the **E trailhead**, drive Hwy 95 S from Radium, or N from Cranbrook, then turn W toward **Invermere**. Go through town, toward Panorama Ski Area. Set your trip odometer to 0 at the bridge where left leads to Panorama. Proceed straight. At 19 km (11.8 mi), where the road curves right and continues toward Jumbo Pass, look for a signed, overgrown, left spur. Hikers will arrive here via that spur.

on foot

   At the BC Parks kiosk, the trail begins on the twin ruts of a grassy old road. Follow it N. In 15 minutes, reach a sign affirming you're on the Earl Grey Pass Trail. About 30 minutes from the trailhead, reach the **W trail register** at 805 m (2640 ft) and attain a view W over Hamill Creek canyon.

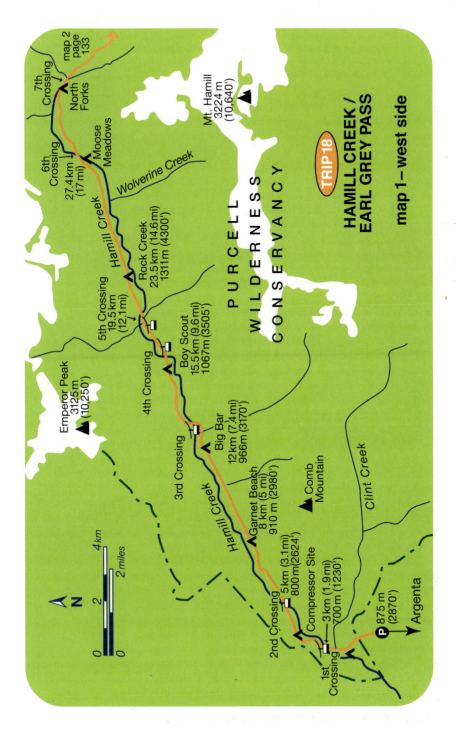

map 1–west side

HAMILL CREEK /
EARL GREY PASS

TRIP 18

PURCELL
WILDERNESS
CONSERVANCY

Mt. Hamill
3224 m
(10,640')

7th
Crossing

North
Forks

map 2
page
133

6th
Crossing
27.4 km
(17 mi)

Moose
Meadows

Wolverine Creek

Hamill Creek

5th Crossing
19.5 km
(12.1 mi)

Rock Creek
23.5 km (14.6 mi)
1311 m (4300')

Boy Scout
15.5 km (9.6 mi)
1067 m (3505')

4th Crossing

Emperor Peak
3125 m
(10,250')

3rd Crossing

Big Bar
12 km (7.4 mi)
966 m (3170')

Hamill Creek

Garnet Beach
8 km (5 mi)
910 m (2980')

Comb
Mountain

Clint Creek

2nd Crossing

5 km (3.1 mi)
800 m (2624')

Compressor Site

3 km (1.9 mi)
700 m (1230')

1st
Crossing

875 m
(2870')

P

Argenta

N

4 km

2 miles

2

2

0

0

The trail then descends 140 m (460 ft) via steep switchbacks to a small, not-very-level campsite near the S bank of **Hamill Creek**, at 665 m (2181 ft). Just beyond the campsite is a bridged crossing of Clint Creek, a major tributary of Hamill. Following Hamill Creek upstream, your general direction of travel will remain ENE for the next 30 km (18.6 mi), and the ascent will remain gentle.

A captivating section of the trip begins about 1 hour from the trailhead, in a sheer-sided, rock-walled gorge where the path hugs the bank of the rip-snorting creek. Reach the **first cable-car crossing** at 3 km (1.9 mi), 700 m (2300 ft).

On the N bank, pass an abandoned mining operation at 3.8 km (2.4 mi), about 1½ hours from the trailhead. You'll see a Pelloton compressor here. Level campsites are nearby. Shortly beyond, pass **McLaughlin Cabin** in a cedar grove at 753 m (2470 ft). Reach the **second cable-car crossing** just after the cabin. On the S bank, at 800 m (2624 ft), soon pass a yellow, metal blaze indicating you've hiked 5 km (3.1 mi) from the trailhead.

After a gradual ascent to 884 m (2900 ft), the trail descends slightly. In an avalanche path thick with cow's parsnip and thimbleberry, attain a view of the valley you're hiking through. Soon enter a lush tributary drainage, rockhop across the stream, then resume through cedar and hemlock forest. At 8 km (5 mi), 910 m (2980 ft), about 3 hours from the trailhead, a yellow, metal blaze marks a left spur descending to the creekside **Garnet Beach campsite**.

At 9 km (5.6 mi) cross an avalanche path affording an impressive view of cliffs and snowfields. The trail is interrupted here by a deep, rough, steep-sided **washout**. If a trail crew has preceded you, they might have brushed out a spur through the greenery. Look for it before the washout; follow it right, then left. It will lead to the easiest place to cross the washout. If no spur is evident, continue on the main trail to the edge of the washout, then ascend right, looking for a place to safely descend to the tributary stream. Rockhop across, climb the far wall, then pick up the trail on the other side. It immediately drops back into forest.

Reach **Big Bar campsite** at 12 km (7.4 mi), 966 m (3170 ft), beneath hemlocks and cedars. It can accommodate two tents, but is best suited to just one. A waterfall is visible on the N side of the valley. Dayhikers who turn around here should be pleased with their accomplishment.

At 13 km (8.1 mi), about 5½ hours from the trailhead, cross a huge log spanning Crazy Creek. About 30 minutes farther, at 1009 m (3310 ft), reach the **third cable-car crossing**. Then, on the N bank, the trail forges through several avalanche paths.

Reach **Boy Scout Camp** at 15.5 km (9.6 mi), 1067 m (3500 ft). Total elevation gain: 402 m (1320 ft). Including time to negotiate the three previous cable-car crossings, backpackers can be here in about 6 hours. Strong dayhikers might make it in 5 hours, which means they should now head for home. There's room here for a couple tents beneath gargantuan cedars, beside a silent creeklet. Hamill Creek is about 20 m/yd distant, so the roar is audible but not overwhelming.

About 10 minutes past Boy Scout Camp, reach the **fourth cable-car crossing**. If it's not functioning, cross on a large log 100 m (110 yd) upstream from the cable-car. Just beyond, on the S bank, cross a bridged tributary beneath a cascade. Near a yellow, metal blaze indicating that you've a hiked a total of 17 km (10.5 mi), a short stretch of trail is submerged. Cross this knee-deep swamp on a slender, slippery log, or circumvent it by thrashing through brush and over deadfall.

At 19.5 km (12.1 mi), above where Hamill Creek cascades steeply, reach the **fifth cable-car crossing**. On the N bank, begin a noticeable ascent. Proceed among more giant cedars. About 2½ hours from Boy Scout Camp, reach **Rock Creek Camp** at 23.5 km (14.6 mi), 1311 m (4300 ft). Immediately before the main trail crosses the log spanning Rock Creek, look for a descending right spur. It quickly leads to two tent sites beside the confluence of Rock and Hamill creeks. The view is N to an alpine cascade.

Giant cedars have now given way to smaller spruce, but as you probe the broader, upper valley, expanded views will help compensate. Near 26.5 km (16.4 mi) a huge avalanche path is on the left, and a grassy, marshy, willowy area is on the right. You're entering prime bear habitat, so make plenty of noise.

At 27.4 km (17 mi), 1381 m (4530 ft), pass a small, unappealing but level campsite just before reaching the **sixth creek crossing**. No more luxurious cable cars. Just a long, skinny footlog (that might not still be in place when you arrive) resembling a horizontal flag pole. It requires the nerve and balance of a tightrope walker. A fall is unlikely to be disastrous, however, because Hamill Creek is a slow-moving pool here, not a whitewater torrent. But if you think you'll end up swimming, do it on purpose: dive in (a few quick strokes will propel you to the far bank) then line your party's packs across. This requires at least 10 m / yd of rope.

On the S bank, work your way through about 80 m (87 yd) of muck. The trail then drifts toward the right (S) side of the grassy, willowy, upper valley. Cairns should help guide you through this rough, rooty, sloppy stretch.

Pass a small lake and see an alpine cascade on the valley's N wall. About 1 hour beyond the lake, reach the **seventh creek crossing**. A footlog spans the first of two Hamill Creek channels. A footlog with a hand cable spans the second. Glacier encrusted peaks are visible from the N bank.

Mt. Hamill, from Slate Peak

Quickly reach Hamill Creek's smaller but still formidable **N forks** at about 35 km (21.7 mi), 1433 m (4700 ft). All are spanned by footlogs. At one crossing, however, where the footlog was extremely wet and slick, we opted for a dry, fallen tree 30 m/yd downstream. Between the last two crossings, there might still be a small, level clearing sufficient for a single tent. Proceed beyond here only if you're confident you can reach the pass (2½ to 3 hours distant for strong hikers) before nightfall. Once the ensuing climb begins, you'll find no level tent sites until near the pass. And fill your water bottles now. The pass is dry. Water is not always available en route—a good reason to hike this stretch in early morning, before the hot summer sun reaches it. A seasonal creeklet 100 m (328 ft) below the W side of the pass might be flowing, but it's not a certainty.

The trail now begins a startling, merciless ascent N—an abrupt initiation to what will be a steady, 823-m (2700-ft) climb in the remaining 8.5 km (5.3 mi) to the pass. Within about 30 minutes, enjoy a brief reprieve before the skyward tilt resumes. The trail now curves SE—your general direction until a final, short, E vault into the pass.

At 1750 m (5740 ft) attain the first truly exhilarating view of the trip. SW, across Hamill Creek Valley's upper reaches, the opposite, 1067-m (3500-ft) wall is festooned with glaciers and spangled with waterfalls. Glimpse more cliffs and glaciers as you ascend. The steep grade eases occasionally, but the trail surface slumps downhill and fails to provide comfortable footing. Alpine larches appear at 2067 m (6780 ft)—visible assurance that you're nearing your goal. The trail bends E into the subalpine zone before cresting **Earl Grey Pass** at 44 km (27.3 mi), 2280 m (7480 ft).

Earl Grey Pass is just a small, grassy gap below treeline. Views are limited. Maneuvering among the trees will enable you to glimpse upper Hamill and Toby creek valleys. Glacier-chested Mt. Hamill is SW. NW of it is 3121-m (10,237-ft) Mt. Lady Grey. ESE is 2961-m (9712-ft) Hyak Mtn. Toby Glacier is partially visible SSE. But after trekking this far, it's cruel and unusual punishment not to see more. So make the short side trip to Slate Peak and feast your soul on the awesome panorama that Earl Grey Pass denies you.

Camping at the pass is not ideal—for you, or the fragile alpine environment. The ground is lumpy and slanted. Disposing of human waste is difficult in the shallow soil. (But it is necessary. Bury it 12 cm / 5.5 inches deep. Pack out used toilet paper with all other trash.) Campfires are too impactful at this elevation. (They leave ugly scars that last years. Look around, you'll see several. Dead wood is scarce and should be left untouched as part of the scenery.) There's no convenient water source. If the previously-described seasonal creeklet below the W side is not flowing, your other options are to melt snow or descend E 136 m (446 ft) to a small cascade that crosses the trail. Still intend to camp at the pass? Pitch your tent on a worn area, rather than begin killing yet another patch of grass. Look for worn tent sites up slope, N of the trail. Others are in and just beyond the band of larches along the E edge of the pass.

Heading N from Earl Grey Pass, able, agile hikers can summit Slate Peak— 1.7 km (1.1) distant—within 1 hour. Start by ascending the bootbeaten path on the right (E) side of the pass. Where the grass stops, work your way up the loose, chunky boulders. Attain the **first knob** at 2482 m (8140 ft). Then drop 43 m (140 ft) over more unstable, awkward boulders before resuming the ascent through

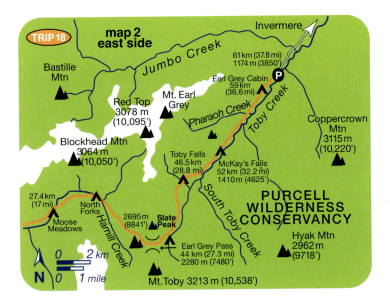

krummholz (stunted, gnarled, tightly-clumped trees) and over slabby slopes to 2695-m (8841-ft) **Slate Peak**. En route, look for lavender Sky Pilot (resembling tiny bottlebrushes), and magenta moss campion.

On a clear day, you'll see countless summits, glaciers, ridges and valleys from Slate Peak. A topo map is necessary if you want to begin interpreting the thrillingly vast, geological chaos surrounding you. The following are but a few of the most obvious features. NW is 3060-m (10,050-ft) Blockhead Mtn. Left (W) of it is 3200-m (10,500-ft) Caldron Peak, backed by 3110-m (10,200-ft) Mt. Quibble—identified by a snow cornice along its left ridge. Farther NW is 3080-m (10,100-ft) Ochre Peak. Beyond these summits, just out of sight, is the impressive Horseshoe Glacier, which is visible from Jumbo Pass (Trip 17). On your side of these summits is Hamill Creek Valley, with which you're now intimately acquainted. NE is Toby Creek valley. Streaking its forested walls are bright-green avalanche paths, with which you'll soon be intimately acquainted. Some 80 km (50 mi) beyond Toby Creek valley is Mt. Assiniboine and its satellite peaks, Mounts Aye and Eon, in the Canadian Rockies. SE is massive Toby Glacier. S is 3212-m (10,538-ft) Mt. Toby.

It takes fleet backpackers about 6 hours to hike the 17 km (10.5 mi) from Earl Grey Pass to the E trailhead. If you depart the pass after 4 p.m., you'll be shaded from hot summer sun. Compared to the trail ascending the W side of the pass, the initial 3 km (1.9 mi) descending E are in better condition and gently graded. After several switchbacks, the trail traverses NE—your general direction the rest of the way. Hop over a **small cascade** at 2150 m (7050 ft). Try not to step on the toads! We counted 16 between the pass and about the 8-km (5-mi) point. This must be their pilgrimage route to Toad Peak.

About 30 minutes below the pass, enter dense forest near 1982 m (6500 ft). Soon cross a large avalanche path adorned with yellow columbine, larkspur,

white valerian, paintbrush, and swirling green Indian hellebore. About 45 minutes below the pass, near 2.5 km (1.6 mi), an unsigned spur descends right to a **campground above Toby Falls**.

At 1747 m (5730 ft), about 1 hour below the pass, cross a small bench-meadow beside a cascade. It has an expansive view, and ample, level ground for a couple tents. Visible N is the pointy summit of 3078-m (10,095-ft) Red Top.

At 1670 m (5480 ft), about 1 hour and 20 minutes below the pass, reach an unbridged creek crossing. Depending on the water level and the springiness of your legs, you might have to wade. About 30 minutes beyond, reach another unbridged creek. This one is larger (knee to thigh deep), swifter, and requires fording but is not dangerous. Then proceed through an oppressive spruce forest before descending steeply through flowery meadows to **Toby Creek**.

At 7.7 km (4.8 mi), 1470 m (4820 ft), about 2½ hours below the pass, the trail re-enters forest. Immediately after, near an old fence, pass a right spur. Stay on the main trail. The spur quickly leads to the Toby Creek horse ford en route to the creek's S fork. About 10 minutes past the spur, traverse an avalanche path lined with aspen. Listen for the roar of McKay's Falls. You'll see it after crossing yet another slide path.

Pass **McKay's Falls** at 8 km (5 mi), 1410 m (4625 ft), about 3½ hours below the pass. A bit farther (about 8 minutes after the trail grazes Toby Creek), a faint right spur leads to a **campsite** with room for several tents on a **creekside gravel flat**. Look for it where there's a swampy pond and a small stand of aspen on the opposite (left) side of the main trail. Visible SW, just above and beyond Earl Grey Pass, is Mt. Toby. Right (N) of the pass is Slate Peak. About 5 minutes past the gravel-flat campsite is a lone tent site among trees and horsetails beside the creek. The E trailhead is now about 2½ hours distant.

About 4½ hours below the pass, reach an **unbridged, major tributary**. The ford is knee to thigh deep but poses no serious risk. About 30 minutes beyond, you must ford another unbridged creek. Shortly after, rockhop across a small stream. The trail proceeds through forest, occasionally broken by more brushy avalanche paths. The openings grant views of the peaks above. While gently descending through a meadow at 15 km (9.3 mi), look left (NW) toward the forest edge for **Earl Grey cabin**. Earl Grey was Canada's Governor General from 1904 to 1911. In 1908 he crossed the Purcell Range via the pass that now bears his name. The cabin was built for his family's vacation in 1909.

At 16 km (9.9 mi), 1220 m (4000 ft), about 15 minutes past Earl Grey cabin, cross the **park boundary** and arrive at the **E trailhead register**. Keep going. The trail quickly reaches a small clearing accessed by an old road. Bush-beater 4WD vehicles can get this far, but all other vehicles will be stopped 1 km (0.6 mi) short of here. The road makes a hairpin turn beside the clearing. Don't descend right. Ascend left and pass an abandoned mine. Then descend the rough, narrow, tightly overgrown road. Reach the signed, **Jumbo Pass Road** where it curves left uphill. Right (downhill) leads to the highway. There's a small, brown EARL GREY PASS TRAIL sign here, at 17 km (10.5 mi), 1174 m (3850 ft). If you've arranged a shuttle, this is where you want to be picked up. If you've parked your vehicle here, it should be near the horse corral, on a spur road just below and W of the trail sign.

TRIP 19
Meadow Mountain

LOCATION	Selkirks, W edge of Goat Range Provincial Park NW of Lardeau
ROUND TRIP	4.2 km (2.6 mi) to first summit
	5.4 km (3.4 mi) to true summit
ELEVATION GAIN	380 m (1246 ft) for first summit
	510 m (1673 ft) for true summit
KEY ELEVATIONS	notch (trailhead parking) 2152 m (7060 ft), first summit 2520 m (8266 ft), true summit 2550 m (8366 ft)
HIKING TIME	1¾ hours for first summit, plus ½ hour for true summit, plus optional excursion beyond road's end
DIFFICULTY	moderate
TRAILHEAD ACCESS	challenging
MAPS	Rosebery 82 K/3, Poplar Creek 82 K/6

Opinion

Love it or hate it, everyone who drives to Meadow Mtn thinks, "This is one hell of a road."

That's because it doesn't stop below treeline, or even in the subalpine zone. The road keeps rampaging through one of the West Kootenay's rare, grand, alpine meadows.

Nearby is glacier-freighted Mt. Cooper, the region's most spectacular peak. No trail approaches it. Hikers spy it only from afar. But the Meadow Mtn road climbs so high and swoops so close, it's as if you're on a Mt. Cooper scenic heli flight.

Even if such a road appalls you, there it is. And there it will remain. Might as well take advantage of it. Get an early-morning start. Drive all the way up. Park near road's end. Roam farther on foot. It's exciting, alpine terrain, but verticality makes it difficult to go far. So…

Drive back down the road part way, to what we call *the notch*. Park there and hike up Meadow Mtn. A steep, bootbeaten route launches you to the summit ridge, where you can follow the rocky, gently rolling, alpine crest northward.

Lingering snowfields on the scalloped east edge of the ridgecrest lend a glacier-walk aura to the experience. And you'll enjoy a constant, 360° panorama punctuated by Mt. Cooper, of course, plus Duncan and Kootenay lakes, and the full sweep of the Purcells.

No West Kootenay summit allows you to wander as long, freely, and easily as is possible on Meadow Mtn. That's because it's not a peak. It's actually a ridge. And few ridges anywhere are this generous to hikers.

So remember while driving the lamentable yet compelling road: You'll want to enjoy Meadow Mtn much longer than the minimum-required hiking time might suggest. Hiking always beats driving. Even here.

Fact

by vehicle

Low-clearance cars will struggle on the road's steep, upper reaches. Moderate clearance is necessary. High clearance is preferable. 4WD is ideal.

In **Kaslo,** reset your trip odometer to 0 at the junction of Hwys 31A and 31N. That's the intersection of "A" Avenue and North Marine Drive, just NW of and uphill from downtown.

0 km (0 mi)

Starting N on Hwy 31N, from the junction with Hwy 31A in Kaslo. Head toward Lardeau and Duncan Lake.

28.4 km (17.6 mi)

Pass the village of Lardeau.

34.5 km (21.4 mi)

Pass the signed turnoff for Argenta, the Purcell Mtns, and Fry Creek Canyon. Cross a bridge over Cooper Creek, then pass the village of Cooper Creek.

38.3 km (23.7 mi)

MacBeth Icefield (Trip 15) is visible right.

38.7 km (24 mi)

Cross a bridge over Meadow Creek.

40 km (24.8 mi)

Turn left onto **Meadow Creek Road**, following the sign for Meadow Creek spawning channel. This turn is across from and immediately before the pub. Reset your trip odometer to 0.

0 km (0 mi)

Starting N on Meadow Creek Road.

2 km (1.2 mi)

Pavement ends. Proceed straight.

2.9 km (1.8 mi)

Bear right. The left fork descends to the spawning channel.

3.8 km (2.4 mi)

Cross a bridged creek.

4.5 km (2.8 mi)

Fork left. Begin ascending steeply.

9.7 km (6 mi)

Bear left on the main road. Pass a cabin (right).

10.6 km (6.6 mi)

Fork right and ascend.

12 km (7.5 mi)

MacBeth Icefield and Duncan Lake are visible.

15.4 km (9.6 mi)

Bear right on Meadow Mtn Road. Left is Cooper Creek Road.

Meadow Mtn summit ridge, Purcells beyond

1

2

3

4

5

19.7 km (12.2 mi)
The road is rougher, steeper.

23.3 km (14.4 mi)
The road climbs sharply for 200 m (220 yd).

23.4 km (14.5 mi)
Cross a stream in a culvert. Clearance and strong torque are necessary ahead. If you're hesitant, park here and walk.

24.1 km (15 mi)
The road is very steep and rough. The left shoulder drops abruptly.

24.9 km (15.5 mi)
Reach a switchback where it's possible to park on the left. But the road ahead is no more difficult than what you've surmounted.

25.4 km (15.8 mi)
Negotiate a trench.

26.3 km (16.3 mi)
Pass a short, right spur. It ascends to an **A-frame cabin** (open to the public for overnight use—first come, first served). The **Meadow Mtn route** begins upslope, behind the cabin. Trailhead parking is in the notch 0.2 km (0.1 mi) ahead.

26.5 km (16.5 mi)
Enter a **notch** at 2152 m (7060 ft). Park here for Meadow Mtn. Otherwise continue driving left.

26.8 km (16.7 mi)
Reach a Forest Service campsite (table, firepit) in a meadow at 2190 m (7185 ft). If continuing to road's end (2.8 km / 1.7 mi farther), consider walking, so you can fully appreciate the alpine environs and constant views.

27.2 km (16.9 mi)
Pass a tarn and another campsite (toilet, firepit).

27.6 km (17.1 mi)
Fork right. The Spokane Glacier on 3094-m (10,151-ft) Mt. Cooper is visible left (SW).

28.4 km (17.6 mi)
The road follows the boundary of Goat Range Provincial Park. You're on a steep, subalpine slope that plunges 1150 m (3772 ft) into McKian Creek Canyon.

29.6 km (18.4 mi)
Reach the last reasonable place to park, at 2256 m (7400 ft). Ignore the steeply descending, left fork. Meadow Mtn is visible right (ESE). To continue, walk the main road NW. It descends into a saddle, climbs, then ends. But you can hike beyond.

photos: *1 Meadow Mtn summit ridge 2 near end of Meadow Mtn Road
3 Mt. Cooper, from road 4 campsite near the notch 5 returning from beyond road's end*

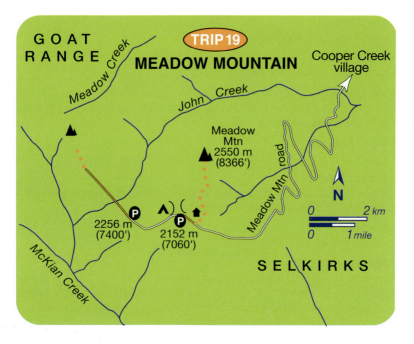

on foot

The bootbeaten route up Meadow Mtn begins at 2170 m (7118 ft), directly behind the **A-frame cabin**. Follow it NNW, into the trees.

In about 4 minutes, ascend into a heathery clearing. Continue ENE, guided by the now sketchy route. Your goal is the ridge above. If you lose the route, beeline upward.

About 15 minutes above the cabin, the ascent eases among scattered trees. Still below the crest, cross a distinctive bench littered with **white rocks**. NNW is a cairn. Continue ascending toward it and beyond.

Note the broken, **black outcrop** (left). It's a helpful landmark on the return (when it should be on your right as you descend). Proceed upward, generally NNE. Reach the **summit ridge** of Meadow Mtn near 2450 m (8036 ft), about 30 minutes from the cabin.

Hamill Creek Valley (Trip 18) is visible ESE. MacBeth Icefield (Trip 15) is NE. In the valley below is Duncan Lake dam. The two summits of Meadow Mtn are N. Glimpse Four Squatters Glacier beyond, just right of the summits.

Proceed left (N), cruising up and down, on or near the summit ridge. After descending into a saddle, ascend a road cleared from chunky, black talus by the local cat-ski operation. It leads to the **first summit**—crowned with communications gizmos—at 2.1 km (1.3 mi), 2520 m (8266 ft). Hiking time: less than 1 hour. The N end of Kootenay Lake is visible SE.

NNE is the 2550-m (8366-ft) **true summit** of Meadow Mtn, at 2.7 km (1.7 mi). It's only 15 minutes farther but requires you to drop into and ascend out of another saddle, adding 130-m (426-ft) of elevation gain to the day's venture. Your reward? An unobstructed N horizon.

TRIP 20
Gwillim Lakes

LOCATION	Valhalla Provincial Park, W of Slocan Lake's S end
ROUND TRIP	11.6 km (7.2 mi), plus 3 km (1.9 mi) to Lucifer Pass
ELEVATION GAIN	1164 m (3818 ft), plus 414 m (1358 ft) to Lucifer Pass
KEY ELEVATIONS	trailhead 1615 m (5297 ft), Drinnon Lake 1950 m (6396 ft) Drinnon Pass 2225 m (7298 ft), Gwillim Creek 1921 m (6301 ft), Gwillim Lakes 2171 m (7120 ft), Lucifer Pass 2585 m (8480 ft)
HIKING TIME	5 hours to 2 days
DIFFICULTY	easy
TRAILHEAD ACCESS	moderate
MAP	Burton 82 F/13

Opinion

Wilderness is precious no matter how people appraise its appearance. A wilderness that nobody ever visits, or even wants to, still contributes ecologically, socially and spiritually to life on earth. So the wilderness of Valhalla Provincial Park has meaning and value regardless that few people venture there, and despite that well-traveled hikers enthusiastically recommend just one of the five trails penetrating the park.

That trail leads to Gwillim Lakes, in the park's southwest corner. It's short enough for a moderate dayhike, but a surfeit of comfortable campgrounds begs you to enjoy a couple days of exceptionally easy backpacking. Every step is a scenic joy. The lakes basin is an exquisite sight and an entertaining destination. No other trip in this book offers such a fulfilling experience so quickly and easily.

The access road is long, but it's broad, brush free, reasonably smooth, suitable for the average 2WD car. Shortly before the road ends, it curves east. Here your eyes will widen and your heart quicken as you gaze up to where you're headed. This is the park's impressive southwest edge. Beyond the trailhead, enticements multiply and expand.

You'll climb through cool, mature forest, then cross a bouldery headwall to reach Drinnon Lake, between Gregorio and Drinnon peaks.

Resuming the ascent, soon cross subalpine Drinnon Pass and enter the park. Small campgrounds at both Drinnon Lake and Pass are attractive, but the superior campground at Gwillim Lakes isn't much farther. From the pass, you'll descend back into forest, cross a bridged creek, and begin the final ascent. Views expand. The trail itself engages your attention as it dances along a rock rib and steep slabs.

Gwillim Lakes basin is a broad, bi-level shelf tucked at about treeline into a rugged, mountainous amphitheatre. Though the campground is large, the tent pads are scattered in a meadow, so you can see in all directions, and you won't be cheek-by-jowl with your neighbours. The separate cooking area has a

Gwillim Lakes basin

wastewater drain and metal food cache. On a hot day, plunging into the gorgeous lakes is irresistible. The surrounding alpine slopes invite a full day's exploration: easy wandering or full-on scrambling. The *on foot* directions explain how to surmount Lucifer Pass and attain a view north into the recesses of the park.

Speedy hikers can reach Gwillim Lakes in a mere two hours. So unless you're probing deeper into the park (it's strictly mountaineering beyond Lucifer Pass), consider dayhiking. It will significantly reduce your impact on the land, as well as your pack's impact on your body. Doughty dayhikers can scramble past the smaller lakes in Gwillim's upper basin, tag Lucifer Pass, and return to the trailhead within ten hours.

Fact

by vehicle

To reach Gwillim Lakes trailhead, drive S from New Denver, or N from Playmor Junction (between Nelson and Castlegar). Below are separate directions for each approach.

From New Denver

Start at the Petro Canada station at the junction of Hwys 6 and 31A in New Denver. Drive S on Hwy 6, along Slocan Lake's E shore, 32.5 km (20.2 mi) to the village of Slocan. (Near the village, ignore the signed turnoff for Drinnon Pass.) Turn right (W) onto Gravel Pit Road. Reset your trip odometer to 0.

0 km (0 mi)
Starting W on Gravel Pit Road. Proceed across the Slocan River bridge.

0.8 km (0.5 mi)
Stay left on Slocan West Road.

1.2 km (0.7 mi)
Cross a bridge over Gwillim Creek.

2.3 km (1.4 mi)
Go right on Little Slocan Road.

13.2 km (8.1 mi)
Reach a junction. Bear left (SW) on the main road for Gwillim Lakes. Right onto
Bannock Burn Road leads to Gimli Ridge trailhead (Trip 21).

20.3 km (12.6 mi)
Reach a junction. Turn right (SW) onto Hoder Creek Road for Gwillim Lakes.
Reset your trip odometer to 0. Directions continue on page 144. Bear left to reach
Little Slocan Lakes campground entry road in just 200 m (220 yd).

From Nelson or Castlegar

Drive Hwy 3A to Playmor Junction, midway between Nelson and Castlegar.
Proceed 15.4 km (9.5 mi) N on Hwy 6. Across from a power station, turn left
(NW) onto Passmore Upper Road. Reset your trip odometer to 0.

0 km (0 mi)
Starting NW on Passmore Upper Road.

0.3 km (0.2 mi)
Cross a bridge over Slocan River. Go left to follow Little Slocan River upstream
along its N bank. Gradually curve N.

3.3 km (2 mi)
Pavement ends.

3.7 km (2.3 mi)
Bear left on Little Slocan Road.

5.3 km (3.3 mi)
Bear right.

7.5 km (4.7 mi)
Proceed straight on the main road.

9 km (5.6 mi)
Stay right.

13.3 km (8.2 mi)
Proceed straight where Koch Creek Road forks left.

16.1 km (10 mi) and 23 km (14.3 mi)
Proceed straight.

25 km (15.5 mi)
Proceed straight (NE) for Gwillim Lakes, as well as for Gimli Ridge (Trip 21). Turn
right and descend to reach Little Slocan Lakes campground in 200 m (220 yd).

25.2 km (15.6 mi)
Reach a junction. For Gwillim Lakes turn left (SW) onto Hoder Creek Road.
Reset your trip odometer to 0 and continue following the directions below. For

Gimli Ridge / Mulvey Basin proceed straight (NE) 7.1 km (4.4 mi), turn left onto Bannock Burn Road, then follow the directions on page 149.

0 km (0 mi)
Starting SW on Hoder Creek Road.

6.5 km (4 mi) and 10.3 km (6.4 mi)
Bear right.

10.6 km (6.6 mi)
Bear right and descend. Notice the huge cedar just before a granite wall.

18.5 km (11.5 mi)
Fork left. Do not ascend right.

18.8 km (11.7 mi)
Fork right. Impressive granite mountains are soon visible.

21.3 km (13.2 mi)
Reach road's end and the Gwillim Lakes trailhead, at 1615 m (5297 ft).

Upon leaving Gwillim Lakes trailhead, when you reach the junction of Hoder Creek and Little Slocan roads, you can (1) turn right to continue retracing your approach, or (2) turn left for Gimli Ridge (Trip 21) and the village of Slocan on Hwy 6, as described here.

0 km (0 mi)
Turning left (NE) from Hoder Creek Road onto Little Slocan Road.

7.1 km (4.4 mi)
Reach a junction. For the village of Slocan on Hwy 6, proceed straight (NE) and continue following the directions below. For Gimli Ridge, turn left onto Bannock Burn Road, then follow the directions on page 149.

Gwillim Lakes campground

18 km (11.2 mi)
Bear left.

19.1 km (11.8 mi)
Cross a bridge over Gwillim Creek.

19.4 km (12 mi)
Go right and cross a bridge over the Slocan River.

20.3 km (12.6 mi)
Reach the village of Slocan and intersect Hwy 6. Turn left (N) for New Denver. Turn right (S) to reach Hwy 3A at Playmor Junction, between Nelson and Castlegar.

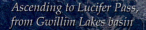
Ascending to Lucifer Pass, from Gwillim Lakes basin

on foot

Directly N of the trailhead is Gregorio Peak. Gwillim Lakes basin is directly N of Gregorio. But to reach the basin, the trail initially heads E, toward Drinnon Peak. The ascent is moderate, steepening as you curve N and cross a boulder slide. The trail is well defined and easy to follow all the way to Gwillim.

Within 1 hour, reach **Drinnon Lake** at 2 km (1.2 mi), 1950 m (6396 ft), beneath granite-walled Drinnon Peak. Just above the lake's S shore is a small campground. You'll find an outhouse, several tent pads, and a metal food cache.

Cross the lake's outlet stream on a sturdy bridge. The trail ascends through open forest, NW then N, to a tiny lake in **Drinnon Pass** at 3.5 km (2.2 mi), 2225 m (7298 ft). There's another small campground here: outhouse, several tent pads, metal food cache. Enter Valhalla Provincial Park at the pass.

Proceeding N of the pass, descend to cross a headwater tributary of **Gwillim Creek** at 1921 m (6301 ft). Figure about 1¾ hours to this point. Soon begin the final 250-m (820-ft) ascent generally NW to the lakes basin.

Part way up, at about 2043 m (6700 ft), the trail is on a rock rib above a steep cliff allowing an aerial perspective of Gwillim Creek valley. N is Gwillim Creek, cascading down from the lakes basin. NE are the craggy Devils Range peaks forming the N wall of the valley. E, beyond Slocan Lake, is Kokanee Glacier Provincial Park.

After the valley overlook, traverse a narrow rockslide beneath steep rock slabs. Just above, the trail levels, entering **Gwillim Lakes basin** at 5.8 km (3.6 mi), 2171 m (7120 ft). Total hiking time: about 2½ hours.

The first of the two main lakes is a few minutes straight ahead (N). On the way, you'll pass a couple campsites, a metal food cache, and a communal cooking area with a wastewater drain. The **campground** has 8 tent pads, mostly scattered to your right (E) in the boulder-strewn alpine meadow. That's also where the outhouse is perched on a platform.

The second main lake is nearby, NW of the first lake, at the same elevation. A smaller third lake is a bit farther NW and about 76 m (250 ft) higher. The two upper basin lakes are N of the first lake and 134 m (440 ft) higher—an easy, off-trail ramble en route to Lucifer Pass, described next.

LUCIFER PASS

ROUND TRIP	3 km (1.9 mi) from Gwillim Lakes campground
ELEVATION GAIN	414 m (1358 ft)
HIKING TIME	3 hours
DIFFICULTY	easy to upper lakes basin, challenging to the pass

Looking N from Gwillim Lakes campground, you can see Lucifer Pass, a narrow arete between Black Prince (left) and Lucifer Peak (right). The pass grants you a view of Rocky Lakes basin (N) and one of the Hird Lakes (farther N).

Between Gwillim Lakes campground and Lucifer Pass is upper Gwillim Lakes basin with two lakes: one small, one long and thin. No established trail continues into the upper basin. Sections of bootbeaten tread are helpful but unnecessary. The one moderately steep, rocky slope is easily overcome.

Continuing beyond the upper basin to Lucifer Pass requires strenuous scrambling. The terrain steepens, and huge, awkward boulders force you to stop and plan your route. But there's no exposure, nothing technical.

From the campground, follow the path around the SE side of the first main lake, then curve N. Ascend the **green chute**, right of an escarpment and waterfall. Work your way up the rocky slope to enter the **upper basin**—134 m (440 ft) above the main basin. The lakes are surrounded by soft, grassy tussocks and scattered boulders. Where you first reach the upper basin, at its S edge, you can survey the entire Gwillim area and scope out other possible explorations.

Drinnon Lake

Onward and upward? Stay right (E) of the upper lakes. Climb NE then N to 2585-m (8480-ft) **Lucifer Pass**. It's between Lucifer Peak (E), and Black Prince (W).

From there you an see it's an arduous, precipitous down-scramble N to the Rocky Lakes and across the valley headwall to the Hird Lakes. Left of and above the Rocky Lakes is Mt. Bor. Right of and beyond Hird Lakes is Urd Peak. Blocked from view, farther down valley, is Evans Lake, the park's largest.

TRIP 21

Gimli Ridge

LOCATION	Valhalla Provincial Park, W of Slocan Lake's S end
ROUND TRIP	9.8 km (6.1 mi)
ELEVATION GAIN	765 m (2510 ft)
KEY ELEVATIONS	trailhead 1750 m (5740 ft)
	saddle 2399 m (7870 ft)
	ridge 2515 m (8250 ft)
HIKING TIME	4¼ to 5 hours
DIFFICULTY	moderate
TRAILHEAD ACCESS	moderate
MAP	Burton 82 F/13

Opinion

Mulvey Basin harbors a vivid-green, lake-splashed meadow so idyllic that satyrs and wood nymphs surely cavort there when nobody's looking. And rarely is anyone looking, because bouncers—menacing, sheer-walled, charcoal hued peaks—refuse entry to hikers.

The old, overgrown trail up Mulvey Creek pierces prime grizzly habitat and halts at a 610-m (2000-ft) headwall that militantly guards the basin above. Climbers might access Mulvey Basin via mountaineering routes, either skirting Wolfs Ears Peak or Gimli Peak. Hikers can follow the Gimli Peak route only as far as Gimli Ridge. But it's worth it: for the view of Mulvey Basin below, and the intimate encounter with Gimli Peak.

Gimli Peak's immensity will dominate your attention en route to the ridge. The peak's black veins give it the look of zebra hide. A profusion of green lichen adds a hint of equatorial lizard skin. Contouring just below the SW face, you might hear rushing water. Is there a stream nearby? No. It's the sound of wind glancing off and swishing across the expanse of vertical rock.

Only when you look south beyond the trailhead does this trip disappoint. In that direction you'll see the tame, forested ridges of the Bonnington Range bubbling down toward Idaho. But the terrain ahead—north toward Gimli Peak, east to Wolfs Ears Peak—more than compensates.

Be aware that the trail to Gimli Ridge dwindles after contouring beneath Gimli Peak's southwest face. Acrophobes should stop there. Beyond, the tread narrows on a steep slope. The final, short ascent to Gimli Ridge requires light, unexposed scrambling. The ridge itself is a slim arete, with only a few awkward boulders for seating. The drop into Mulvey Basin is abrupt. Most hikers, however, will find all this exhilarating yet safe.

Approaching Gimli Ridge

Fact

by vehicle

From the Petro Canada station at the junction of Hwys 6 and 31A in **New Denver**, drive S on Hwy 6. Follow Slocan Lake's E shore 32.5 km (20.2 mi) to the village of Slocan. (Near the village, ignore the signed turnoff for Drinnon Pass.) Turn right (W) onto Gravel Pit Road. Reset your trip odometer to 0.

From **Playmor Junction** (midway between Nelson and Castlegar, where Hwy 6 departs Hwy 3A) drive N on Hwy 6. Proceed 45.5 km (28.2 mi) to the village of Slocan. Turn left (W) onto Gravel Pit Road. Reset your trip odometer to 0.

0 km (0 mi)
Starting W on Gravel Pit Road. Proceed across the Slocan River bridge.

0.8 km (0.5 mi)
Stay left on Slocan West Road.

1.2 km (0.7 mi)
Cross a bridge over Gwillim Creek.

2.3 km (1.4 mi)
Go right on Little Slocan Road.

13.2 km (8.1 mi)
Reach a junction. For Gimli Ridge, turn right (NW) onto Bannock Burn Road, reset your trip odometer to 0, and continue following the directions below. Left (SW) on the main road leads to Hoder Creek Road at 20.3 km (12.6 mi), where right (SW) leads to Gwillim Lakes trailhead (Trip 20). Bear left at 20.3 km (12.6 mi) to reach Little Slocan Lakes campground entry road in just 200 m (220 yd).

0 km (0 mi)
Starting NW on Bannock Burn Road. In 100 m (110 yd), bear right. At 200 m (220 yd), bear right again and descend briefly.

Mulvey Basin, from Gimli Ridge

8.4 km (5.2 mi)
Proceed straight.

10.5 km (6.5 mi)
Curve right on the main road and ascend steeply.

12.5 km (7.8 mi)
Bear left.

12.7 km (7.9 mi)
Curve sharply back, heading toward jagged peaks.

12.9 km (8 mi)
Reach road's end and the Gimli Ridge trailhead, at 1750 m (5740 ft).

on foot

Follow the trail N through a brushy clearcut. Within 10 minutes turn left, cross a creek, and enter forest. The trail is distinct, the ascent moderate. Your general direction of travel is N, toward Gimli Peak.

After about 40 minutes of steady climbing, the grade eases. Pass big, embedded boulders. Gain a view of the alpine basin ahead. Soon after, the ascent steepens again along a narrow, **subalpine rib** granting views on both sides.

The trail fades above treeline. Traces of bootbeaten path and common sense will lead you left (NW), up the **rocky, grassy slope**, through a patch of beige gravel.

At about 1½ hours, reach a 2399-m (7870-ft) **saddle on the S shoulder of Gimli Peak**. There's a stone windblock on top, and a green plastic toilet on the W slope.

Proceed N toward Gimli Peak, staying just left (W) of the shoulder's crest. A few cairns will guide your ascent. Clamber over **stone blocks** covered with black-and-green lichen. Near the top of talus, a sketchy path is visible. It switchbacks tightly, approaching Gimli's sheer SW face.

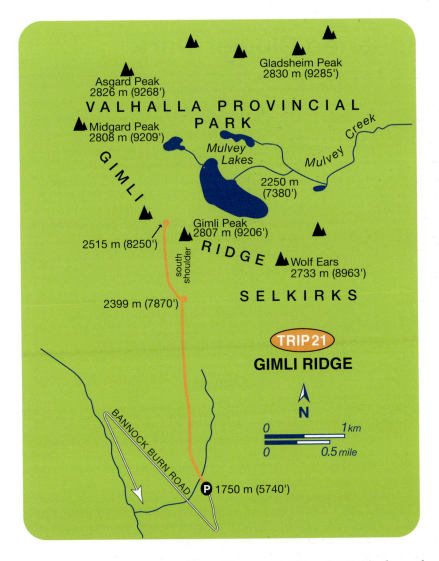

About 30 minutes above the saddle, near 2470 m (8100 ft), the path descends briefly, working N around the **vertical face** to a grassy bench about one meter wide. Where the path ends, the route is still obvious: up, directly ahead, over chunky boulders.

Just 15 minutes of mild scrambling will earn you a perch on 2515-m (8250-ft) **Gimli Ridge**, immediately W of Gimli Peak, about 4.9 km (3 mi) from the trailhead.

More than 305 m (1000 ft) below you, N and NE, are the Mulvey Basin lakes. The steep, icy descent from the ridge into the basin requires climbing skills and equipment. Across the basin N is Asgard Peak. NE is Gladsheim Peak.

TRIP 22, 23, 24, 25
Kokanee Glacier Park

LOCATION	Selkirks, W of Kootenay Lake between Nelson and Kaslo
DISTANCE	9.2-km (5.7-mi) round trip to Kokanee Lake 31-km (19.2-mi) circuit for optimal backpack
ELEVATION GAIN	405 m (1328 ft) for round trip to Kokanee Lake 986 m (3233 ft) for optimal backpack circuit
KEY ELEVATIONS	Gibson Lake trailhead 1565 m (5133 ft), Kokanee Lake 1970 m (6462 ft), Kaslo Lake 1957 m (6420 ft) Kokanee Glacier Cabin 1965 m (6445 ft), upper Sapphire Lake 2262 m (7419 ft), Mt. Giegerich 2449 m (8033 ft), S end of Glory Basin 2400 m (7872 ft) Helen Deane Lake 1975 m (6478 ft)
HIKING TIME	3 hours for Kokanee Lake 3 days / 2 nights for optimal backpack
DIFFICULTY	easy to Kokanee, Kaslo, Sapphire, and Helen Deane lakes, moderate to Mt. Giegerich or Glory Basin
TRAILHEAD ACCESS	easy
MAPS	Kokanee Peak 82 F/11, Slocan 82 F/14

Opinion

If the West Kootenay wilderness were a swimming pool, the core area of Kokanee Glacier Provincial Park would be the shallow end.

It's less intimidating, more inviting, because the primary trail entering the park's core—from Gibson Lake trailhead, to Kaslo Lake—is well constructed, gently graded, regularly maintained, frequently signed. Few West Kootenay trails possess these attributes.

And the core area's primary trail leads to a palace of a backcountry hut: Kokanee Glacier Cabin. Imagine a multi-millionaire's Whistler chalet plunked down on the shore of Kaslo Lake. It certainly blunts the sharp edge of the savage West Kootenay, making it less severe, more merciful.

Kokanee Park's core area is also more beautiful than much of the West Kootenay. Or rather, you'll find the region's beauty in higher concentration here. It's not just a *park* in the geopolitical sense. Numerous lakes and extensive alplands make it truly park-like.

Inviting + merciful + beautiful = popular. Thus Kokanee Park's core area does not afford solitude. It hosts a steady stream of hikers. Solitude is among the distinguishing and most appealing traits of the West Kootenay wilderness. But don't expect to find it here.

Five of the trips in this book begin on the primary trail entering Kokanee Park's core area: Kokanee & Kaslo Lakes (Trip 22), Sapphire Lakes / Mt. Giegerich

photos: *1 Kaslo Lake, Kokanee Glacier Cabin far shore 3 Kokanee Lake 2 & 4 Kokanee Glacier Cabin 5 Queens Cup*

Stream en route to Griffin Lake

(Trip 23), Glory Basin (Trip 24), Helen Deane Lake (Trip 25), and The Keyhole (Trip 26).

The first four of those trips lead to and beyond Kaslo Lake and—ideally—require a two-night stay, so we've grouped them together here. The Keyhole spur veers off the primary trail well before Kokanee Lake and—ideally—is a dayhike unto itself, so we describe it separately.

For the Kaslo Lake-and-beyond options, here's our advice:

22 Kokanee and Kaslo Lakes

From Gibson Lake trailhead, a pedestrian highway leads 4.6 km (2.9 mi) to Kokanee Lake: brilliant cobalt, in a sharp-sided notch. You'll traverse a steep slope above the west shore. Beyond, you'll enter the basin cradling Keen, Garland and Kaslo lakes. You'll reach Kaslo Lake campground, near the southeast shore, at 8 km (5 mi). Kokanee Glacier Cabin is above the northeast shore, at 8.5 km (5.3 mi).

Carrying a full backpack, hiking at a moderate pace, you'll reach the cabin in 2½ hours. So, carrying only a daypack, it's easy to tour all these lakes in a single day. But don't do it, unless you're unable to devote more time here.

Three days is the minimum requirement for maximal enjoyment: one day to hike in; one day to continue up to Sapphire Lakes, plus either Mt. Giegerich or Glory Basin; one day to hike out; the afternoon you hike in, or the morning you hike out, you can visit Helen Deane Lake.

Basing yourself at Kaslo Lake for a couple nights, you must decide: campground or cabin? The campground has eight tent sites (available first come, first served), an outhouse, bear-proof food storage, and a wastewater drain. It's notoriously buggy.

The timber frame, post-and-beam cabin has 20 bunks, running water, a full kitchen (fridge and stoves), a spacious dining room, plus indoor toilets and showers. It's famously luxurious.

Kokanee Lake

You'll pay significantly more at the cabin, but you'll be significantly more comfortable. Staying at the cabin also eliminates a tent and sleeping pad from your pack weight. This is the only deluxe, public accommodation in the West Kootenay backcountry. Take advantage of it. Opt for the campground only if you can't reserve space at the cabin.

See page 158 for Kokanee and Kaslo Lakes (Trip 22) on foot directions.

23 Sapphire Lakes / Mt. Giegerich

Kokanee Lake is an impressive sight. Kaslo Lake, with its campground and cabin, is a convenient base. But the compelling destination here is high above Kaslo Lake's west shore: the alplands extending from Griffin Creek, south to Lemon Pass, Sapphire Lakes, and Glory Basin; and above Griffin Lakes to Mt. Giegerich.

This pocket of poetic beauty invites you to wander, sit, admire, resume… meander, stop, meditate, continue… explore, pause, gaze, and carry on. Here you'll hike along streams, past tarns, among granite boulders, through meadows and rock gardens. Visually, it's intriguing. Atmospherically, it's soothing. Never is it taxing.

Well, depending on your fitness and experience level, you might find Mt. Giegerich taxing. But it's mellow compared to most summits. Some call it an "easy scramble." We think of it as simply a short, off-trail detour to a fine viewpoint where you can overlook the alplands and see far beyond.

Lower Sapphire Lake

See page 161 for Sapphire Lakes / Mt. Giegerch (Trip 23) on foot directions.

Glory Basin

24 Glory Basin

Glory Basin is an austere, alpine groove just above and south-southeast of Sapphire Lakes. Ringed by Sunset Mtn, Outlook Mtn, and Mt. John Carter, it seems a world apart: virginal, ethereal. It comprises slabs, pools, trickles, moss beds, and the occasional, tenacious wildflower.

The easiest way to appreciate Glory Basin is on a round trip via Sapphire Lakes, starting and ending the day at Kaslo Lake—either the campground or cabin.

A more challenging and fulfilling option is to visit Glory Basin on a loop: starting at Kaslo Lake, ascending past Sapphire Lakes, returning to Kaslo Lake via the Commission Creek route.

You have but one day for Kokanee Park? The weather forecast is solid gold? You're a swift, determined dayhiker? Consider an aggressive circuit. Start early at Gibson Lake trailhead, stride past Kokanee Lake, round Kaslo Lake, march to Sapphire Lakes, probe Glory Basin, exit the alplands via the Commission Creek route, then troop back to the trailhead. You'll see it all in a single sortie between sunrise and sunset.

Before attempting the loop or the circuit, however, be aware that the Commission Creek route is a plummeting descent through a rocky gorge that lacks a defined trail. It entails navigation and constant boulder-hopping. Toughened hikers find it a fun, exciting shortcut. But if you've rarely strayed off-trail, don't start experimenting here. It's safest to return the way you came.

See page 162 for Glory Basin (Trip 24) on foot directions.

25 Helen Deane Lake

You pitched your tent at the campground, or fluffed your bag in your bunk at the cabin. You've eaten dinner, done the dishes, yet sunset is still a couple hours away. And someone asks, "Wanna go for a walk?" "Sure," you say, "to Helen Deane Lake."

It's an easy, 45 minutes from the cabin on Kaslo Lake. The round trip elevation gain is only 162 m (531 ft). The setting is pretty: an undulating, subalpine bench. En route you'll pass the 120-year-old Slocan Chief Cabin, now an interpretive centre.

Helen Deane is also the logical, dayhike destination for the less capable or motivated among a family or group comprising a broad range of ages, abilities or interests. If you're a strong, keen hiker, however, file Helen Deane in the "maybe, if there's time" category.

See page 164 for Helen Deane Lake (Trip 25) on foot *directions.*

Fact

before your trip

Be aware that dogs and bikes are not allowed in Kokanee Park.

If you hope to stay at Kokanee Glacier Cabin, make reservations well in advance with the Alpine Club of Canada: info@alpineclubofcanada.ca, or (403) 678-3200.

If you intend to pitch your tent at Kaslo Lake, bring cash to pay the camping fee. And if you intend to cook, bring a stove, because campfires are prohibited.

If you're staying overnight in the park, bring chicken wire to wrap around your vehicle. (See photo page 26.) It will prevent porcupines from munching the tires, hoses and fan belts. Secure it with rocks and pieces of wood. Seriously. You don't want to return to the trailhead and find your vehicle has been disabled. In the past, chicken wire has been available at Gibson Lake trailhead. But bring your own, to be sure you have enough to adequately protect your vehicle.

Helen Deane Lake

by vehicle

In **Nelson**, from the middle of the orange bridge spanning Kootenay Lake's west arm, drive Hwy 3A NE 20 km (12.4 mi). Or, in **Balfour**, from the turnoff to the Kootenay Lake ferry terminal, drive Highway 3A SW 11.7 km (7.3 mi). From either approach, turn E onto the unpaved road signed for Kokanee Glacier Provincial Park. Reset your trip odometer to zero.

0 km (0 mi)
Starting E on the unpaved road to Kokanee Park, from Hwy 3A.

4.2 km (2.6 mi)
Cross the Busk Creek bridge.

7.2 km (4.5 mi)
Proceed straight on the main road. Ignore the descending left fork.

10.2 km (6.3 mi)
Cross the Sunset Creek bridge.

11.5 km (7.1 mi)
Pass the Kokanee Cedars (Trip 49) trailhead (left).

16 km (10 mi)
Bear right and enter the spacious, Gibson Lake trailhead parking lot. Elevation: 1565 m (5133 ft). There's a day-use shelter here, as well as picnic tables, outhouses, and a kiosk.

on foot

TRIP 22 KOKANEE & KASLO LAKES

ROUND TRIP	17 km (10.5 mi) to Kokanee Glacier Cabin
ELEVATION GAIN	524 m (1718 ft)
HIKING TIME	4½ to 5 hours

For Kokanee & Kaslo Lakes (Trip 22), Sapphire Lakes / Mt. Giegerich (Trip 23), Glory Basin (Trip 24), and Helen Deane Lake (Trip 25), the directions are initially the same, as follows:

Depart the NE corner of Gibson Lake trailhead, right of the kiosk, on a **former road**. Ignore the trail descending from the day-use shelter to the lake.

Begin a moderate ascent N. Soon switchback right (SE). In 15 minutes, at 1670 m (5478 ft), immediately before a culvert, bear left onto the signed trail and ascend N. The road continues straight (SSE). About 5 minutes farther, the trail curves left to rejoin the road. Proceed generally NW.

At 1770 m (5806 ft), after hiking about 30 minutes, turn left onto trail, leaving the former road behind. You'll hike generally NNW all the way to Kaslo Lake. Streams tumbling down the valley walls are now audible. Impressive cliffs are visible. Soon enter the **subalpine zone**. At 40 minutes, overlook Gibson Lake (left / S).

At 3.5 km (2.2 mi), about 1 hour from the trailhead, pass through a **narrow draw**. Just beyond, look up (right / NNE) to see The Keyhole (Trip 26), on the crest of the valley wall. About 150 m (165 yd) farther, at 1975 m (6480 ft), the unsigned **Keyhole trail** forks right and ascends N. Proceed straight (NNW) on the primary trail, contouring for the next 0.75 km (0.5 mi).

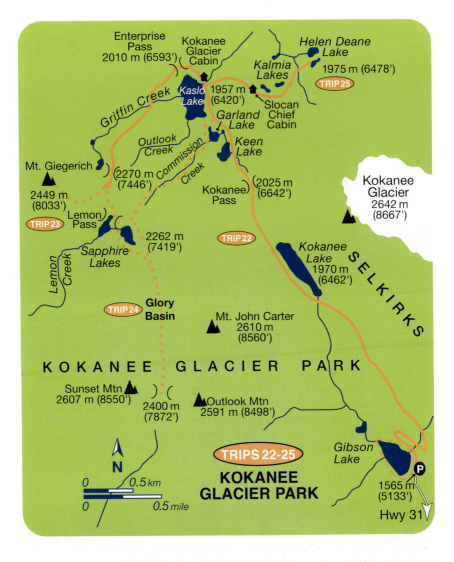

Overlook Kokanee Lake ahead (NNW) after hiking about 1¼ hours. A brief descent lands you at the S end of **Kokanee Lake** at 4.6 km (2.9 mi), 1970 m (6462 ft), about 1½ hours from the trailhead.

The trail continues NNW, contouring about 24 m (80 ft) above the **lake's SW shore**. Views are constant. Cross an enormous rockslide spilling down the NE flank of Mt. John Carter.

Beyond Kokanee Lake, cruise NNW through broad meadows. Crest Kokanee Pass at 2025 m (6642 ft). Then descend along beautiful, mossy creeklets, passing above the NE shore of small Keen Lake at 7.4 km (4.6 mi), 1993 m (6537 ft).

Still heading NNW, the trail passes above the NE shore of small **Garland Lake** at 7.8 km (4.8 mi), 1970 m (6462 ft).

Kokanee Glacier Cabin on Kaslo Lake,
from Enterprise Pass. The Pyramids beyond.

If you intend to hike the Glory Basin loop or circuit, pause here and observe. Left (SW) is Commission Creek gorge—the descent route from Sapphire Lakes. You'll follow the creek downstream to the W shore of Garland Lake, then skirt the N shore to rejoin the trail near where you now stand.

Resuming NNW beyond Garland Lake, the trail passes above the SE shore of larger **Kaslo Lake** at 8 km (5.3 mi), 1963 m (6439 ft). A signed, left spur leads SSW to the **campground**. The primary trail continues N, above Kaslo lake's E shore.

Reach a signed **junction** above the **NE end of Kaslo Lake**, at 8.45 km (5.2 mi), 1963 m (6439 ft), about 2½ hours from the trailhead. Left (W) leads to **Kokanee Glacier Cabin** at 8.5 km (5.3 mi), 1965 m (6445 ft), then continues to Sapphire Lakes / Mt. Giegerich (Trip 23), and Glory Basin (Trip 24). Right (NE) leads to Slocan Chief Cabin and Helen Deane Lake (Trip 25).

Griffin Lake

TRIP 23 SAPPHIRE LAKES / MT. GIEGERICH

ROUND TRIP	8.6 km (5.3 mi) to upper Sapphire Lake
	9.8 km (6.1 mi) to Mt. Geigerich
ELEVATION GAIN	347 m (1138 ft) to upper Sapphire Lake
	526 m (1725 ft) to Mt. Geigerich
HIKING TIME	2¾ to 3 hours for upper Sapphire Lake
	3¼ to 3½ hours for Mt. Geigerich

Follow the directions in Trip 22 to the signed **junction** above the **NE end of Kaslo Lake**, at 8.45 km (5.2 mi), 1963 m (6439 ft), about 2½ hours from the trailhead.

Turn left (W). Reach **Kokanee Glacier Cabin** at 8.5 km (5.3 mi), 1965 m (6445 ft). Beyond the W corner of the building (front, left, when facing away from the entry steps), pick up the trail signed for Sapphire and Tanal lakes. Subsequent distances begin at the cabin.

A 10-minute ascent generally NW leads to a junction at 0.3 km (0.2 mi), in 2010-m (6593-ft) **Enterprise Pass**. Nearing the pass, overlook Kaslo Lake and glimpse Kokanee Glacier SE.

The Enterprise Creek trail descends right (NW) from the pass, reaching Tanal Lake in 1.8 km (1.1 mi). For Sapphire Lakes and Glory Basin, turn left (SW). About 8 minutes above the pass, a tiny gap (right / NW) grants a view of Tanal Lake far below, in Enterprise Creek Valley.

Ascending the Griffin Creek drainage SW toward Griffin Lake, the trail narrows and becomes rougher. Kokanee Glacier is partially visible left (SE). Behind you (NE) is dark, stark, Sawtooth Ridge NE.

At 2220 m (7282 ft), the trail negotiates impressive, granite boulders, above and E of shallow **Griffin Lake**. A deep, turquoise channel snakes through the drainage. Continue the gentle ascent S to a 2270-m (7446-ft) **saddle** at 3.3 km (2 mi). Mt. Giegerich is the gentle peak right (WSW).

Mt. Giegerich

The summit calls you? Pause in the saddle and plot your freelance ascent. The most gradual route is evident. In general, leave the trail by angling right (SW). High on the mountain's shoulder, near 2380 m (7806 ft), curve right (NW). Near 2420 m (7938 ft), bear right (N) to the 2449-m (8033-ft) summit of **Mt. Giegerich**. Distance from the saddle: 1.6 km (1 mi). Distance from the cabin on Kaslo Lake: 4.9 km (3 mi). The panorama includes the Valhallas (W), and the Purcells (E). Overlook Glory Basin SSE, and an unnamed tarn perched high on the mountain's SW arm.

If returning directly to Kaslo Lake, descend by retracing your steps to the trail in the saddle. If continuing to Sapphire Lakes or Glory Basin, descend by retracing your steps to about 2380 m (7806 ft), then dropping generally W to intersect the trail between the saddle (left / N) and Sapphire Lakes (right / S).

Sapphire Lakes

Continuing S from the 2270-m (7446-ft) saddle at 3.3 km (2 mi), the trail descends gradually into broad, subalpine **Lemon Pass**. Follow it across an open expanse toward a stand of subalpine fir. Sheltered among the trees is a green, plastic toilet. Just beyond and slightly below is **lower Sapphire Lake**, at 4 km

Smuggler's Ridge, near Helen Deane Lake

(2.5 mi), 2245 m (7365 ft), near the SW end of the pass. Just past the lake's SW end, the outlet stream plunges into Lemon Creek Valley.

Hiking cross-country now, rockhop around the NE end of lower Sapphire Lake. From the SE shore, angle left (SE) and ascend. Jump the creek linking the lower and upper lakes. Pass a cascade-fed pool. At 4.3 km (2.7 mi), 2262 m (7419 ft), reach the NW shore of **upper Sapphire Lake**. Glory Basin is above and beyond the far (SSE) end of the lake.

TRIP 24 GLORY BASIN

ROUND TRIP	14.6 km (9.1 mi) from Kokanee Glacier Cabin
LOOP	14 km (8.7 mi) returning via Commission Creek
CIRCUIT	29.6 km (18.4 mi) from Gibson Lake, returning via Commission Creek
ELEVATION GAIN	485 m (1590 ft) for round trip, 462 m (1515 ft) for loop, 977 m (3204 ft) for circuit
HIKING TIME	5¼ hours for round trip, 5 hours for loop 9½ hours for circuit

Follow the directions in Trip 22 to the signed **junction** above the **NE end of Kaslo Lake**, at 8.45 km (5.2 mi), 1963 m (6439 ft), about 2½ hours from the trailhead.

Turn left (W). Reach **Kokanee Glacier Cabin** at 8.5 km (5.3 mi), 1965 m (6445 ft). From there, follow the directions in Trip 23 to **upper Sapphire Lake**. It's at 4.3 km (2.7 mi), 2262 m (7419 ft), above the SE edge of Lemon Pass.

Glory Basin is above and beyond the far (SSE) end of the lake. To explore the trail-less, alpine basin, round the right (W) shore of upper Sapphire Lake. Then ascend SSE. Ahead is 2610-m (8560-ft) Mt. John Carter, which forms the basin's left (E) wall.

At 2320 m (7610 ft), you're about midway into **Glory Basin**. Proceed S into the basin's upper reaches. Between 2607-m (8550-ft) Sunset Mtn (right / W), and 2591-m (8498-ft) Outlook Mtn (left / ESE), is a 2400-m (7872-ft) **unnamed pass**. This is the **S end of Glory Basin**, at 7.3 km (4.5 mi). Beyond (SW) is Nilsik Creek Valley.

Upon exiting Glory Basin, you can, of course, retrace your steps to Kaslo Lake via Griffin Lake and Enterprise Pass. Or you can vary the return by opting for the Commission Creek route. It allows you to loop back to Kaslo Lake, or complete a circuit ending back at Gibson Lake trailhead.

Commission Creek Route

The Commission Creek route will shorten your distance: slightly if returning to Kaslo Lake, substantially if returning all the way to Gibson Lake. But it doesn't necessarily make for an easier day. It's a plummeting descent through a rocky gorge that lacks a defined trail. Attempt it only if you have off-trail confidence born of experience.

For the Commission Creek route, retrace your steps from the **unnamed pass** (S end of Glory Basin) at 7.3 km (4.5 mi), to the N end of **upper Sapphire Lake**, at 10.3 km (6.4 mi), 2245 m (7365 ft). Do not continue N to the saddle through which you previously arrived here. Instead, turn right (NE) and descend the open, grassy, lower reaches of **Lemon Pass**.

Watch for sections of bootbeaten path and occasional cairns. Initially hike on the left (NW) bank of **Commission Creek**, but cross to the right (SE) bank farther down. Follow the creek downstream. Keep descending NE. In general, stay more right than left.

Approaching Garland Lake, go left (N), off the last boulder field. Descend the final 23 m (75 ft) in **forest**. There might still be a few cairns in this jumbled

Upper Glory Basin

area. Round the N shore of Garland Lake. Then angle right (E), across the meadow between Kaslo and Garland lakes. Intersect the park's primary **trail** at 13.3 km (8.2 mi), 1970 m (6462 ft), above the NE shore of small **Garland Lake**.

You're now on familiar ground. Turn left (NNW) to complete a loop, reaching Kokanee Glacier Cabin at 14 km (8.7 mi). Turn right (SSE) to complete the 29.6-km (18.4-mi) circuit starting and ending at Gibson Lake trailhead.

TRIP 25 HELEN DEANE LAKE

ROUND TRIP	5 km (3.1 mi)
ELEVATION GAIN	162 m (531 ft)
HIKING TIME	1½ hours

Follow the directions in Trip 22 to the signed **junction** above the **NE end of Kaslo Lake**, at 8.45 km (5.2 mi), 1963 m (6439 ft), about 2½ hours from the trailhead.

Turn right (NE). Ascend over the gentle shoulder of **Smuggler's Ridge** at 2050 m (6724 ft). Continue E to the 120-year-old **Slocan Chief Cabin**, now an interpretive centre. Kokanee Glacier is visible right (SE). A couple minutes beyond, pass the tiny **Kalmia Lakes**. About 10 minutes farther NE, 2.5 km (1.6 mi) from the junction near Kaslo Lake, reach **Helen Deane Lake** at 1975 m (6478 ft).

Descending Commission Creek route

Before retracing your steps back to Kaslo Lake, resume N another 6 minutes to overlook Keen Creek Valley.

TRIP 26
The Keyhole

LOCATION	Kokanee Glacier Provincial Park, Selkirks, W of Kootenay Lake, between Nelson and Kaslo
ROUND TRIP	11 km (6.8 mi)
ELEVATION GAIN	1144 m (3752 ft)
KEY ELEVATIONS	Gibson Lake trailhead 1565 m (5133 ft), Keyhole fork 1975 m (6480 ft), Keyhole 2709 m (8885 ft)
HIKING TIME	5 to 6 hours
DIFFICULTY	challenging
TRAILHEAD ACCESS	easy
MAP	Kokanee Peak 82 F/11

Opinion

A pedestrian highway pierces the popular core area of Kokanee Glacier Provincial Park. About one hour along is an unsigned fork few hikers notice. Here, a rough but serviceable trail tilts skyward, climbing the valley wall beneath Esmeralda Peak.

But it's only a spur, and it soon stops at an abandoned mine. Above is seriously steep, rugged terrain. No trail could possibly ascend such a chaos of boulders. But confident scramblers do—all the way to a tiny cleft in the ridgecrest separating Kokanee Creek Valley from Kokanee Glacier.

That's the Keyhole. Inserting yourself into it, however, is anticlimactic. Though you're on the edge of Kokanee Glacier, much of the ice is not visible. The ridges and peaks within view aren't much higher than the Keyhole, so they fail to impress.

You find gymnastic challenge to be its own reward? Scrambling exhilarates you even more than a culminating panorama? You measure happiness with an altimeter? The Keyhole will make you very happy, very quickly.

Most hikers won't enjoy and shouldn't attempt the Keyhole. Park rangers tell of novices who've struggled up, looked back, and lost their nerve. Their common sense numbed by fear, they attempted to traverse the glacier, hoping to loop back to the trail. Big mistake.

The glacier is deceptive. It might appear to offer a smooth, gentle, downhill cruise, but it's treacherous. Don't try it without the requisite skills and equipment.

Fact

by vehicle

In **Nelson**, from the middle of the orange bridge spanning Kootenay Lake's west arm, drive Hwy 3A NE 20 km (12.4 mi). Or, in **Balfour**, from the turnoff to the Kootenay Lake ferry terminal, drive Highway 3A SW 11.7 km (7.3 mi). From either approach, turn E onto the unpaved road signed for Kokanee Glacier Provincial Park. Reset your trip odometer to zero.

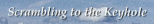

0 km (0 mi)
Starting E on the unpaved road to Kokanee Park, from Hwy 3A.

4.2 km (2.6 mi)
Cross the Busk Creek bridge.

7.2 km (4.5 mi)
Proceed straight on the main road. Ignore the descending left fork.

10.2 km (6.3 mi)
Cross the Sunset Creek bridge.

11.5 km (7.1 mi)
Pass the Kokanee Cedars (Trip 49) trailhead (left).

16 km (10 mi)
Bear right and enter the spacious, Gibson Lake trailhead parking lot. Elevation: 1565 m (5133 ft). There's a day-use shelter here, as well as picnic tables, outhouses, and a kiosk.

on foot

Depart the NE corner of Gibson Lake trailhead, right of the kiosk, on a **former road**. Ignore the trail descending from the day-use shelter to the lake.

Begin a moderate ascent N. Soon switchback right (SE). In 15 minutes, at 1670 m (5478 ft), immediately before a culvert, bear left onto the signed trail and ascend N. The road continues straight (SSE). About 5 minutes farther, the trail curves left to rejoin the road. Proceed generally NW.

At 1770 m (5806 ft), after hiking about 30 minutes, turn left onto trail, leaving the former road behind. You'll hike generally NNW all the way to Kaslo Lake. Streams tumbling down the valley walls are now audible. Impressive cliffs are visible. Soon enter the **subalpine zone**. At 40 minutes, overlook Gibson Lake (left / S).

At 3.5 km (2.2 mi), about 1 hour from the trailhead, pass through a **narrow draw**. Just beyond, look up (right / NNE) to see The Keyhole on the crest of the valley wall.

About 150 m (165 yd) farther—at 3.65 km (2.3 mi), 1975 m (6480 ft)—the unsigned **Keyhole trail** forks right and ascends N. The primary trail proceeds straight (NNW), soon arriving at Kokanee Lake (Trip 22).

Need further help identifying the Keyhole fork? Look for a white drainage pipe beneath the primary trail, and a large solid boulder (left). If you cross a milled-lumber footbridge over a creeklet, you've gone about 15 m / yd too far.

Departing the primary trail, ascend N onto the **steep, open, rocky, heathery slope**. Though narrow, rough, and steep, the Keyhole trail is distinct.

After a long traverse, switchback right (NE), ignoring a faint, left spur. At 4.8 km (3 mi), 2305 m (7560 ft), **reach the end of trail** near a former mine site. The Keyhole is still far above (NE).

Beyond trail's end, a bootbeaten path continues climbing through the increasingly rocky terrain. About 5 minutes past the sign, cross to the NE side of a **stream**.

From here on, you're freelancing. But the Keyhole is visible, so just take aim and work out the easiest line of ascent. A few cairns and scraps of

bootbeaten route offer navigational assistance. You'll soon be scrambling more than hiking.

Above 2400 m (7872 ft), the distant view W includes the Valhallas. Nearby, above you, the 2764-m (9066-ft) Pyramids are NNW. The Keyhole is still NE. Rising immediately right (S) of the Keyhole is 2789-m (9148-ft) Esmeralda Peak.

Returning to the immediate chore, negotiate huge, awkward boulders. The final pitch is very steep but entails no exposure. Solid hand- and footholds make the left side of the draw easier.

Top out in **the Keyhole** at 5.5 km (3.4 mi), 2709 m (8885 ft). Just as it seems you've escaped the sign-happy park core, you're greeted by yet another sign. This one states the obvious, confirming that you have indeed arrived at your destination.

Trail leading to the Keyhole scramble

Kokanee Glacier is immediately in front of you, E and N. Precisely what you can see depends on how far you can wander, and that will depend on the ice and snow conditions you encounter.

By mid summer, enough snow should have melted to allow you to boulder hop left (N) and attain a broader view. Dark, stark Sawtooth Ridge rises above the far side of the glacier. Distant N is Mt. Brennan (Trip 12). Scramblers unfazed by exposure can continue ascending and see much more.

TRIP 27
Woodbury Cabin

LOCATION	Kokanee Glacier Provincial Park, Selkirks
	W of Kootenay Lake, between Nelson and Kaslo
ROUND TRIP	16 km (10 mi)
ELEVATION GAIN	809 m (2654 ft)
KEY ELEVATIONS	road's end trailhead 1341 m (4400 ft)
	Woodbury cabin 2150 m (7054 ft)
HIKING TIME	5 to 6 hours
DIFFICULTY	moderate
TRAILHEAD ACCESS	moderate
MAP	Slocan 82 F/14

Opinion

The Woodbury Creek trail is an all-or-nothing proposition.

Hike to Woodbury cabin, perched high in the upper reaches of the drainage, and you'll enjoy a grand view of Woodbury Glacier splayed across the north face of Glacier View Peak. En route to that climactic vista, however, the needle on your scenery meter probably won't budge from zero. The lower reaches of the Woodbury drainage just aren't very engaging.

Still, that ta-da! moment justifies this hike, for two reasons:

(1) It's a more impressive sight than Kokanee Glacier. The provincial park's namesake is bigger, but the hiker-accessible viewpoints of it reveal only the edges of the ice. At Woodbury cabin, your perspective of Woodbury Glacier is bang on.

(2) That ta-da! will be the first of many if you press onward and upward to complete the Woodbury-to-Silver-Spray traverse (Trip 28), which is *the* compelling reason to hike here.

From Woodbury cabin, the traverse route leads to Silver Spray cabin. Vast views are constant because it's mostly above treeline. It's an exhilarating adventure—if you're capable.

The prerequisites are experience travelling cross-country, skill at navigating with map and compass, confidence on steep, rough terrain, and physical endurance. For safety and enjoyment, you'll also need fair weather. Read Trip 28 for details.

You're simply dayhiking? It's important to compare the Woodbury and Silver Spray (Trip 29) trails, because they begin at the same trailhead.

Hiking to Woodbury cabin is noticeably easier, because the ascent is gradual. The forest understory is lush. Wildflowers are prevalent, but so is deadfall and brush.

The Silver Spray trail climbs steeply. It requires more concentrated effort but grants you an alpine ramble—across grassy slopes studded with slabby rocks—before reaching the cabin.

Woodbury Glacier

Surveying the world from Silver Spray cabin, nothing your eyes light upon is as impressive as Woodbury Glacier, yet the immediate terrain is more varied, intriguing, and beautiful.

At Silver Spray, you can wander among nearby tarns, scramble on granite slabs, or ascend another 30 minutes on a cairned route: past the remains of the Violet Mine to the col between Sunrise Mtn and Mt. McQuarrie.

From Woodbury, even if you're not continuing the traverse, you can follow the Moonlight Peak trail in that direction, probing the steep, bouldery basin above the cabin. Or you can explore cross-country to an unnamed tarn about 1 km (0.6 mi) distant.

The cabins themselves are quite different. Woodbury is older, smaller, darker, and—lacking recent maintenance—might be less appealing than your tent. It's at the upper edge of the subalpine zone, sheltered by trees. Silver Spray is modern, spacious, airy, bright. It's just above treeline, in the alpine zone.

You crave solitude? You'll likely find it on the Woodbury Creek trail. Silver Spray is much more popular.

You've only one day to invest here? Opt for Silver Spray. Most people agree it's a more fulfilling dayhike.

Fact

before your trip

The Alpine Club of Canada (ACC) maintains Woodbury cabin. Reservations and fees are required. Visit www.alpineclubofcanada.ca for details. The cabin sleeps eight and is equipped with a wood stove, a propane cook stove, and propane lights. Propane and bucked-up wood are provided. Bring your own sleeping pad, cookware, and dishware.

At the Woodbury / Silver Spray trailhead, porcupines have disabled vehicles by chewing on tires, brake linings, hoses, and electrical wiring. Prevent this by bringing enough chicken wire to encircle your car. Use it to erect a porcupine-proof barricade. See photo page 26.

by vehicle

From the junction of Hwys 31 and 3A, at the Kootenay Lake ferry terminal in **Balfour**, drive N on Hwy 31. At 25.5 km (15.8 mi) turn left (W) onto the unpaved road signed for Kokanee Glacier Provincial Park. Reset your trip odometer to 0.

Nearing the Woodbury-Silver Spray trailhead

From the Kaslo Creek bridge on the S edge of **Kaslo**, drive S on Hwy 31. At 11.3 km (7 mi) turn right (W) onto the unpaved road signed for Kokanee Glacier Provincial Park. Reset your trip odometer to 0.

0 km (0 mi)
Starting W on the unpaved road, departing Hwy 31.

1.1 km (0.7 mi)
Fork left. The road is level, then descends.

2.4 km (1.5 mi)
Fork right at a three-way junction. The road then curves left, following Woodbury Creek upstream through a canyon.

4.4 km (2.7 mi)
Cross a bridge.

7.3 km (4.5 mi)
Cross a bridge.

7.8 km (4.8 mi)
Bear left. The road is steeper, rockier.

11.5 km (7.1 mi)
Just after crossing a bridge, reach a fork at 1494 m (4900 ft). Left ascends to Sunset Lake. Right descends 1.3 km (0.8 mi) to the Woodbury/Silver Spray trailhead. Assess before continuing. If the road ahead appears too rough or overgrown, park at this fork (thoughtfully leaving room for other vehicles) and begin hiking here.

12.8 km (7.9 mi)
Reach the reach road's end trailhead parking area at 1341 m (4400 ft).

on foot

Hikers heading to Woodbury or Silver Spray cabins start on the same trail. From the road's end trailhead (1341 m / 4400 ft), it departs near the kiosk, leads W, and is initially level, heading upstream above the S bank of Woodbury Creek.

At 1365 m (4478 ft), about 10 minutes from the trailhead, cross a **bridge** to the NW bank of **Woodbury Creek**. The trail proceeds left (SW) upstream. Sections of boardwalk speed your progress.

Cross a bridge to the W bank of **Silver Spray Creek** about 15 minutes from the trailhead, at 1390 m (4560 ft).

Reach a signed **junction** at 1.6 km (1 mi), 1400 m (4593 ft), about 20 minutes from the trailhead. For Woodbury cabin, bear left (SW) and resume upstream on the still generally level trail. Right (NW) ascends to Silver Spray cabin (Trip 29).

En route to Woodbury cabin, numerous footbridges span tributary streams. Trailside greenery is profuse, sometimes obscuring the trail. The easy ascent gradually steepens.

Near 1500 m (4921 ft), after hiking about 45 minutes, Glacier View Peak is visible ahead (WSW). Above 1750 m (5741 ft) the trail is eroded, narrower, rougher. At 1850 m (6070 ft) Woodbury Glacier is visible left (S) on the N face of 2753-m (9030-ft) Glacier View Peak.

The final approach is steep, switchbacking generally NNW. Easily rockhop across a creeklet. At 8 km (5 mi), 2150 m (7054 ft), the trail levels in the small, stream-riddled bench occupied by **Woodbury cabin**. Strong, determined hikers arrive here about 2½ hours after departing the trailhead.

Follow the boardwalk beyond (SW) of the cabin to find the **water-source creeklet**. It's just past the signposted trail to Moonlight Peak, which you'll ascend if hiking the Woodbury-to-Silver-Spray traverse (Trip 28).

Woodbury cabin was built in 1984. Sturdily designed to deflect avalanches, it has withstood direct hits. Nevertheless, the ACC does not allow winter bookings.

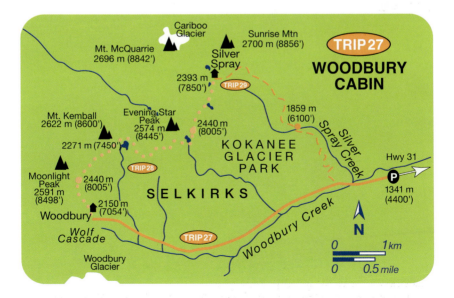

The scenery from nearby the cabin is impressive. It includes Woodbury Glacier on Glacier View Peak (S), Wolf Cascade (the incipient Woodbury Creek) plummeting into the valley after draining the glaciated basin, and 2591-m (8498-ft) Moonlight Peak (NW).

From the cabin, it's possible to explore cross-country (SW, then W) about 1 km (0.6 mi) to a tarn perched on a bench at 2341 m (7680 ft).

Trail to Woodbury cabin.
Cow parsnip (white), arnica
(yellow), and aster (lavender)

TRIP 28
Woodbury-to-Silver-Spray Traverse

LOCATION	Kokanee Glacier Provincial Park, Selkirks
	W of Kootenay Lake, between Nelson and Kaslo
ONE-WAY TRIP	approximately 8 km (5 mi)
ELEVATION CHANGE	approximately 693 m (2273 ft) gain
	and 450 m (1476 ft) loss
KEY ELEVATIONS	Woodbury cabin 2150 m (7054 ft), highpoint (ridges on
	Moonlight and Evening Star peaks) 2440 m (8005 ft)
	Silver Spray cabin 2393 m (7850 ft)
HIKING TIME	5½ to 7 hours one way
DIFFICULTY	very challenging
TRAILHEAD ACCESS	moderate
MAP	Slocan 82 F/14

Opinion

The West Kootenay is a wild creature, loosely penned by two-lane highways and small settlements. This book details most of the established trails here: opportunities to reach your hand between the bars of the cage, as it were, and safely stroke the head of the beast. The Woodbury-to-Silver-Spray Traverse is different. It's an invitation to step into the cage and look the beast in the eye, briefly encountering it on its own terms.

The traverse is day two of a three-day, two-night backpack trip. The first leg—Woodbury cabin (Trip 27)—can be a dayhike. The third leg—Silver Spray cabin (Trip 29)—can also be a dayhike. But the optimal way to see this area, and the only way to complete the traverse, is to backpack the three-day loop described here.

The loop is optimal because dayhikers bound for either cabin spend most of their time below treeline. Only in the subalpine and alpine zones—in the vicinity of the two cabins, and on the traverse between them—are the views frequent and extensive. Even then, the scenery is not thrilling. Other pockets of West Kootenay high country are more impressive.

Here, the thrill isn't so much visual as visceral. Traverse day is payday. The reward is in the doing, and in the sense of accomplishment afterward, because this is an exciting, challenging route.

Rarely level, often steep, the traverse route bounces over ridges, swings past tarns, dekes through trees and krummholz, crosses streams, meadows and boulder fields. It grants frequent views of peaks near and distant. And it affords a glimpse of Kootenay Lake far below. Plus, it's bookended by substantial, cabins where you can relax, cook, eat, and sleep in comfort.

"Exciting" and "challenging," however, are accurate only if you're a keen, strong, fleet hiker, and a capable, confident, cross-country routefinder. If you're anything less, you could find the traverse frightening and overwhelming. If

*Large tarn at 2271 m, across from
Woodbury Glacier on Glacier View Peak*

you're anything more, for example an experienced mountaineer, you might find it mundane and easy.

In addition to the requisite fitness and skills, you'll need a compass and the 1:25 000 topo map. You'll also need an ice axe, unless someone you trust has recently completed the traverse and assured you it's snow-free.

Accurate navigation on rough, trail-less terrain is the key to success here. But anyone can make an error, and an accident is always possible. So don't rely on the cabins for shelter. If benighted midway, you'll need enough gear to bivouac. Be prepared to survive—warm and dry—through a cold, wet night. And be sure someone reliable knows when to expect your "mission safely accomplished" phone call.

We describe the loop clockwise, though the other direction is viable. Silver Spray cabin and its immediate setting are more open and scenic than the Woodbury cabin and setting, so hiking clockwise—first to Woodbury, then to Silver Spray—feels climactic.

On day two, depart the Woodbury cabin early. On the traverse, think "endurance." Strive for the most aggressive pace you can enjoyably maintain all day, because routefinding becomes vastly more difficult—perhaps impossible—after sunset.

Fact

before your trip

See Trip 27, page 171, about making reservations at Woodbury and Silver Spray cabins, and porcupine-proofing your vehicle at the trailhead.

by vehicle

See Trip 27, page 172, to reach the road's end, trailhead parking area at 12.8 km (7.9 mi), 1341 m (4400 ft).

on foot

From the road's end trailhead, ascend the Woodbury Creek drainage (see Trip 27 *on foot* for details) to the small, stream-riddled bench occupied by **Woodbury cabin** at 8 km (5 mi), 2150 m (7054 ft). Strong, determined hikers arrive here about 2½ hours after departing the trailhead.

Entering the 2430-m notch

Follow the boardwalk beyond (SW) of the cabin to the signpost indicating the trail to Moonlight Peak. Turn right (NNW) and ascend among larch and alpine fir.

Surging above treeline into a **bouldery draw**, the trail is distinct, easy to follow. Reach 2440 m (8005 ft) about 40 minutes above the cabin. Though the trail keeps climbing left (NNW) toward the summit of 2591-m (8498-ft) Moonlight Peak, abandon it here to begin the cross-country traverse to Silver Spray cabin.

Turn right and work your way NNE across big boulders. Your immediate goal is **Moonlight Peak's SE ridge**, a mere 8 minutes distant. Aim for the left (upper) and easiest-to-reach of two, prominent notches on the ridgecrest.

When you're in the **notch**, at 2430 m (7972 ft), you'll know it's the correct one if (a) the right (E) wall is festooned with lime lichen, and (b) the scree chute down the far side affords a reasonable descent route. Ahead (NNE), towering above the basin you're about to enter, is a sharp peak: 2622-m (8600-ft) Mt. Kemball.

From the notch, carefully drop N via the scree chute into the **basin below Mt. Kemball**. As the grade eases, angle right (NE) across boulders and perhaps lingering patches of compacted snow. Eventually reach grass, but stay high, near 2287 m (7500 ft).

Ascend into open, subalpine forest and cross **Mt. Kemball's SE shoulder** at about 2250 m (7382 ft). Looking back, the chute you descended from the notch is now an alarming sight, appearing to be vertical.

Curve left (N) around the shoulder to begin entering the next basin. Cross two, heathery, 2300-m (7546-ft) ribs. Hop a creeklet. Contour N until you can ease down to the **large tarn** at 2271 m (7450 ft), about 2½ hours from Woodbury cabin.

Round the tarn's left (N) shore, then contour right (SSE) around the E shore. The view right (SSW), across the tarn to Glacier View Peak, is reminiscent of a famous view in Washington's North Cascades: across Image Lake to Glacier Peak.

Another S-trending ridge is the next obstacle. Nip over it by ascending to about 2316 m (7600 ft), then curve left (N) until you can comfortably descend into the **next basin** where you'll rockhop a creek near 2286 m (7498 ft).

Descending the scree chute, from the 2430-m notch

This basin harbours a **small tarn**. It's at 2295 m (7530 ft), near the far (E) wall, initially obscured from view by a curtain of trees. Find it by ascending E out of the creek drainage. Round the left (N) shore.

Having hiked about 3 hours from Woodbury cabin, depart the small tarn's E shore and begin a strenuously steep ascent E on grass and rock. Surmount the **S ridge of Evening Star Peak** at 2415 m (7923 ft), well shy of the 2574-m (8445-ft) summit.

From the ridgecrest, Sunset Lake is visible right (SE), across the Woodbury drainage. A sliver of Kootenay Lake is visible down-valley (E). The Purcell Range rises beyond it.

Note the tarn below, in the basin you're about to enter. The traverse route does not descend nearly that far. You'll soon skirt a tarn, but it's left (NNE), in the basin's upper reaches, still out of sight.

Snake through a few boulders to begin plummeting directly off the ridgecrest. Angle left (NE), negotiating hard pan and loose scree. Bottom-out near 2377 m (7797 ft) and cross a boulder-choked stream. Ascend the gentle slope ahead (NNE), skirting the S and E shores of a **tarn** (possibly ice covered) beneath Evening Star Peak's SE face.

Gain the **SE ridge of Evening Star Peak** at 2408 m (7898 ft), about 4¼ hours from Woodbury cabin. The crest is rough, shaggy, punctuated with boulders and krummholz. The E side of the ridge is nearly vertical, plunging into a tarn-less basin. Do not attempt to descend here. Go left, following the crest NNW.

Soon arrive at a notch that appears to offer an escape (right / NE) off the ridge. It's dangerous: seriously steep, riddled with loose rock. Ignore it. Continue along the crest 2 minutes farther. You'll find a much more accommodating **exit ramp** (again, right / NE) at 2440 m (8005 ft). Stairstep down on heather and rock among a few larch.

As the grade eases, bear left (NNE), descending on chunky boulders. But you need not struggle to contour here. It's easier to cross the next ridge slightly

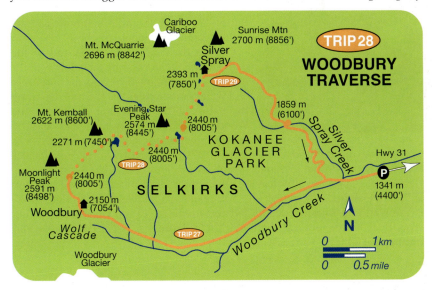

Sunrise Mtn, immediately north of Silver Spray cabin

Woodbury Traverse route

lower than is possible. So drop to about 2347 m (7698 ft), then angle right (NE) and ascend on rock and grass.

At about 2377 m (7797 ft), crest a **SE-trending ridge**—a distant arm of 2696-m 8842-ft Mt. McQuarrie. Immediately below (NE) is a long, slender tarn in a narrow defile. Ahead (NNE), about 0.8 km (0.5 mi) distant, the roof of Silver Spray cabin is visible among rock outcrops.

After an easy descent on boulders and grass, pass the left (NW) end of the **long, slender tarn** at 2362 m (7750 ft), about 5½ hours from Woodbury cabin.

Ascending N from the tarn, you might notice cairns leading to your destination. If not, proceed N, rolling over meadow and rock. Hop a creeklet. Within 15 minutes reach **Silver Spray cabin** at 2393 m (7850 ft). It's among tarns, in a small, alpine basin beneath the S face of 2700-m (8856-ft) Sunrise Mtn.

Total hiking time from Woodbury cabin to Silver Spray cabin is difficult to estimate due to people's widely varying speeds on rough, untracked terrain requiring map-and-compass navigation. From our experience, however, we know it's possible for hikers carrying full packs and moving at a determined pace to complete the traverse within 7 hours. Our hiking time was 5¾ hours. We spent an additional hour resting, eating, gazing, and photographing.

From the cabin door steps, follow the path around the front of the cabin (beneath the dining-area windows) to find the outhouse and **water-source creeklet**. The trail departing the cabin at the door steps leads to the Woodbury/Silver Spray trailhead. It soon curves right, dropping generally SE.

To reach the trailhead, you'll descend 1052 m (3451 ft) in 7 km (4.3 mi). It takes about 1½ hours. Within 15 minutes you'll see evidence of the 2003 forest fire.

About 70 minutes after leaving Silver Spray cabin, reach a signed **junction** at 5.4 km (3.3 mi), 1400 m (4593 ft). You're now on familiar ground. Right (SW) is the trail you initially descended to Woodbury cabin. Go left, following Woodbury Creek downstream. Within 20 minutes, reach the **road's end trailhead** at 7 km (4.3 mi), 1341 m (4400 ft).

TRIP 29
Silver Spray Cabin

LOCATION	Kokanee Glacier Provincial Park, Selkirks
	W of Kootenay Lake, between Nelson and Kaslo
ROUND TRIP	14 km (8.7 mi)
ELEVATION GAIN	1052 m (3451 ft)
KEY ELEVATIONS	road's end trailhead 1341 m (4400 ft)
	Silver Spray cabin 2393 m (7850 ft)
HIKING TIME	5 to 6 hours
DIFFICULTY	moderate
TRAILHEAD ACCESS	moderate
MAP	Slocan 82 F/14

Opinion

Silver "spraying" from the earth must have been an enticing image to miners. The trail they constructed up Silver Spray Creek in the early 1900s certainly suggests so. It's strictly business, tilting anxiously skyward. But if you're as fit as a prospector, you'll enjoy the challenge and find it rewarding.

Dayhikers who start early can emerge above treeline by lunch, then devote the afternoon to relaxation or exploration in an alpine niche as beautiful as any in the Selkirks. Backpackers can spend the night here in relative luxury. Silver Spray cabin, perched on the edge of the upper basin, is handsome, spacious, comfortably equipped.

Strong hikers reach Clover Basin and enter the subalpine zone in just over two hours, moderate hikers in three. From there to Silver Spray cabin, perhaps another 45 minutes, the journey is scenic. Alpine larch, child-sized brooks, pocket meadows, and slabby boulders create a high-altitude-park atmosphere. Nearby cliffs are reminiscent of the famous Bugaboos.

The cabin hunkers against a low ridge from which you can appreciate your accomplishment. Ringing the basin above you are (counterclockwise) Sunrise Mtn, Mt. McQuarrie, and Evening Star Peak. In the distance, down Woodbury Creek drainage, is Kootenay Lake. On the east shore is the village of Riondel, with Bluebell Mtn above it. Tam O'Shanter Creek canyon is left (north of the village). Beyond are the Purcells.

Following cairns, you can continue above Silver Spray cabin, past the remains of the Violet Mine, to the col between Sunrise Mtn and Mt. McQuarrie. It takes about 30 minutes one way. The view from the col is less impressive than from near the cabin, but go regardless. It's a fine alpine ramble, allowing you to fully relish the alpine prize you worked so hard to attain.

Sunrise Mtn, immediately north of Silver Spray cabin

The most compelling reason to visit Silver Spray cabin, however, is the Woodbury-to-Silver-Spray traverse (Trip 28). It's an exhilarating adventure—if you're capable. The prerequisites are experience travelling cross-country, skill at navigating with map and compass, confidence on steep, rough terrain, and physical endurance. For safety and enjoyment, you'll also need fair weather.

The journey begins on the trail to Woodbury cabin (Trip 27), where you'll spend the first night. On day two, you'll traverse to Silver Spray cabin, staying in the alpine and upper subalpine zones the entire time, enjoying constant, distant views. On day three, you'll hike down the Silver Spray trail to the trailhead. Read Trip 28 for details.

Fact

before your trip

See Trip 27, page 171, about making reservations at Silver Spray cabin, and porcupine-proofing your vehicle at the trailhead.

by vehicle

See Trip 27, page 172, to reach the road's end, trailhead parking area at 12.8 km (7.9 mi), 1341 m (4400 ft).

on foot

Hikers heading to Woodbury or Silver Spray cabins start on the same trail. From the road's end trailhead (1341 m / 4400 ft), it departs near the kiosk, leads W, and is initially level, heading upstream above the S bank of Woodbury Creek.

At 1365 m (4478 ft), about 10 minutes from the trailhead, cross a **bridge** to the NW bank of **Woodbury Creek**. The trail proceeds left (SW) upstream. Sections of boardwalk speed your progress.

Cross a bridge to the W bank of **Silver Spray Creek** about 15 minutes from the trailhead, at 1390 m (4560 ft).

Reach a signed **junction** at 1.6 km (1 mi), 1400 m (4593 ft), about 20 minutes from the trailhead. For Silver Spray cabin, go right (NW). Left (SW) continues upstream to Woodbury cabin (Trip 27).

In either direction, soon confront evidence of the 2003 forest fire. Kokanee Park tries to keep both trails clear, but wind easily topples burned trees, so expect to negotiate deadfall.

The ascent to Silver Spray cabin is steep. Following Silver Spray Creek upstream, your overall direction will remain NW to the cabin.

At 1692 m (5550 ft), after hiking about 1 hour, cross a boulder field. Looking right (E), down the Woodbury drainage, you can see the valley cradling Kootenay Lake. The lake itself is not yet visible, but the Purcell Range is, rising beyond. Pontiac Peak is S, above Sunset Lake and Scranton Basin.

Descending from Silver Spray cabin

Resuming through forest, the trail bends left (W) and the ascent eases at 1800 m (5900 ft), about 1½ hours from the trailhead. Cross a bridge spanning the creek at 1859 m (6100 ft). Glimpse granitic outcroppings above, ringing **Clover Basin**.

Enter the subalpine zone at 2104 m (6900 ft), after hiking about 2¼ hours. The meadows are scattered with larch, subalpine fir, and whitebark pine. Your hard work is paying off. Views are now constant. The terrain is intriguing. The trail narrows, crossing bouldery, heathery slopes laced with brooks.

A scenic, final surge into the alpine zone leads to **Silver Spray cabin** at 7 km (4.3 mi), 2393 m (7850 ft). Strong hikers arrive within 3 hours. Looming immediately N is 2700-m (8856-ft) Sunrise Mtn. NW is 2688-m 8819-ft Mt. McQuarrie. SW is 2574-m (8445-ft) Evening Star Peak.

The original Silver Spray cabin was built in 1903 to house men mining silver at the nearby Violet Mine. The new cabin, built in 1994, is the result of 5,000 hours of volunteer labour and $70,000 of donated materials.

From the cabin door steps, follow the path around the front of the cabin (beneath the dining-area windows) to find the outhouse and **water-source creeklet**.

Continuing to the col (NNW) between Mt. McQuarrie and Sunrise Mtn requires another 30 minutes of steep hiking. Elevation gain: 150 m (492 ft). From the cabin, follow the path S. It soon curves right, around the S shore of a tarn, then ascends N.

About 40 m (130 ft) above, pyramidal Mt. Loki (Trip 30) is visible right (E) in the Purcells. Scanning the range S, you'll see Haystack Mtn (Trip 33).

Soon pass the former **Violet Mine**. Stone foundations of a blacksmith shop still stand. The miners bunked below, in the original Silver Spray cabin. Just above is 2543-m (8340-ft) **McQuarrie/Sunrise col**, where the view includes Satisfaction Peak at the far end of Caribou Ridge (NNE).

Near Silver Spray cabin

Mt. Loki

LOCATION	Purcells, E of Kootenay Lake, NNE of Riondel
ROUND TRIP	10.2 km (6.3 mi)
ELEVATION GAIN	1151 m (3775 ft)
KEY ELEVATIONS	trailhead 1620 m (5314 ft)
	Portman Notch 2140 m (7019 ft)
	scrambling begins 2275 m (7462 ft)
	summit 2771 m (9090 ft)
HIKING TIME	7 to 8 hours
DIFFICULTY	challenging
TRAILHEAD ACCESS	challenging
MAP	Kaslo 82 F/15

Opinion

Mt. Loki is so prominent—lancing the sky above the other peaks crowding Kootenay Lake's east shore—that anyone driving Hwy 31 between Nelson and Kaslo on a clear day will see it.

And Mt. Loki is so topical—bubbling up in conversations among mountain-minded Kooteneers—that visiting hikers soon hear of it and decide they too want to summit this landmark peak.

It's the local equivalent of the jut-jawed sheriff every outlaw comes gunning for. And it's a very worthy goal—if you're a fit, experienced scrambler.

This is a deceiving ascent. The distance is short, the directions brief. You need simply follow the trail, then continue up the summit ridge. Yet the elevation gain is substantial, much of it on steep, untracked terrain, some of it exposed.

Handholds are necessary to maintain balance on a few pitches, so Loki is a scramble, not just an arduous hike. Don't underestimate the demands and associated risks, and don't overestimate your capabilities. Come prepared for a challenge. And expect to be richly compensated for your effort.

The top-of-the-world view from the summit of Mt. Loki encompasses as much of the West Kootenay as it's possible to see with your feet still on the ground. From Kaslo, Loki looks reasonably far. But from Loki, it appears you could hit Kaslo with a frisbee if your disc caught a pillowy updraft. Here, the fiord-ness of Kootenay Lake is obvious. And the West Kootenay's world-apart atmosphere makes visceral sense when you're eye-level with the thousand peaks isolating the region.

Mt. Loki's relative accessibility is a recent development. Only a few years ago, the summit was so far from the nearest road that few people had tagged it, and very few of those managed to do so in a single day. Logging (sigh) has now creeped upslope from Kootenay Lake, granting a high-elevation trailhead.

The trail, however, is not an endowment from a benevolent logging company, or the gift of a visionary, land-management poobah. It's the unauthorized creation of local hikers who recognized the loggers had inadvertently opened a door.

Lake below Mt. Loki

Pulaskis and shovels flying, the hikers quickly built a trail from the new logging road, toward Portman Notch, on Loki's summit ridge. Voilà. No more all-day ascent. Now it's a mere 90-minute hike to the summit-ridge scramble, which makes Loki a daytrip—even if you're coming from Nelson and must ride the Kootenay Lake ferry both ways.

But don't rush back to the east shore unless you must. The Riondel campground is beautiful. The campsites are shaded by cedars. The broad, pebble beach invites you to swim and relax. The next day, you can summit Mt. Crawford (Trip 31), where we shot this book's front-cover photo in which Mt. Loki breaks the horizon.

Fact

before your trip

If you're coming from Kaslo or Nelson, search "Kootenay Lake ferry schedule" on Google, so you'll know the optimal connections. From Balfour, the first departure is 6:30 a.m. From Kootenay Bay, the last departure is 10:20 p.m.

by vehicle

From the **Kootenay Bay** ferry terminal on the E shore of Kootenay Lake, ascend N on Hwy 3A. At 1.1 km (0.7 mi) fork left onto Riondel Road and reset your trip odometer to 0.

From **Creston**, drive N on Hwy 3A. It follows the E shore of Kootenay Lake. Proceed through the hamlet of Gray Creek and the village of Crawford Bay. The highway ascends out of Crawford Bay, then descends. Just before the final descent to the Kootenay Bay ferry terminal, fork right onto Riondel Road and reset your trip odometer to 0.

Mt. Loki, from Kaslo

0 km (0 mi)
Starting N on Riondel Road from Hwy 3A.

8.9 km (5.5 mi)
Follow the main road curving left into Riondel.

9.2 km (5.7 mi)
Turn right onto Eastman Ave, also signed for the campground.

13.1 km (8.1 mi)
Cross the bridge over Tam O'Shanter Creek. Pavement ends.

13.2 km (8.2 mi)
You're now on Powder Creek FS road.

14 km (8.7 mi)
Continue straight where Chatter Creek Road forks right.

15.8 km (9.8 mi)
Pass the parking area for Pebble Beach (left).

16.4 km (10.2 mi)
Continue straight where Loki South Road forks right.

17.6 km (10.9 mi)
Cross the bridge spanning Loki Creek.

18.6 km (11.5 mi)
Continue straight where Loki North Road forks right.

19.1 km (11.8 mi)
Turn right onto Portman Creek Road.

24 km (14.9 mi)
Fork left.

25 km (15.5 mi)
Fork right.

28.7 km (17.8 mi)
Reach the trailhead at 1620 m (5314 ft). It's signed
Mount Loki via Portman Notch.

on foot

The trail departs the right (uphill / SE) side of
the road. It briefly leads E, then curves right (SE)
and steepens.

At 1892 m (6206 ft), about 40 minutes from the
trailhead, proceed along the bottom of a **rockslide**.
Soon pass a bog (right) in the upper (creek-less)
reaches of the **Portman Creek drainage**. Here the trail
climbs E to Portman Notch.

Attain **Portman Notch** at 2.6 km (1.6 mi), 2140 m
(7019 ft), about 70 minutes from the trailhead. The
notch is an E-W groove atop the Portman Creek
drainage. It's the ingress granting hikers easy access
to Mt. Loki's summit ridge.

From the notch, the trail contours ENE into a
saddle at 3.1 km (1.9 mi). Here, the land slopes
away left (N) and right (S), and it's apparent you're
on the summit ridge.

The summit and the ridgecrest route to it—ESE
then curving directly E—are visible as you forge into

*Starting up
the summit ridge
from the saddle*

*Mt. Loki's false and true summits
from west-ridge approach*

the **alpine zone**. The trail dwindles to a route. Encounter big, sharply inclined, lichen-covered slabs at 2275 m (7462 ft). Hands-on **scrambling begins here**. Work through boulders above, then more slabs.

Surmount the false summit, pierce the rockbands, bypass the gendarmes. Top out on 2771-m (9090-ft) Mt. Loki at 5.1 km (3.2 mi), about 4 hours from the trailhead.

The 360° panorama comprises Kootenay Lake and nearly all the major mountains ringing it. The Purcell Range extends S and N. The Selkirks span the W horizon. The sheer, granite peaks called the Leaning Towers are NE. The highest of the towers, 3040-m (9974-ft) Hall Peak, is 21.5 km (13.3 mi) distant. Visible below are the alpine lake at the base of Mt. Loki's soaring, E wall, and the village of Kaslo, on Kootenay Lake's far shore (NW). Twin peaked, glacier laden, 3094-m (10,151-ft) Mt. Cooper is NW.

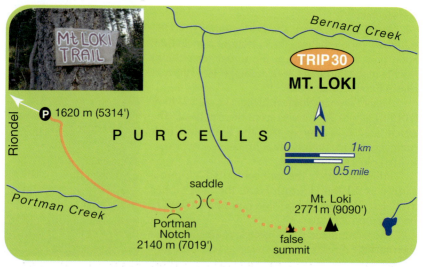

TRIP 31
Mt. Crawford / Plaid Lake

LOCATION	Purcells, E of Kootenay Lake, NE of Crawford Bay
ROUND TRIP	4.6 km (2.9 mi) to summit, 7.6 km (4.7 mi) to lake
	8.4 km (5.2 mi) to summit and lake
ELEVATION GAIN	519 m (1702 ft) to summit, 690 m (2263 ft) for lake
	864 m (2834 ft) for summit and lake
KEY ELEVATIONS	trailhead 1820 m (5970 ft), saddle 2165 m (7100 ft)
	summit 2339 m (7675 ft), lake 1820 m (5970 ft)
HIKING TIME	2 hours for summit, 3 hours for lake
	4 hours for summit and lake
DIFFICULTY	moderate to lake, mildly challenging to summit
TRAILHEAD ACCESS	moderate until challenging, steep, final approach
MAPS	Kaslo 82 F/15, Crawford Bay 82 F/10

Opinion

Mt. Crawford is the most colourful summit in the West Kootenay. It wears a cape of brilliant, rust-hued quartzite[1] that dazzles like a Folies Bergère costume. On a clear, fall afternoon, when it's illuminated by low-angle light, this Big Rock Candy Mountain[2] will keep even the most well-traveled hikers staring, admiring, and—in vain—scouring their memories for a comparable peak.

This trail is also the shortest of any leading to the top of a significant West Kootenay mountain. The access road climbs high. The subalpine trailhead allows you to swiftly pierce the remaining forest and attain expansive views. The trail efficiently rides a ridgecrest directly to the summit block. On top, you'll see much of the southern Purcells. You'll get a close-range, seemingly eye-level look at Mt. Loki (Trip 30). And you'll overlook Plaid Lake from a Titan's perspective.

Of the two destinations here—Mt. Crawford and Plaid Lake—make the mountain your prime objective. It's an easier, quicker, more scenically rewarding hike. If you have time and energy, descend to the lake after you summit. Bear in mind, you won't fully appreciate Mt. Crawford unless you at least begin descending toward the lake, because that's where you'll see most of the quartzite that makes the west face uniquely beautiful.

The vaguely Scottish *Plaid Lake* is thematically related to the obviously Scottish *Tam O'Shanter Creek*, which drains the lake. In the early 1900s, the lake and creek were vitally important to the Bluebell mine[3], in Riondel, near where the creek enters Kootenay Lake.

---

1   Quartzite is a hard metamorphic rock that was originally sandstone until subjected to heat and pressure, usually during tectonic compression. Pure quartzite is generally white or gray but can be pink or red. Hard and angular, quartzite was often used as railway ballast. Colourful quartzite is used for roofing tiles, flooring, and stairs. During the Stone Age, quartzite was an inferior alternative to flint.

2   *Big Rock Candy Mountain* is a song written in the 1890s about the joys of hobo life.

3   The Bluebell mine produced silver, zinc and lead. It operated from 1895 to 1929, and again from 1950 to 1972. It has the longest history of any mine in British Columbia.

Ascending Mt. Crawford

To keep the mine's water-powered ore concentrator running through the fall and winter, when creek levels dropped, the miners built a rock dam at Plaid Lake. Each winter, two men lived in a cabin near the lake's north shore, where they regulated the creek flowing into a pipeline. The miners below signaled their water needs to the men up at the lake by detonating dynamite.

If you descend to the lake, and you hike around the west shore, you'll see the remains of the hand-built rock dam and channel way.

Fact

before your trip

Be aware that—starting at the Kootenay Bay ferry terminal on the E shore of Kootenay Lake—driving to the trailhead entails 30 minutes on pavement, plus 50 minutes on unpaved backroads.

by vehicle

From the **Kootenay Bay** ferry terminal on the E shore of Kootenay Lake, ascend N on Hwy 3A. Bear right (E) at 1.1 km (0.7 mi) where Riondel Road forks left. At 4.7 km (2.9 mi) enter the village of Crawford Bay. Pass the school (right), the gas station (right), and the motel (left). Just before the church, turn left (N) onto Wadds Road and reset your trip odometer to 0.

From **Creston**, drive N on Hwy 3A. It follows the E shore of Kootenay Lake. Reset your trip odometer to 0 in the hamlet of Gray Creek, as you pass the Gray Creek Store (left). Proceed N. At 5.9 km (3.7 mi) cross the bridge over Crawford Creek. Proceed through the village of Crawford Bay. At 7.6 km (4.7 mi)—between the church and the motel—turn right (N) onto Wadds Road and reset your trip odometer to 0.

0 km (0 mi)
Starting N on Wadds Road. Follow it NE.

2.6 km (1.6 mi)
Reach a T-junction. Turn left (N) onto Crawford Creek Road (paved). Ignore the unpaved right fork.

4.7 km (2.9 mi)
Pass the dump. Pavement ends. Proceed generally E.

5.3 km (3.3 mi)
Bear right on the main road.

10.1 km (6.3 mi)
Reach a junction. Fork left onto Crawford-Hooker Road.

11.3 km (7 mi)
Fork left onto Plaid Lake Road. Slow down. Watch for water bars (trenches dug across the road to prevent erosion). Begin a switchbacking ascent generally NW. About half way up, huckleberry bushes are profuse.

11.9 km (7.4 mi)
Bear right, ignoring a minor, left fork.

13.7 km (8.5 mi)
Cross the base of a clearcut.

14.8 km (9.2 mi)
The ascent steepens.

15.3 km (9.5 mi)
The edge of the road drops steeply right, granting a view across heavily-logged Crawford Creek Valley.

15.8 km (9.8 mi)
Reach a fork at 1580 m (5184 ft). There's ample room to park and turn around here, if you want to stop driving. Whether you continue by vehicle or on foot, ignore the main road left. Turn right onto Plaid Lake Road, which narrows and steepens, climbing 240 m (788 ft) in less than 1 km (0.6 mi). Strong hikers can dispatch that final ascent in 20 minutes.

16.6 km (10.3 mi)
Reach the trailhead parking area at 1820 m (5970 ft).

on foot

The trail ascends left (W). Ignore the deteriorating road, which continues straight (N) and descends.

The grade is moderate for about 5 minutes, then steepens sharply. Your destination—Mt. Crawford—is soon visible right (N). In mid-September, blueberries are rife here.

At 2035 m (6675 ft), about 30 minutes along, attain a view SW of Kootenay Lake's west arm and the Nelson Range beyond. The profile of Kokanee Glacier Provincial Park (W) improves as you ascend. The village of Crawford Bay is visible below (SW).

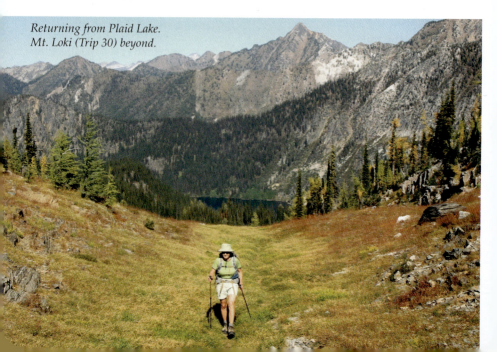

Returning from Plaid Lake.
Mt. Loki (Trip 30) beyond.

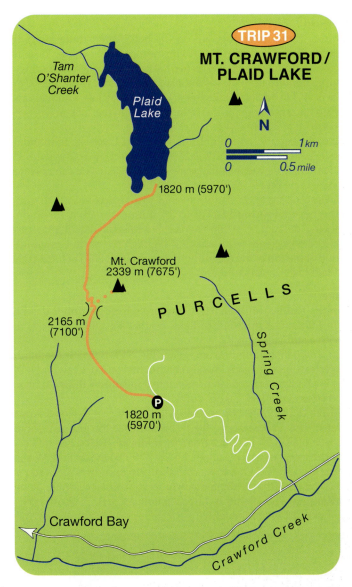

The trail rises N along the crest of **Mt. Crawford's S ridge**. About 35 minutes from the trailhead, a saddle is visible about 5 minutes ahead. Look NNE, right of the saddle. Note the vertical depression—between a black outcrop and a steeper slope—that obviously serves as the ascent route from the saddle to the summit of Mt. Crawford.

Reach the **saddle** at 1.9 km (1.2 mi), 2165 m (7100 ft), within 45 minutes of the trailhead. Decision time. You can continue right, ascending NE on the bootbeaten route along Mt. Crawford's S ridge, aiming for the summit. Or you can follow the trail left, descending the saddle's NW slope, heading for Plaid Lake.

Mt. Crawford

Continue right, ascending NE on the bootbeaten route along the upper reaches of Mt. Crawford's S ridge. As it steepens into a **chute**, loose rock gives way to scree and dirt. Zig and zag as necessary to achieve solid footing.

About 15 minutes from the saddle, reach the **summit ridge** at 2300 m (7544 ft). Plaid Lake is visible below (N). Right (SE) is your goal, just 5 minutes away. Work your way up the large, angular, quartzite boulders to the 2339-m (7675-ft) **summit of Mt. Crawford** at 2.3 km (1.4 mi).

Visible N—beyond and slightly left of Plaid Lake—is pyramidal, 2771-m (9090-ft) Mt. Loki (Trip 30). NNW is 2896-m (9500-ft), ice-crowned Mt. Brennan (Trip 12). Having achieved an aerial view of Plaid Lake, you can now gauge your desire to hike to its shore.

After descending to the saddle, even if you've decided not to visit the lake, it's worthwhile detouring just 10 to 15 minutes in that direction. On the switchbacking descent, you can marvel at a spectacular display of quartzite boulders (rose and cream, with mustard highlights) on Mt. Crawford's W face. Turn around at the top of the **meadowy draw**, at about 2075 m (6806 ft), where the S end of Plaid Lake is visible NE.

Plaid Lake

From the **saddle**, high on Mt. Crawford's S ridge, you'll descend 345 m (1132 ft) in 1.9 km (1.2 mi) to Plaid Lake. So that's a 3.8-km (2.4-mi) round-trip detour, with a stiff climb on the way out.

Begin a switchbacking descent, generally NW. Beneath the **boulder field** (cream and rose quartzite with mustard highlights) on Mt. Crawford's W face, the trail leads N among scattered larch, then into a **meadowy draw**. At about 2075 m (6806 ft), the S end of Plaid Lake is visible NE.

Continue descending NE beneath Mt. Crawford's N slope. Approach the lake's inlet stream. Follow above the W bank. Reach the grassy, S shore of **Plaid Lake** at 1820 m (5970 ft). Distance from the trailhead: 3.8 km (2.4 mi).

From the inlet stream, it's about 1.5 km (0.9 mi) around the W shore to the **rock dam** at the lake's N end. It was built in 1926 to control the water entering a gravity-feed pipeline that generated power for the ore concentrator at the Bluebell mine, in Riondel. The stream is Tam O'Shanter Creek. It flows NW, reaching Kootenay Lake just N of Riondel.

Kootenay Lake, from trail to Mt. Crawford

TRIP 32
Gray Creek Pass Summits

LOCATION	Purcells, E of Kootenay Lake, SE of Crawford Bay
ROUND TRIP	8.6 km (5.3 mi) for N and S summits
ELEVATION GAIN	796 m (2610 ft) for N and S summits
KEY ELEVATIONS	trailhead 1982 m (6500 ft), N summit 2348 m (7700 ft)
	1st S summit 2146 m (7040 ft)
	2nd S summit 2235 m (7330 ft)
HIKING TIME	3 to 4 hours for N and S summits
DIFFICULTY	moderate
TRAILHEAD ACCESS	moderate
MAP	Crawford Bay 82 F/10

Opinion

Are you comfortable on trailless terrain? Willing to do some light scrambling? If so, spend a few happy hours ascending the minor summits flanking Gray Creek Pass.

In either direction, a mere 30 to 45 minutes of exertion will earn you an aerial perspective of the eastern half of the West Kootenay. You'll overlook fiord-like Kootenay Lake. Beyond, in the Selkirk Range, you'll see the peaks of Kokanee Glacier Provincial Park. Farther north, Mt. Brennan (Trip 12) breaks the horizon.

Each route offers a different experience, so hike both. The north route is easier and allows you to assess the possibilities to the south. The south route is steeper, rougher, and allows you to ramble longer before encountering a sharp descent. But both routes are short. Together they ask of strong hikers no more than about three hours. Only if you're a cocksure mountain goat should you proceed beyond the stopping points described below.

Inexperienced at off-trail hiking and scrambling? Gray Creek Pass is a relatively safe place to give it a go. Exposure—the risk of a hazardous fall—is minimal. And both summits are so close to Gray Creek Pass Road that it should be difficult to get lost.

Fact

by vehicle

If you're coming from Nelson or Kaslo, catch the Kootenay Lake ferry at Balfour. Reset your trip odometer to 0 upon disembarking the ferry at **Kootenay Bay**, on the lake's E shore. Drive E on Hwy 3A to Crawford Bay, then S. At 12.3 km (7.6 mi) pass Gray Creek store and slow down. About 150 m (165 yd) beyond, turn left (E) onto Oliver Road (before the Gray Creek bridge). Again reset your trip odometer to 0.

If you're coming from **Creston**, reset your trip odometer to 0 at the junction of Hwys 3 and 3A, at the N end of town. Drive N on Hwy 3A, along the E shore of Kootenay Lake, 72 km (44.6 mi) to the community of Gray Creek. About 150 m

South ridgecrest above Gray Creek Pass

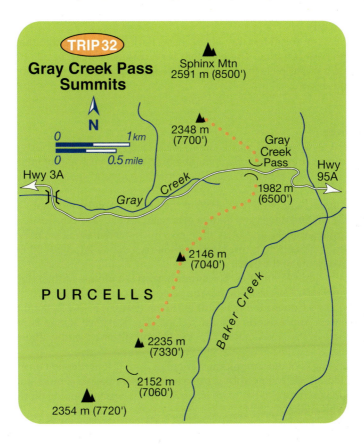

(165 yd) after crossing the Gray Creek bridge, turn right (E) onto Oliver Road (before reaching Gray Creek store). Again reset your trip odometer to 0.

0 km (0 mi)
Starting E on Oliver Road (known locally as the Gray Creek Pass Road). Pavement ends.

0.3 km (0.2 mi)
Turn right and cross a bridge over Gray Creek.

0.4 km (0.25 mi)
Stay left and ascend. The road immediately switchbacks left. Stay on the main road, passing minor spurs.

1.3 km (0.8 mi)
Bear left on Gray Creek Pass Road and descend slightly. Pass a sign stating distances: Marysville 84 km, Kimberley 88 km. Resume ascending.

7 km (4.3 mi)
Bear right and proceed through the snow gate.

18 km (11.2 mi)
Arrive at 1982-m (6500-ft) Gray Creek Pass. Park here to hike to either of the Gray Creek Pass summits. There's room for a couple vehicles beside the road. There's also a one-vehicle pullout on the left, just before the sign warning of the steep grade ahead.

on foot

North Route
From where the road crests Gray Creek Pass, you can see your goal: the rounded, alpine summit NW. Begin hiking from the one-vehicle pullout just N of the steep-grade sign. Head generally N, following spits and spats of trail through open forest.

It's immediately evident you're on the **crest of a narrow ridge**. Within 5 minutes, the crest broadens and your goal is again visible, so you're not dependent on the vanishing trail. Proceed NW through a thick stand of small larch. Within 20 minutes, enter subalpine forest laced with berry bushes. At about 30 minutes, you'll be ascending in the open.

Top out within 45 minutes. The **summit cairn** is a minute farther, right (NE), at 1.3 km (0.8 mi), 2348 m (7700 ft). You're now 366 m (1200 ft) above the road. Kootenay Lake's Crawford Bay is visible 1811 m (5940 ft) below. Beyond the bay, the lake's west arm extends toward Nelson. The Kokanee Range is NW. Mt. Brennan (Trip 12) is NNW, about 67.5 km (42 mi) distant. Nearby, directly N is Sphinx Mtn.

Continuing N of the summit cairn entails a 75-m (246-ft) descent on a rugged thumb of loose rock, followed by a steep ascent. Most people should stop at the cairn. When you return to the road, angle SE. You'll begin dropping off the ridge crest if you head directly S.

Before leaving the N summit, study the ridge SSW of the pass. Planning your route is easiest from here. See the 10-m (33-ft) cliff at a dip in the ridge? If it appears too difficult for you to negotiate, drop into forest on the NNE side of the ridge, contour SE, then ascend to the low dip in the ridge that has a thin line of larches. From there it's possible to follow the ridge S for another hour.

South Route
Begin hiking from the one-vehicle pullout just N of the steep-grade sign. Cross the road and ascend a short trail to a crude A-frame shelter. Then head SW into forest.

Drop into a shallow draw. Cross a rocky rib. Drop deeper into the next forested draw. Aim for the **white talus slope** ahead. Skirt left of a rockslide. About 15 minutes from the road, reach a second rockslide. From there, ascend to the ridge.

Reach the **first summit** at 2146 m (7040 ft). Visible SE is Haystack Mtn (Trip 33). ESE is 2866-m (9400-ft) Snowcrest Mtn.

Resuming SSW along the ridgecrest, drop to 2057 m (6750 ft), then ascend. Reach the 2235-m (7330-ft) **second summit** at 3 km (1.9 mi).

Beyond is a commitment: a steep 83-m (272-ft) descent into forest, followed by a 201-m (660-ft) ascent. Most people should, and will want to, turn around at the second summit.

TRIP 33
Haystack Mountain

LOCATION	Purcells, Kianuko Provincial Park
	E of Kootenay Lake's S end, N of Creston
ROUND TRIP	6 km (3.7 mi) to lake, 8.4 km (5.2 mi) to summit
ELEVATION GAIN	358 m (1174 ft) to lake, 976 m (3200 ft) to summit
KEY ELEVATIONS	trailhead 1707 m (5600 ft), lake 2065 m (6773 ft)
	summit 2683 m (8800 ft)
HIKING TIME	2½ to 3 hours for lake, 5½ to 6 hours for summit
DIFFICULTY	easy to lake, moderate to summit
TRAILHEAD ACCESS	moderate due only to distance
MAP	Boswell 82 F/7

Opinion

Welcome to Kianuko Provincial Park. You're now among the very few who've heard of it. And only a fraction of those have been there. It's so obscure, you'll likely have it all to yourself.

The park is north of Creston, east of Kootenay Lake's south shore. It straddles the height of land between Sanca and Meachen creeks. This is the unofficial divide separating the two Kootenay regions: West and East.

A pleasant, easy-striding trail follows Sanca Creek upstream to an unnamed, small, shallow, marshy, but pretty, subalpine lake in the park's northwest corner.

Immediately beyond the lake is Haystack Mtn, whose chunky, black boulders invite scramblers on a spirited romp. Attain the summit, and you'll overlook a dozen, small, cobalt lakes ensconced in the southern Purcells.

Upon reaching the lake and assessing Haystack Mtn, even if you decline the invitation to scramble, don't stop. Turn left at the lake and wander deeper into the basin. There's no trail, but the going is easy, nearly level, through open forest. If the sun's shining and the bugs are genial, select a satisfactory throne beside the creek or in the meadow and declare yourself the temporary, benevolent monarch of this tiny, tranquil realm.

Hikers who ask more—of themselves and the scenery—will press on toward Haystack Mtn. After resuming the ascent, however, it's tempting to stop on the ridgecrest, still well below the summit, because (a) the final scramble looks formidably vertical from there, and (b) the aerial view of the lake now seems reward enough. Both assumptions are wrong. Keep going.

The scramble is steep, but it's not vertical. The blocky boulders are small platforms offering solid footing. And there are many more lakes visible from above. The summit's 360° panorama surpasses the limited view from the ridgecrest and is well worth the effort. Just be careful nearing the top, where the rock is looser and apt to shift.

Haystack Mtn, from unnamed lake
in the subalpine basin

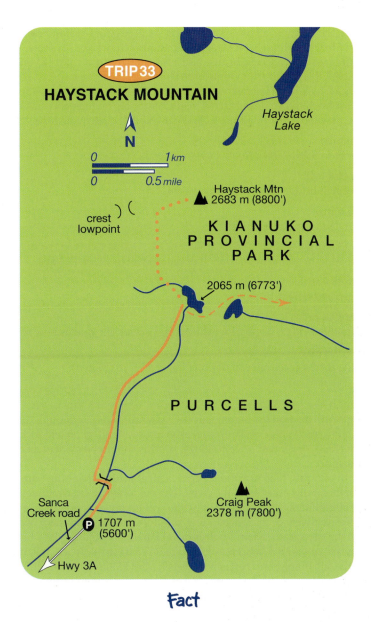

TRIP 33

HAYSTACK MOUNTAIN

Haystack Lake

N

0　　　　　　1 km

0　　　　　0.5 mile

▲ Haystack Mtn
2683 m (8800')

crest
lowpoint

K I A N U K O
P R O V I N C I A L
P A R K

2065 m (6773')

P U R C E L L S

Craig Peak
2378 m (7800')

Sanca
Creek road

Ⓟ 1707 m
(5600')

Hwy 3A

Fact

by vehicle

From the **Kootenay Bay** ferry terminal on the E shore of Kootenay Lake, reset your trip odometer to 0 and ascend N on Hwy 3A. Bear right (E) at 1.1 km (0.7 mi) where Riondel Road forks left. At 4.7 km (2.9 mi) proceed through the village of Crawford Bay. At 12 km (7.4 mi) proceed through the hamlet of Gray Creek. At 27 km (16.7 mi) pass Lockhart Provincial Park. At 43 km (26.7 mi) turn left (E) onto Sanca Creek Road. This is immediately N of Sanca Creek bridge. Reset your trip odometer to 0.

From the junction of Hwys 3 and 3A on the N edge of **Creston**, reset your trip odometer to 0 and drive N on Hwy 3A along Kootenay Lake's E shore. At 34 km (21.1 mi) cross Sanca Creek bridge and immediately turn right (E) onto Sanca Creek Road. Reset your trip odometer to 0.

Sanca Creek Road has been in good condition for several years—better than most West Kootenay trailhead access roads. Assuming maintenance has kept pace with the inevitable deterioration, a 2WD car should be adequate here.

0 km (0 mi)
Starting E on Sanca Creek Road. Pavement ends.

7.4 km (4.6 mi)
Cross a small bridge. Begin a steady ascent.

9 km (5.6 mi)
Fork left and continue ascending.

9.3 km (5.8 mi)
Proceed straight on the main road. It remains level to 12 km (7.4 mi).

13.5 km (8.4 mi)
Fork right and cross a bridge.

14.8 km (9.2 mi)
Cross another bridge. Begin a switchbacking ascent. The road is now rougher.

17 km (10.5 mi)
Reach the road's end trailhead parking lot, at 1707 m (5600 ft).

on foot

Depart the far (NE) end of the trailhead, beside the kiosk. After initially heading NNE, the trail leads generally NE, ascending gently through cool forest.

In quick succession: rockhop a creeklet, cross a footlog, go left, rockhop two more creeklets, cross two more footlogs. All this should be evident, because the trail is distinct.

At 10 minutes, 1750 m (5740 ft), cross a **steel bridge spanning Sanca Creek**. The trail then pulls away from the creek. The moderate ascent continues.

At 20 minutes, 1810 m (5937 ft), cross yet another footlog over a creeklet. Attain the first view of the surrounding summits. Glimpse Haystack Mtn (NNE) through the trees. Enter **Kianuko Provincial Park** at 48 minutes, 1980 m (6494 ft). The view expands. At 3 km (1.8 mi), 2065 m (6773 ft), arrive at a **small, unnamed lake** in the subalpine basin beneath Haystack Mtn. Hiking time: about 1¼ hours.

Numerous larch trees turn the basin electric yellow in autumn. There's a toilet (green, plastic throne) in the trees NW of the lake. Haystack Mtn is NNE, immediately beyond the lake. The optimal route to the summit begins in the obvious, grassy chute.

Where the trail enters the basin, it's possible to follow it right, around the lake. It continues NE, then curves E and descends. It's rarely hiked, probably in poor condition, scenically bereft. Passing several more small lakes, including Carrot Lake, it heads generally N, crosses forested Sanca Pass, then forks at a campsite. Right proceeds NE to Meachen Creek Road. Left leads generally W to Haystack Lake. Most hikers forgo that trudge, preferring to overlook the lake from Haystack Mtn.

To ascend Haystack Mtn, begin on the **bootbeaten path angling left (N) at the lake**. The path soon fades, but hiking cross-country through this open, rolling, subalpine forest is easy. (Note landmarks so you can return via the same, efficient route.) Your immediate goal is the ridgecrest (N). There are several ways to attain it.

The simplest route, and the one we recommend, is via the broad, **grassy chute**. It's steep but hikeable and leads directly to the **ridgecrest**. Near the top, angle right, into the trees, to avoid the steepest pitch.

Another way to gain the ridgecrest from the basin is to veer left (NW) well before reaching the grassy chute. Right of a rockslide spilling from the crest lowpoint, locate a path switchbacking upward. A few cairns might still guide you onto this path from near a creeklet at the bottom of the slide. But the path doesn't surmount the ridge. You'll have to scramble the last bit. It also lands you lower on the crest, and farther from Haystack Mtn, than does the grassy chute.

However you assault the ridge, turn right (NE) on top and **follow the crest** toward Haystack's bouldery W face. The ascent eases temporarily, the crest widens, and the trees dwindle. Enter a broad, grassy, **alpine saddle** beneath the peak.

The final ascent is strenuous but straightforward: a 40-minute scramble on big, chunky, black boulders, to the 2683-m (8800-ft) **summit of Haystack Mtn.** Swift hikers arrive here in about 2¾ hours, having covered 4.2 km (2.6 mi) from the trailhead.

The 360° view comprises about a dozen, small lakes. Haystack Lake (NE) is the biggest. Most are unnamed. Also visible are Akokli Mtn (W), Mt. Godwin (SW), Craig Peak (S), White Grouse Mtn (NE), and Snowcrest Mtn (N).

Haystack Mtn

TRIP 34
Toad Mountain

LOCATION	Purcells, SSW of Nelson
ROUND TRIP	8 km (5 mi)
ELEVATION GAIN	625 m (2050 ft)
KEY ELEVATIONS	trailhead 1850 m (6070 ft), first unnamed summit 2110 m (6923 ft), second unnamed summit 2132 m (6995 ft), Toad Mtn 2209 m (7247 ft)
HIKING TIME	3 to 4 hours
DIFFICULTY	moderate
TRAILHEAD ACCESS	moderate
MAP	82 F/O6

Opinion

Every city that isn't topographically destitute has a quintessential hike.

Phoenix, Arizona, has Camelback Mountain. Auckland, New Zealand, has Rangitoto Island. Barcelona, Spain, has Montserrat. Nelson, British Columbia, has Toad Mountain.

Some will contest that pronouncement. They'll argue Pulpit Rock (Trip 51) is *the* Nelson, B.C. trail.

We agree that every hiker who visits Nelson should scamper up Pulpit and overlook the town. But Pulpit doesn't boost you nearly high enough to see Nelson in its full, raucously mountainous context. Toad does.

Besides, Toad is a genuine hike, whereas Pulpit has an urban/social/gym atmosphere. On Pulpit, you're sure to encounter other people intently dashing up and down for a quick workout, or sauntering, jabbering, oblivious to their surroundings. On Toad, we've seen moose and grizzlies, but never people.

Toad is a captivating ridgewalk. After a steep ascent through forest, the trail surmounts an unnamed summit, follows a narrow crest to a second unnamed summit, then continues along another crest to Toad. Beyond the first summit, views are constant. So are ups and downs, but they're never severe.

You'll see Nelson and Kootenay Lake's west arm, far, far below. You'll also see Nelson's beloved ski area: Whitewater. And you'll see a big chunk of the southern Purcell and Selkirk ranges.

While the Toad Mtn trail is engaging and the horizon impressive, the immediate surroundings are unremarkable. Toad and its cohorts are minor mountains, where roads and clearcuts are part of the scenery. That's why it's possible for crack mountain bikers to ride from the top of Toad all the way into Nelson—a remarkable feat, to be sure, but one that proves this is not seriously vertical terrain.

As for the name "Toad," its origin is a real-life cliché. A prospector, Charlie Townsend, sat down here to fill out his location notice for a mining claim. Upon reading the words "situated on," he looked up, saw a toad, and wrote "Toad Mountain."

TOAD MT. →

Vantage point at 1933 m

Charlie was among the first of a swarm. Gold and silver were discovered near Nelson in 1867. When silver was mined near Toad Mtn in 1886, Nelson boomed. The mine—the remains of which you'll see near the trailhead—was called *the Silver King*. The population of the adjacent mining camp swelled to 190 in 1898.

For two decades, the Silver King provided Nelson smelters with more silver ore than did any other West Kootenay mine. All this mineral wealth spawned the construction of two railways, which transformed Nelson from a boomtown into a regional transportation and distribution centre.

Thus the granite heritage buildings that today make Nelson one of Canada's most handsome towns are, in a sense, a gift of Toad Mtn. And Toad's status as Nelson's premier hike is based on history in addition topography.

Fact

by vehicle

0 km (0 mi)
Near the SW edge of Nelson, at the junction of Hwys 6 and 31, drive toward Salmo on Hwy 6.

3.7 km (2.3 mi)
Pass signs for "Silver King S.H." and "Nelson Waldorf School."

6.4 km (4 mi)
Pass the "Leaving Nelson" sign. Slow down. Just 100 m (110 yd) beyond, turn right onto Giveout Creek Road. If you reach Cottonwood Lake Park (right), you've gone too far and must turn around.

0 km (0 mi)
Reset your trip odometer to 0. Proceed onto unpaved Giveout Creek Road.

0.7 km (0.4 mi)
Bear right. Ignore the left fork.

1.6 km (1 mi)
Curve left, onto Gold Creek Road.

2.2 km (1.4 mi)
Switchback right. Ignore the left spur.

4 km (2.5 mi)
Pass a small cabin (right).

4.7 km (2.9 mi)
Switchback left. Ignore the right fork.

5.6 km (3.5 mi)
Ignore the 4 km sign. (That's the distance from the start of the Gold Creek Road.)

6.5 km (4 mi)
Fork left on the main road.

6.7 km (4.2 mi)
The road is briefly level.

7 km (4.3 mi)
Fork right. Just beyond, proceed straight, ignoring the right fork.

7.2 km (4.5 mi)
Bear left. Ignore the right spur.

7.3 km (4.5 mi)
Fork right and ascend. The road is rougher now.

8 km (5 mi)
The road steepens.

8.2 km (5.1 mi)
After a level respite, the road switchbacks through a bushy cutblock.

9.3 km (5.8 mi)
Continue straight. Ignore the steeply ascending left fork.

10.3 km (6.4 mi)
Fork left and ascend at the top of the cutblock.

10.8 km (6.7 mi)
Toad Mountain is visible ahead.

11 km (6.8 mi)
Stay on the main road. Ignore the left fork.

11.6 km (7.2 mi)
Pass the Silver King Mine tailings. Ascend left. Ignore the descending right fork. Toad Mountain is visible right (SSW).

11.8 km (7.3 mi)
Pass a shed (left). Switchback left (NE) and ascend. (The trailhead parking is directly above, after the next switchback, so if you want to stop driving, you can park here, on the right.)

12.5 km (7.8 mi)
Stop and park here, where the road is broad and level, at 1850 m (6070 ft). Ahead the road is steep, often muddy, and allows no room to park.

on foot
Follow the road SSW. Ignore two forks ascending left. In about 10 minutes, just as the road levels on a crest, watch for a trail (possibly signed) on the right.

The road continues SE to a small lake. But abandon the road here, at 1873 m (6145 ft). Follow the **trail** right (SW), ascending into forest.

At 1933 m (6342 ft) the trail ascends left (S) of outcrops. Attain a vantage point. Whitewater Ski Area is visible left of E. The Valhallas are NNW. The peaks near Kokanee Glacier are just right of N.

Keep to the trail as it vaults over an outcrop, veers right, then switchbacks sharply left. At 1975 m (6480 ft) glimpse Kootenay Lake's west arm (left / NNE).

Watch for where the trail ascends steeply over bedrock. It then veers left, drops slightly, then curves right NNW and ascends among more outcrops.

At 2025 m (6644 ft), about 25 minutes from the trailhead, Nelson is visible below. You can even identify Pulpit Rock (Trip 51) above the N shore of Kootenay Lake's west arm.

About 40 minutes from the trailhead, crest the **first summit** at 2110 m (6923 ft). The orange bridge spanning Kootenay Lake's west arm near Nelson is visible below. Turn around, and you'll see Toad Mtn just right of W. It's now apparent the rest of the hike will be on a ridgecrest: from this first summit, left over a second summit, then right to Toad Mtn.

From the first summit, follow the trail left (SW), undulating along the crest. Drop to 2078 m (6818 ft) before surmounting the **second summit**, 20 minutes from the first, at 2132 m (6995 ft). The actual highpoint is a minute farther left (SE), but no matter.

Turn right and continue following the ridgecrest trail WNW. It drops to 2076 m (6811 ft), then ascends NW, gradually curving N. Top out on 2209-m (7247-ft) **Toad Mtn** at 4 km (2.5 mi), about 45 minutes from the second summit. You've now hiked about 1¾ hours from the trailhead.

A triangular, wood foundation affords comfortable seating. A few noteworthy landmarks within the vast panorama are Nelson (NNE), the Valhallas (distant NNW), the Seven Summits (Trip 35 / WNW), and Red Mtn (SW).

From Toad Mtn, swift hikers can descend to the trailhead in 1 hour and 10 minutes.

Ore car

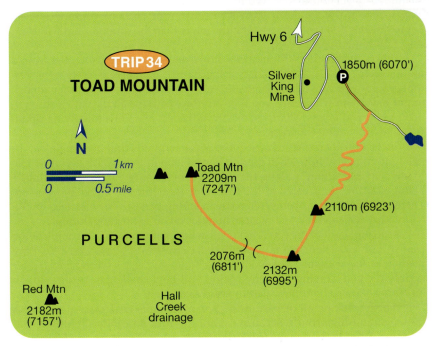

TRIP 35
Seven Summits

LOCATION	Monashees, NW of Rossland
ONE WAY TRIP	30.4 km (18.9 mi)
ELEVATION CHANGE	732-m (2400-ft) gain, 1128-m (3700-ft) loss
KEY ELEVATIONS	N trailhead 1575 m (5166 ft)
	highpoint 2200 m (7216 ft)
	Old Glory junction 1805 m (5920 ft)
	S trailhead 1412 m (4630 ft)
HIKING TIME	9 hours or overnight
DIFFICULTY	moderate
TRAILHEAD ACCESS	easy
MAP	Rossland-Trail 82 F/4

Opinion

Ridges rule. Trails following their crests offer summit scenery—continuously yet effortlessly. And the Seven Summits trail is the Big Kahuna of ridgewalks in the southern West Kootenay. Your cruising altitude will be approximately 1980 m (6500 ft)—slightly lower than the summits, but within an easy, half-hour ascent of each.

This is the southern Monashees, however—obviously concocted from a milder recipe than was the range farther north. No tabasco sauce here. The topography you'll overlook is gentle. And the occasional view of a cutblock might make you wince. But you'll be striding, perhaps all day, often through open forest and grassy clearings, mostly at the elevation of a low-flying cloud. It can be a levitating experience.

Fit, fast hikers can scorch the entire Seven Summits trail in a single day. In late June and early July, when the sun lingers long in the sky, it's even possible to tag a couple summits along the way. Just make sure you're well hydrated before starting. And carry at least three or four litres of water per person. There's only one water source en route: a spring beneath the east face of Old Glory Mtn, which you won't want to hunt for if you're hustling through.

At a moderate pace, you'll have to backpack if you want to complete the trail in one go. There are no established campsites. Follow *Leave No Trace* guidelines. But without a mountain-biking buddy to cache a second day's water supply for you, staving off dehydration will be a challenge. Yes, mountain bikers are allowed here. Stay alert to avoid a collision.

Whether hiking all or part of the Seven Summits trail, start at the north trailhead and hike south, because overall the trail descends slightly in that direction. Want to shorten the trip? Hike south only as far as the Old Glory trail junction, at 13.7 km (8.5 mi). Then descend Hanna Creek's south fork drainage 3.5 km (2.2 mi) to Hwy 3B, where your total one-way distance will be 17.2 km

Southern horizon, from Seven Summits trail

(10.7 mi). Ascending Old Glory (see photo page 217) from the saddle on Unnecessary Ridge would add 5 km (3 mi), plus an extra 395 m (1295 ft) of elevation gain. Hitchhiking back to your vehicle shouldn't be difficult.

Fact

by vehicle

To reach the **S trailhead**, start at the junction of Hwys 22 and 3B in Rossland. Reset your trip odometer to 0 at the Mine Museum, on the W side of town, then follow the directions below.

0 km (0 mi)
Starting W on Hwy 22.

0.4 km (0.25 mi)
Turn right onto the Old Cascade Hwy. Pavement ends at 0.8 km (0.5 mi). Continue on gravel.

12.6 km (7.8 mi)
Crest Record Ridge at the 12-km marker. The trailhead parking area is on the right, at 1412 m (4630 ft).

To reach the **N trailhead**, start at the junction of Hwys 22 and 3B in Rossland. Reset your trip odometer to 0 at the Mine Museum, on the W side of town, then follow the directions below.

0 km (0 mi)
Starting N on Hwy 3B.

4 km (2.5 mi)
Pass through Red Mountain Resort.

South end of Seven Summits trail, near Record Ridge

9.8 km (6.1 mi)
Hanna Creek trailhead is on the left. There are pullouts for parking on both sides of the highway. (The Plewman and Old Glory trails—Trip 36—start here. Both intersect the Seven Summits trail and therefore offer shortcut exits.)

20 km (18.3 mi)
Reach Nancy Greene Summit, also known as Strawberry Flats. The paved trailhead parking area is on the left, at 1575 m (5166 ft). The trail will eventually begin here. Look for a sign. If you don't see one, begin by briefly walking the highway as described below.

on foot

From the paved trailhead parking area, walk N on Hwy 3B about 300 m (328 yd) toward Nancy Greene Lake. Turn left onto the wide gravel road entering the highway maintenance yard. In 100 m (110 yd) descend right following the Seven Summits trail sign. You're still on a road and will be for about the next 40 minutes. It swings SW, out of the way, before curving S and ascending.

At 1.8 km (1.1 mi), proceed straight, ignoring the left fork. The road is 2WD passable to 2.2 km (1.4 mi), where there's room for two vehicles to park. But if hitchhiking between trailheads, you'd probably have to walk this stretch of road at day's end anyway. Beyond 2.5 km (1.6 mi) the road ascends steeply and deteriorates. Even with 4WD it might be impassable. At 3.4 km (2.1 mi), 1790 m (5880 ft), the road ends in a **basin** beneath Mt. Lepsoe. There's parking for up to five vehicles.

At the granite slabs here, the road narrows to trail and ascends right (W) through a regrowing cutblock. In 5 minutes, follow boardwalk through a wet area, then cross a **bridged creek**. Ascend S among alpine fir. Fluorescent green blazes sporadically mark the trail. Attain views after 30 minutes. Continue

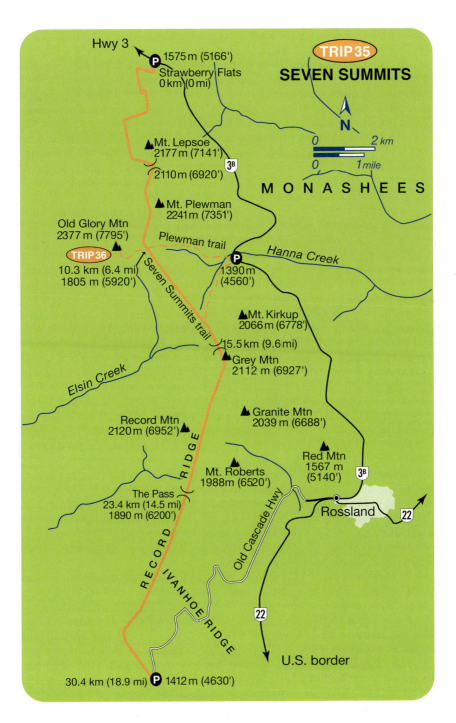

Hwy 3

P 1575 m (5166')
Strawberry Flats
0 km (0 mi)

TRIP 35
SEVEN SUMMITS

N

0   2 km
0   1 mile

M O N A S H E E S

▲ Mt. Lepsoe
2177 m (7141')

3ᴮ

2110 m (6920')

▲ Mt. Plewman
2241 m (7351')

Old Glory Mtn
2377 m (7795')

Plewman trail

Hanna Creek

TRIP 36

P
1390 m
(4560')

10.3 km (6.4 mi)
1805 m (5920')

Seven Summits trail

▲ Mt. Kirkup
2066 m (6778')

15.5 km (9.6 mi)
▲ Grey Mtn
2112 m (6927')

Elsin Creek

▲ Granite Mtn
2039 m (6688')

Record Mtn
2120 m (6952') ▲

RIDGE

▲ Red Mtn
1567 m
(5140')

3ᴮ

The Pass
23.4 km (14.5 mi)
1890 m (6200')

▲ Mt. Roberts
1988 m (6520')

Old Cascade Hwy

Rossland

22

22

RECORD   IVANHOE RIDGE

U.S. border

P 1412 m (4630')
30.4 km (18.9 mi)

climbing steadily for a couple kilometers across the slope beyond the basin's W rim. The forest opens, revealing Old Glory Mtn.

At 6.4 km (4 mi), 2110 m (6920 ft), on a **saddle** S of Mt. Lepsoe, the Columbia River is visible down the Elgood Creek drainage. To reach the 2180-m (7150-ft) summit of Mt. Lepsoe, turn left (N) here and ascend off-trail 0.5 km (0.3 mi) past silver snags and across grassy slopes. The trail curves W into the **alpine zone**. About 10 minutes farther, the peaks of Valhalla Provincial Park are visible NNE.

At 7.7 km (4.8 mi) reach the Seven Summits trail **highpoint**: 2200 m (7216 ft). For the next 3 km (1.9 mi), enjoy a scenic traverse on the W side of **Mt. Plewman**. The trail crosses three passes overlooking nearby basins and ranges to the E. Open slopes afford vast views from NE to SE. The Columbia River Canyon is below. The Canadian Rockies are beyond. Old Glory Mtn is SSW.

From 2150 m (7052 ft), an easy, moderately steep, off-trail ramble will earn you a 360° panorama atop Mt. Plewman. Whether you ascend via the SW or NW ridge, you'll gain 90 m (300 ft) in 0.6 km (0.4 mi).

Resuming S, the Seven Summits trail bobs over a knoll, traverses the E face of **Unnecessary Peak**, then intersects the Plewman trail (Trip 36) at 10.3 km (6.4 mi), 2110 m (6920 ft). You overlook the long, forested slope the trail descends. The **Plewman trail**—left (N), then generally E—descends 720 m (2360 ft) in 5 km (3.1 mi) to Hwy 3B. Unless exiting here, proceed S on the Seven Summits trail along rocky escarpments atop **Unnecessary Ridge**. Old Glory Mtn, capped with a white meteorological building, is visible right (W), across Esling Creek basin.

Drop slightly to a **junction** 100 m / 110 yd farther, on the SW slope of Unnecessary Ridge. The Seven Summits trail proceeds straight (SE). Want to make the sidetrip to Old Glory Mtn (Trip 36)? Turn right (W). Descend 50 m (164 ft) into Esling Creek basin. Curve SW. Traverse Old Glory's E slope, then curve onto its more moderate summit ridge. You'll gain 345 m (1130 ft) in 2.5 km (1.6 mi) to the 2377-m (7795-ft) summit. The view extends up the Monashees and down into Idaho. After summitting, retrace your steps to the junction on the SW slope of Unnecessary Ridge.

Continuing SE on the Seven Summits trail, enjoy a 1.6-km (1-mi) ridge-top ramble for about 30 minutes before the trail begins descending. At 13.7 km (8.5 mi), 1805 m (5920 ft), reach a junction amid a large clearing in a **saddle**. Left (NE) is the **Old Glory trail** (Trip 36)—a former road. It descends Hanna Creek's S fork drainage—415 m (1360 ft) in 3.3 km (2.1 mi)—to Hwy 3B. Unless exiting here, proceed SE on the Seven Summits trail. It ascends across a long, steep, lightly-treed slope, toward Grey Mtn.

At 15.5 km (9.6 mi), 1942 m (6370 ft), enter the **saddle** between Mt. Kirkup and Grey Mtn. From here, the off-trail ascent of 2066-m (6778-ft) Mt. Kirkup gains 124 m (408 ft) in 1.3 km (0.8 mi). The route is N, then NE up the ridge.

Resuming S, the Seven Summits trail rises onto the **W shoulder of Grey Mtn** for another 1 km (0.6 mi). At 2052 m (6730 ft), you can veer off-trail and ascend 60 m (200 ft) in 300 m (328 yd) to the summit of Grey Mtn.

From the SW shoulder of Grey Mtn, descend seven switchbacks to the Long Squaw ski run at **Red Mountain Resorts Ski Area**. Ascend Long Squaw for 150 m (165 yd) to a deep gully. Enter the gully and ascend S. Twelve switchbacks top-out on **White Wolf Ridge**, at 1991 m (6530 ft). You've now hiked 19.1 km (11.8 mi) from the N trailhead.

Proceed S along the ridge. Beyond the heli-pad, a traverse leads to **Record Notch** at 20.3 km (12.6 mi). Then a brief, switchbacking ascent concludes atop the N end of **Record Ridge**, at 21.4 km (13.3 mi), 2027 m (6650 ft). Another off-trail ascent beckons: N to 2120-m (6952-ft) Record Mtn, gaining 92 m (302 ft) in 1 km (0.6 mi).

To continue on the Seven Summits trail, switchback down the W side of Record Ridge. A long, scenic traverse leads to **The Pass**, at 23.4 km (14.5 mi), 1890 m (6200 ft). It's a broad saddle with a prominent outcrop to the S. Cross the ridge here and descend into a series of **meadows**. If you're desperate for water, look for a **spring** in the upper meadow, in an alder patch next to a static pool. Beneath the meadows, the trail traverses through forest.

At 24.7 km (15.3 mi), 1668 m (5470 ft), turn S at the base of a rock rib. The next 1.5 km (0.9 mi) is relatively level, often open, occasionally on smooth bedrock. The main Seven Summits trail descends W, off the ridge, then swings around the W side of **Rock Knob**. It's also possible to follow an older, steeper, rockier trail over the knob. This more scenic alternative ascends 50 m (164 ft) and rejoins the main trail in 1 km (0.6 mi). Either way, once the knob is behind you, proceed S.

At 28 km (17.3 mi), 1650 m (5412 ft), hike through meadows punctuated by big trees for about 1 km (0.6 mi). After a brief plunge into forest, intersect a **road**. The S trailhead is now just 1.5 km (0.9 mi) farther.

Follow the road through forest and a few large clearings. Immediately to the W, a section of trail (signed at each end) parallels the middle 0.75 km (0.5 mi) of the road. Approaching the S trailhead, the road briefly divides; bear right.

Soon arrive at the **S trailhead**. The elevation here is 1412 m (4630 ft). Excluding sidetrips, your total distance from the N trailhead is 30.4 km (18.9 mi).

Rossland

TRIP 36
Old Glory Mountain

LOCATION	Monashees, NW of Rossland
CIRCUIT	16.8 km (10.4 mi)
ELEVATION GAIN	1114 m (3654 ft)
KEY ELEVATIONS	trailhead 1390 m (4560 ft)
	Unnecessary Ridge 2110 m (6920 ft)
	summit 2377 m (7795 ft)
HIKING TIME	6 to 7 hours
DIFFICULTY	moderate
TRAILHEAD ACCESS	easy
MAP	Rossland-Trail 82 F/4

Opinion

Standing atop Old Glory Mountain will give you the perspective of a deity. You'll gaze down upon the world and feel… disappointment. That's because the summit affords a more glorious vantage than the surrounding scenery deserves. Too many effete hills. Not enough burly peaks.

Nevertheless, summitting a mountain and surveying the horizon is always exciting. Even if they are only hills, you'll see them in every direction, range upon range, layered thick as a child's collage, well into Washington and Idaho. And you'll get there by way of a long, triangular circuit, 10 km (6.2 mi) of which is above treeline.

You'll ascend through a pleasing forest; traverse a sunny, grassy, south-facing slope; cross two, inviting, subalpine basins; and walk the crest of Unnecessary Ridge. Completing the loop, instead of hiking out and back, allows you to appreciate the entire ridge. It's called *Unnecessary*, but it's an essential part of the trip.

Here in the southwest corner of the West Kootenay, clear summer days can be hot. Even in a shady forest, it can feel like someone left the thermostat on high. So start this trip early to avoid sweltering under the midday sun while ascending that south-facing slope. Bring a hat. Pack cool, airy clothing. Start well hydrated. And carry at least three liters of water per person.

From the late 1940s through the early 60s, the meteorological station crowning Old Glory was manned constantly. The crew used horses to pack in supplies via Hanna Creek. But this was the distant outback then. Hwy 3B did not exist. Reaching Old Glory was an arduous journey, especially in winter when they had to snowshoe all the way from Red Mtn ski lodge. Kind of makes hiking here in summer—on a trail, from the nearby highway, with no threat of tribulation—seem like a rather feeble undertaking, doesn't it? Oh well, enjoy your good fortune.

Old Glory Mtn, from Unnecessary Ridge

Fact

by vehicle

In **Rossland**, start at the junction of Hwys 22 and 3B. Reset your trip odometer to 0 at the Mine Museum, on the W side of town, then drive N on Hwy 3B. Reach the Hanna Creek trailhead at 10 km (6.2 mi), 1390 m (4560 ft). It's the old road probing the forest (left). Park at the bottom of this road, or in the small pullout on the right (N) side of the highway. There's another pullout 0.3 km (0.2 mi) ahead (right).

At the **Nancy Greene Lake** junction of Hwys 3 and 3B, reset your trip odometer to 0. Then drive SE on Hwy 3B. A big U-bend crosses the Hanna Creek culvert at 18 km (11.2 mi) then curves SE again. Reach the Hanna Creek trailhead at 18.7 km (11.6 mi), 1390 m (4560 ft). It's the old road probing the forest (right). Park at the bottom of this road, or in the small pullout on the left (N) side of the highway.

on foot

A brown signpost marks the Old Glory trail on the S side of the highway. Follow it uphill. In a minute reach a signed junction. For the most direct route to Old Glory Mtn, go right on the Plewman trail and cross a stream. Left also leads to Old Glory Mtn, but it's long, tedious, more tolerable on the descent.

The **Plewman trail** quickly leads to a clearing where a derelict school bus rusts in peace. A road exits the clearing and drops to the highway; don't follow it. Instead, turn left and ascend the trail into selectively-cut forest. The grade remains gentle while the trail parallels the highway. Pass several giant cedars whose trunks measure 3 m/yd in diameter. About 10 minutes from the trailhead, pass a right spur that leads 40 m (44 yd) out to the highway.

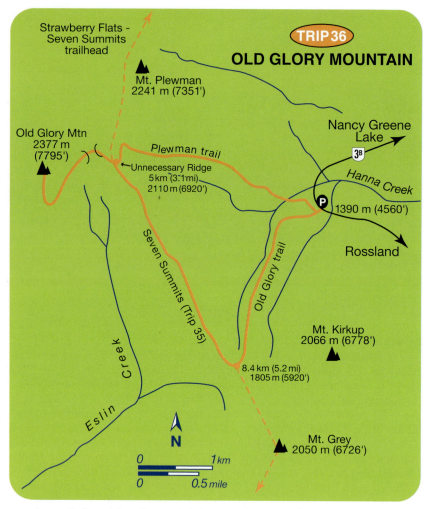

Strawberry Flats -
Seven Summits
trailhead

TRIP 36

OLD GLORY MOUNTAIN

▲ Mt. Plewman
2241 m (7351')

Nancy Greene
Lake

Old Glory Mtn
2377 m
(7795')
▲

Plewman trail

← Unnecessary Ridge
5 km (3.1 mi)
2110 m (6920')

Hanna Creek

P
1390 m (4560')

Rossland

Seven Summits (Trip 35)

Old Glory trail

Eslin Creek

Mt. Kirkup
2066 m (6778')
▲

8.4 km (5.2 mi)
1805 m (5920')

N

0 ____ 1 km
0 ____ 0.5 mile

Mt. Grey
▲ 2050 m (6726')

Ascend through a beautiful forest of cedars, hemlocks and alders. Thimbleberry bushes are abundant. Near 1 km (0.6 mi) cross a huge, log bridge over **Hanna Creek**. In a few minutes, cross another branch of the creek and start a moderate ascent NW on the S-facing slope. Highway traffic is no longer audible. The trees are now smaller. The trail stays just inside the forest edge, beneath a clearcut.

Near 3 km (1.9 mi), 1805 m (5920 ft), cross a couple creeks—dry in summer. The grade is moderate into **Plewman Basin**. The forest is now more open, allowing grass and lavender fleabane to flourish.

Near 3.5 km (2.2 mi) Mt. Plewman is visible right (N). At 4.5 km (2.8 mi) the trail turns S. Intersect the Seven Summits trail (Trip 35) atop **Unnecessary Ridge** at 5 km (3.1 mi), 2110 m (6920 ft). You've now ascended 720 m (2360 ft) from the highway. Most hikers will be here within 2 hours.

Weathered, silver snags punctuate the ridge. By early autumn, the foliage is red and maroon. Old Glory Mtn, capped with a white meteorological building, is visible W, across Esling Creek Basin.

From where you arrive atop Unnecessary Ridge, right (N) on the Seven Summits trail leads 10.3 km (6.4 mi) to Hwy 3B at Nancy Greene Summit. Left (S) leads 20 km (12.4 mi) to the Old Cascade Hwy at Record Ridge.

Follow the Seven Summits trail left (S) along rocky escarpments. Drop slightly to a **junction** on the SW slope, at 5.1 km (3.2 mi). The sidetrip to Old Glory Mtn departs here. After summitting, you'll return to this junction. You can then turn left (N) to retrace your steps through Plewman Basin, or right (SE) to continue along the ridge and loop back to the trailhead.

Don't be put off by what looks like a precarious, razorback route along Old Glory's summit ridge. The final ascent is on a comfortably safe, moderately graded trail. But first you must drop 50 m (164 ft) into Esling Creek Basin.

Starting from the junction on the SW slope of Unnecessary Ridge, follow the trail descending generally W across a dry, rocky grassy slope. From where you bottom-out in **Esling Creek Basin**, it's a 345 m (1130 ft) climb to the summit. The trail curves SW across the base of Old Glory Mtn. It gradually steepens, traversing Old Glory's E slope. Eventually curve N around the S shoulder onto the broad **summit ridge**.

After hiking 2.5 km (1.6 mi) from Unnecessary Ridge, surmount 2377-m (7795-ft) **Old Glory Mtn**. Total distance from the trailhead: 7.6 km (4.7 mi). The view extends up the Monashees and down into Idaho.

Upon returning to the junction on the SW slope of Unnecessary Ridge, your total distance will be 10.1 km (6.3 mi). Go right (SE) to loop back to the trailhead. Enjoy a 1.6-km (1-mi) ridge-top ramble for about 30 minutes before the trail begins descending SE.

At 13.5 km (8.4 mi), 1805 m (5920 ft), reach a junction amid a large clearing in a **saddle**. The Seven Summits trail ascends SE toward Grey Mtn. Don't follow it. Instead go left (NE) on the **Old Glory trail**—a former road. It descends **Hanna Creek's S fork drainage**—415 m (1360 ft) in 3.3 km (2.1 mi)—to Hwy 3B. The initial 45 minutes can be annoying if the alders haven't been cleared recently.

At 16.8 km (10.4 mi) reach the **signed junction** where the Plewman and Old Glory trails initially parted. You're now on familiar ground— just a minute above **Hwy 3B**. Bear right to reach your vehicle at the **trailhead**.

Thimbleberry

TRIP 37
Shedroof Divide

LOCATION	Salmo-Priest Wilderness
	Washington Selkirks, E of Metaline Falls
ROUND TRIP	14.4 km (8.9 mi)
ELEVATION GAIN	762 m (2500 ft)
KEY ELEVATIONS	N Shedroof Divide trailhead 1800 m (5900 ft)
	shoulder of Shedroof Mtn 1951 m (6400 ft)
HIKING TIME	4 hours
DIFFICULTY	moderate
TRAILHEAD ACCESS	easy, but long
MAPS	USGS Salmo Mtn (for round trip)
	Helmer Mtn, Continental Mtn

Opinion

Shedroof Divide forms the west side of Upper Priest River Valley. The Shedroof trail flirts with the crest of the divide, caresses four small peaks, enjoys an occasional dalliance with meadowy slopes, but is ultimately seduced by forest much of the way. Where vantage points reveal sweeping panoramas, the flaccid scenery fails to arouse.

Still, this is a good choice for a through-trip. Going the full 29-km (18-mi) distance in one, 10-hour dayhike might spark an adrenaline rush you otherwise wouldn't experience here. Try running it. The trail's smooth surface is conducive to a light, fast adventure. Like most ridge trails, however, this one doesn't maintain a constant elevation. Ups and downs amplify the challenge. The other obstacles are (1) arranging a vehicle shuttle, and (2) staying hydrated. Water is scarce on this dry ridge mid-July through September.

Most people, opting for a casual, out-and-back dayhike, should start at the north trailhead and turn around near the shoulder of Shedroof Mtn, at about 7.2 km (4.5 mi). That's where the ridgecrest first plummets, and the trail dutifully follows. By then you've pretty much seen the best the ridge has to offer anyway.

Specifically, what will you see from the ridge? There are valleys on both sides. East is Idaho's Selkirk Crest (Trips 38-41)—too distant to be impressive. West are Washington's eastern most mountains—too unimpressive to be memorable.

Fact

before your trip

Keep in mind that while the border crossing at Nelway is open daily, it's closed from midnight to 8 a.m.

by vehicle

From **Nelson**, drive S on Hwy 6 to Salmo. Proceed S on Hwy 3/6 to the border crossing at Nelway. From the US customs building, drive 16.5 km (10.2 mi) S into Washington. Turn left (E) onto paved Sullivan Lake Road, signed for Pend Oreille County Road 9345. This turnoff is by a yellow highway sign: Hill, Low

Shedroof Divide

Speed, Curves For 2 Miles. It's just N of the town of Metaline Falls. If you're coming from the S, this turn is 3.3 km (2 mi) NE of the middle of the Pend Oreille River bridge.

0 km (0 mi)
Starting E on Sullivan Lake Road.

5.2 km (3.2 mi)
Pass Mill Pond historic site.

7 km (4.3 mi)
Proceed straight on Sullivan Creek Road where Road #2212 forks left.

7.6 km (4.7 mi)
Go left on Road #22. This is also Road #2220. It's signed for Salmo Mtn (21 mi / 34 km) and E Sullivan campground (0.25 mi / 0.4 km).

8.3 km (5.1 mi)
Go straight, passing the campground. Pavement ends.

14.5 km (9 mi)
Stay on the main road for the Shedroof Divide trailheads.

17.3 km (10.7 mi)
Cross a bridge and reach a 3-way junction. Go far left (NE) on Road #2220 toward Salmo Mtn for the N Shedroof Divide trailhead. Far right (SE) on #22 leads to the Grassy Top Mtn and S Shedroof Divide trailheads in about 12.5 km (7.8 mi); directions continue below.

19.8 km (12.3 mi)
Bear right on the main road, where a rough road forks left.

28 km (17.4 mi)
Proceed straight on the main road. The narrow spur forking right leads to Shedroof Cutoff Trail #511.

38 km (23.6 mi)
Bear right on the main road through a pass. The rough road forking left (NW) climbs to the summit of Salmo Mtn.

38.5 km (23.9 mi)
Reach the **N Shedroof Divide trailhead**. The spacious, road's end parking area is at 1800 m (5900 ft). Trails leading to N Shedroof Divide, Salmo Basin, and Snowy Top Mtn depart the road, not the upper lot. The long, discouraging descent to S Salmo River via Trail #506 starts at the first kiosk, just before the parking area.

For the Grassy Top Mtn and S Shedroof Divide trailheads, turn SE onto Road #22 at the 17.3-km (10.7-mi) 3-way junction above. Reset your trip odometer to 0 and follow the directions below.

0 km (0 mi)
Starting SE on Road #22, toward Pass Creek Pass.

3.7 km (2.3 mi)
Proceed straight on the main road where a spur forks left.

12.2 km (7.6 mi)
Reach the trailhead for Grassy Top Mtn (Trail #503) on the right, at 1646 m (5400 ft). The trail is 7 m (20 ft) before (W of) the sign. *On foot* directions for Grassy Top continue below. Proceed on the main road for the S Shedroof Divide trailhead.

12.4 km (7.7 mi)
Proceed through tiny Pass Creek Pass.

12.7 km (7.9 mi)
Reach the **S Shedroof Divide trailhead** (Trail #512) on the left, across from a brown sign, at 1677 m (5500 ft). No parking here. There's a two-vehicle pullout 100 m (110 yd) farther. The trail ascends beside a small outcrop, continues steeply to the ridgecrest, then traverses the E flank of Round Top Mtn.

on foot

For **N Shedroof Divide**, start on Salmo Divide Trail #535. It continues from road's end, below the parking area. Pass the barricade and proceed on level road. S Salmo River Valley is visible N. Little Snowy Top Mtn is NE.

At 1.6 km (1 mi), about 15 minutes from the trailhead, proceed S on Trail #535. A sign here states distances to Shedroof Mtn (4.9 km / 3 mi) and Snowy Top Mtn (12.9 km / 8 mi). Begin a moderate ascent.

At 1878 m (6160 ft), about 30 minutes from the trailhead, the trail levels. Soon traverse an **open slope**. Salmo Mtn is visible NW. Leola Peak and its attendant ridges are W across Sullivan Creek Valley. Crowell Ridge is SW.

At 1921 m (6300 ft), about an hour from the trailhead, curve right and descend 244 m (800 ft) into a **saddle**. There's a campsite here, at 5 km (3 mi), 1677 m (5500 ft), and a junction with **Trail #512**. Left leads to Snowy Top Mtn. Go right to continue along Shedroof Divide.

Crest a shoulder of **Shedroof Mtn** at 6.4 km (4 mi), 1951 m (6400 ft). Descend about 60 m (200 ft), then regain that elevation ascending to the next saddle. You're now at 7.2 km (4.5 mi), about 1¾ to 2 hours from the trailhead parking area. Upper Priest Lake and the N shore of Priest Lake are visible. The ridgecrest plummets here. Out-and-back hikers should turn around.

If you've arranged a vehicle shuttle and are hiking one-way, you've got 21.8 km (13.5 mi) to go. The trail undulates SW along Shedroof Divide. It traverses the flanks of Thunder, Helmer, Mankato, and Round Top mountains before dropping

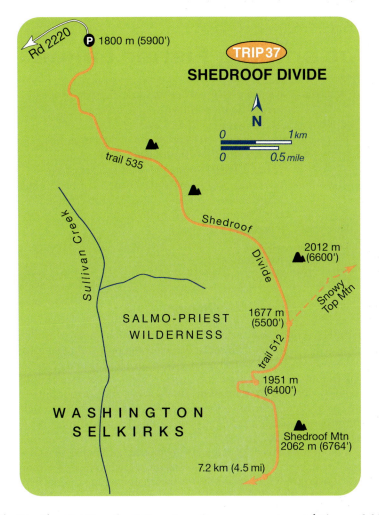

to the S trailhead at Pass Creek Pass. In early summer, water might be available at four points: NW of Shedroof Mtn, near the junction of Trails 512 and 535; just N of Thunder Mtn; 1.6 km (1 mi) N of Helmer Mtn; and just S of Helmer Mtn.

You'll encounter several junctions along Shedroof Divide Trail #512. For example, Trail #511 (about 1.6 km / 1 mi S of Shedroof Mtn) and Trail #526 (NE of Helmer Mtn) fork right and descend the W slope to Gypsy Meadows, on Road #2220. Four other trails descend the E slope. Ignore them all. Keep following Trail #512 generally SSW along the crest.

Grassy Top Mtn

Trail #503 descends S, immediately crosses Pass Creek, then ascends SW through dense forest. Near 1.6 km (1 mi) the well-maintained trail levels in open forest and fields of beargrass. Priest Lake is visible SE; beyond is the Selkirk Crest (Trips 37-39). Bear left (S) on Trail #503 at the junction where Trail #533 forks right. Curve SE to surmount 1906-m (6253-ft) Grassy Top Mtn at 6.4 km (4 mi).

TRIP 38
Trout and Big Fisher Lakes

LOCATION	Kaniksu National Forest, Idaho Selkirks
	NW of Bonners Ferry
ROUND TRIP	9.6 km (6 mi) to Trout Lake
	15.2 km (9.4 mi) to ridge above Big Fisher Lake
ELEVATION GAIN	446 m (1463 ft) to Trout Lake
	761 m (2496 ft) to ridge above Big Fisher Lake
KEY ELEVATIONS	trailhead 1651 m (5415 ft), Trout Lake 1937 m (6352 ft)
	ridge above Big Fisher Lake 2252 m (7385 ft)
	Big Fisher Lake 2052 m (6732 ft)
HIKING TIME	3 to 5 hours
DIFFICULTY	easy
TRAILHEAD ACCESS	easy, but long
MAP	USGS Pyramid Peak

Opinion

Aristotle's school was called *peripatetic*, which meant thinking and discoursing while walking. Nietzsche believed the only valuable ideas were *laufenden*—those conceived while walking. So grab a buddy and go for a walkie talkie. The trail to Trout and Big Fisher lakes is ideal, because neither the path nor the scenery demand concentration. Yet the lakes and surrounding forested ridges are comely enough to buoy your emotions. Who knows, you might solve a nagging problem, hatch a brilliant plan, or chart a new life course—before returning to the trailhead.

You'll be in forest most of the way—primarily subalpine fir and spruce, interspersed with berry bushes—but it opens up, allowing views for about 2 km (1.2 mi) each way. Trout Lake is lovely. It's in subalpine forest, beneath modest, granite cliffs. Take a break from your peripatetic discourse, clamber onto the mammoth boulder that reaches into the lake, and snack on the carob-and-apricot cookies you baked the night before.

Continuing all the way to Big Fisher Lake is unnecessary. The best view of it is from the ridgecrest above, before the trail drops to the shore. But wandering farther out the trail-less crest will enable you to survey Parker Ridge, across Parker Creek Valley. That's where backpackers should go for more vistas and solitude than Trout or Big Fisher lakes provide. You can reach Parker Ridge from Pyramid Pass, as described below.

Fact

before your trip

For current conditions, visit http://www.fs.usda.gov/activity/ipnf/recreation/hiking, or stop at the Bonners Ferry Ranger District office, in Bonners Ferry, Idaho. It's on the S side of town, on the W side of Hwy 2/95.

Big Fisher Lake

by vehicle

Follow the directions for Pyramid and Ball lakes (Trip 39). The Trout and Big Fisher lakes trip shares the same trailhead, at 1651 m (5415 ft).

on foot

Follow **Trail #13**. It starts at the lower end of the parking area, just downhill from the signpost, on the NW side of the road. It initially leads N, then veers left, ascending generally W via moderately graded switchbacks.

Reach a **signed junction** at 0.8 km (0.5 mi), 1799 m (5900 ft). Go right (NNW) on **Trail #13** for Trout and Big Fisher lakes, and Pyramid Pass. Left (W) on Trail #43 leads to Pyramid and Ball lakes (Trip 39).

Reach a **signed junction** at 2 km (1.25 mi), 1866 m (6120 ft). There's a creeklet here. Go right (ENE) on **Trail #41** for Trout and Big Fisher lakes. Left ascends initially W, then N to Pyramid Pass and accesses Parker Ridge (skip below for directions).

At 1920 m (6300 ft), about 30 minutes from the trailhead, attain views S over forested Trout Creek Valley and beyond to rocky ridges. Ascend through outcroppings. Kootenay River Valley is visible E. Cross several creeklets—probably dry by late summer. At 2017 m (6615 ft), the Pyramid Lake cirque is visible SW.

From this highpoint before Trout Lake, the trail contours generally E, granting views for the next 1 km (0.6 mi). Though the scenery is unremarkable, the hiking is pleasant. From where the trail begins a gradual descent N, competent scramblers can strike out cross-country WNW along the ridge above Trout Lake, ascending to a 2287-m (7500-ft) peaklet.

Reach **Trout Lake** at 4.8 km (3 mi), 1937 m (6352 ft), about 1½ hours from the trailhead. It's in subalpine forest, beneath modest, granite cliffs.

Proceed NE for Big Fisher Lake. The trail resumes a moderate ascent, traversing a densely treed ridge. At 2095 m (6870 ft) the grade eases in grassy

TRIP 38

TROUT AND BIG FISHER LAKES

Long Canyon Creek

Parker Lake

Parker Creek

KANIKSU NATIONAL FOREST

IDAHO SELKIRKS

Long Mtn Lake

ridge 2252 m (7385')

Big Fisher Lake 2052 m (6732')

2287 m (7500')

Trout Lake 1937 m (6352')

Bonners Ferry

1866 m (6120')

634

Trout Creek

Pyramid Peak 2242 m (7355')

P 1651 m (5415')

Pyramid Lake

N

TRIP 39

Ball Lakes

0   1.5 km
0   1 mile

forest. At 7.6 km (4.75 mi)—about 45 minutes from Trout Lake—reach the trail's 2252-m (7385-ft) **highpoint** on the ridge overlooking Big Fisher Lake. Creston and Mt. Thompson are visible NE, across Kootenay River Valley.

The trail drops 194 m (635 ft) off the E side of the ridge. It reaches **Big Fisher Lake** at 8.5 km (5.25 mi), 2052 m (6732 ft), in a granite cirque beneath Fisher Peak. Descending to the lake is unnecessary unless you intend to camp there.

For a better view, turn left and ascend N about 10 minutes along the grass-and-heather crest. Maneuver through trees to attain a view W across upper Parker Creek Valley to Parker Ridge.

Pyramid Pass and Parker Ridge

From the **signed junction** at 2 km (1.25 mi), 1866 m (6120 ft), ascend **Trail #13** initially W, then N. It ascends moderately through heavy timber.

In about 20 minutes, reach 2046-m (6710-ft) **Pyramid Pass**. From here, the trail drops 98 m (320 ft) in 1 km (0.6 mi) to a fork. Left plumbs the depths of Long Canyon. Go right (NNE) on **Trail #221** and begin a stiff ascent.

After gaining **Parker Ridge** at 2146 m (7040 ft), head N. Where the trail fades, proceed along the crest. Watch for a spur descending right (E) to Long Mtn Lake. After traversing **Long Mtn**, follow the crest NE. The crest trail leads 8.1 km (5 mi) from Pyramid Pass to 2337-m (7670-ft) **Parker Peak**.

Calypso orchids

TRIP 39
Pyramid and Ball Lakes

LOCATION	Kaniksu National Forest, Idaho Selkirks NW of Bonners Ferry
ROUND TRIP	8 km (5 mi)
ELEVATION GAIN	358 m (1174 ft) to lake, 976 m (3200 ft) to summit
KEY ELEVATIONS	trailhead 1651 m (5415 ft) Pyramid Lake 1845 m (6052 ft) Upper Ball Lake 2045 m (6708 ft)
HIKING TIME	2½ to 3 hours
DIFFICULTY	easy
TRAILHEAD ACCESS	easy, but long
MAP	USGS Pyramid Peak

Opinion

Most people aren't up for exuberant sports. They'd rather paddle-boat with the swans. For many, even a simple hike is just too darned demanding. But what if they tried the flawlessly engineered, impeccably maintained trails in northern Idaho? Compared to the scrappy paths north of the border, these are pedestrian glideways. If a paddle-boater is ever going to enjoy hiking, it'll be here.

The trail to Pyramid Lake is short and comfortably graded. The lakeshore is forested, but the cirque walls lend nobility to the scene. The trail continuing to Ball Lake briefly tilts skyward, allowing you to overlook Pyramid Lake and appreciate the surrounding ridges. The final stretch to Ball is virtually level. It too is a pretty, subalpine lake in a rocky setting, but it's less impressive than Pyramid. Smaller and humbler yet is Lower Ball Lake, just beyond and below Upper Ball.

Previously overrun and abused by a horde of backpackers, Pyramid and Ball lakes are now closed to camping. Good. The trail is so short that these are obviously dayhike destinations. The lakes remain popular. On a sunny Saturday, the 12-vehicle parking lot can fill by 11 a.m. Unless you go midweek, you'll have to start very early or late to avoid continually tipping your hat to a steady stream of paddle-boaters.

Robust hikers can tag Pyramid and Ball lakes within a couple hours. So why not include nearby Trout and Big Fisher lakes (Trip 38) on the day's agenda? Another option, if you're an experienced mountain goat, is to veer off-trail atop the Pyramid cirque wall, scramble over Pyramid Peak to Pyramid Pass, then pick up the trail descending southeast back to the parking area.

Fact

before your trip

For current conditions, visit http://www.fs.usda.gov/activity/ipnf/recreation/hiking, or stop at the Bonners Ferry Ranger District office, in Bonners Ferry, Idaho. It's on the S side of town, on the W side of Hwy 2/95.

Upper Ball Lake

by vehicle

From **Creston**, drive S on Hwy 21. Enter Idaho at the Rykerts-Porthill border crossing. Reset your trip odometer to 0 at the US customs building. Proceed S. At 16.2 km (10 mi), in the hamlet of Copeland, turn right (W) onto the National Forest access road. It's just N of a bar, and 1.6 km (1 mi) N of the Hwy 1/95 junction. Reset your trip odometer to 0.

0 km (0 mi)
Starting W on the National Forest access road. It's signed for Copeland Bridge and Westside Road.

0.7 km (0.4 mi)
Proceed on pavement.

1.1 km (0.7 mi)
Cross the Kootenai River bridge.

3.9 km (2.4 mi)
Reach a T-intersection. Turn left (S) onto Westside Road #417.

11.1 km (6.9 mi)
Turn right (W) onto Trout Creek Road #634 and reset your trip odometer to 0. Skip the next section describing the S approach, then continue following the directions below.

In **Bonners Ferry, Idaho**, drive to the intersection of First and Riverside streets, on the N edge of the historic downtown. Reset your trip odometer to 0.

0 km (0 mi)
Starting W on Riverside Street, from the First Street intersection.

0.2 km (0.1 mi)
Cross railroad tracks. Follow the sign for Kootenai National Wildlife Refuge.

0.8 km (0.5 mi)
Pass the mill.

5.6 km (3.5 mi)
Bear right.

5.8 km (3.6 mi)
Bear left and cross a bridge.

6.2 km (3.8 mi)
Pass two wildlife refuge parking lots as you drive through the wetlands.

8.1 km (5 mi)
Bear right (N) at the base of a slope, where a county road forks left (S) toward Snow Creek Road.

8.6 km (5.3 mi)
Pass the wildlife refuge visitor center and cross Myrtle Creek bridge.

10.5 km (6.5 mi)
Reach a junction. Proceed straight (N) on Westside Road—still paved. Myrtle Creek Road #633 forks left (W) to the Two Mouth Lakes trailhead (Trip 40).

19 km (11.8 mi)
Proceed straight on gravel. Slow down to prevent sliding off the steep shoulder.

24.2 km (15 mi)
Turn left (W) onto Trout Creek Road #634 and reset your trip odometer to 0.

From either approach above, proceed onto Trout Creek Road #634 and follow the directions below.

0 km (0 mi)
Starting W on Trout Creek Road #634. It ascends moderately through mixed forest.

7.3 km (4.5 mi) and 8.4 km (5.2 mi)
Proceed straight on the main road. Ignore the forks.

9.5 km (5.9 mi)
Pass extraordinary, trailer-sized boulders.

10 km (6.2 mi)
Proceed straight on the main road. Left leads to Russell Peak Trail #12. It's less rewarding than the hike to Pyramid and Ball lakes, or the other Idaho trips in this book.

14.5 km (9 mi)
Arrive at the trailhead parking area for Pyramid and Ball lakes, as well as Trout and Big Fisher lakes (Trip 38). Elevation: 1651 m (5415 ft). The road ends 200 m (220 yd) farther at a turn-around loop. Just off the loop are a couple tentsites in the trees. Park in the loop only if you're camping.

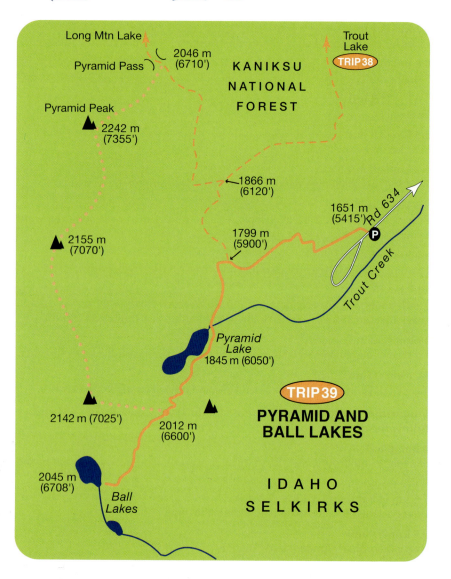

Long Mtn Lake

2046 m (6710')
Pyramid Pass

KANIKSU

NATIONAL

FOREST

Trout Lake

TRIP 38

Pyramid Peak

▲ 2242 m (7355')

1866 m (6120')

1651 m (5415')

Rd 634

P

▲ 2155 m (7070')

1799 m (5900')

Trout Creek

Pyramid Lake 1845 m (6050')

TRIP 39

PYRAMID AND BALL LAKES

▲ 2142 m (7025')

▲ 2012 m (6600')

IDAHO

SELKIRKS

2045 m (6708')

Ball Lakes

on foot

Follow Trail #13. It starts at the lower end of the parking area, just downhill from the signpost, on the NW side of the road. It initially leads N, then veers left, ascending generally W via moderately graded switchbacks.

Reach a signed junction at 0.8 km (0.5 mi), 1799 m (5900 ft). Go left (W) on Trail #43 for Pyramid and Ball lakes. Right (NNW) is Trail #13 to Trout and Big Fisher lakes (Trip 38), and Pyramid Pass.

Just after the junction, cross a bridged creek. Continue the gentle ascent. Reach Pyramid Lake at 1.6 km (1 mi), 1845 m (6052 ft). The shore is treed, but the lake is in a rocky cirque. The area has obviously been abused. Please contribute to restoration by treading lightly.

Where Pyramid Lake is first visible from the trail, about 20 m/yd from the shore, a left fork crosses the bridged outlet stream. That's the way to Ball Lake. Follow it S, away from Pyramid Lake. Soon attain an excellent view NE down Trout Creek Valley, which you ascended in your vehicle.

The trail then turns SW and switchbacks steeply up the SE wall of the Pyramid Lake cirque. Gain an aerial perspective of Pyramid Lake. Pyramid Peak and Pass are visible (N), as are the ridges that wrap around toward Trout and Big Fisher lakes (NE, but hidden from view).

About 40 minutes after leaving Pyramid Lake, surmount the cirque wall at 2012 m (6600 ft). From here, competent scramblers can strike out cross-country to Pyramid Peak and Pass. Skip below the next paragraph for details.

From the cirque wall at 2012 m (6600 ft), the trail continues SSW, forking in about 10 minutes. Right quickly reaches Upper Ball Lake, in a cliffy gorge, at 4 km (2.5 mi), 2045 m (6708 ft). Left leads 0.8 km (0.5 mi) to Lower Ball Lake at 2014 m (6606 ft). Within 5 minutes, Lower Ball is visible 12 m (40 ft) below the trail. It's hugged by forest in a rocky crevasse and is smaller than Upper Ball.

To reach Pyramid Peak and Pass from the cirque wall at 2012 m (6600 ft), hike cross-country (WNW) along the crest to the first, 2142-m (7025-ft) peak. Keep following the crest N over the second, 2155-m (7070-ft) peak. Drop NW to a 2055-m (6740-ft) pass, then resume N to the 2242-m (7355-ft) summit of Pyramid Peak.

From Pyramid Peak, descend NE to 2046-m (6710-ft) Pyramid Pass where you'll intersect the trail. Go right (SE). At the junction where left leads NE to Trout Lake, go right (S). At the junction where right (W) leads to Pyramid Lake, go left 15 minutes to the trailhead.

Trout Lake (Trip 38)

TRIP 40
Two Mouth Lakes

LOCATION	Kaniksu National Forest, Idaho Selkirks
	W of Bonners Ferry
ROUND TRIP	11.3 km (7 mi)
ELEVATION GAIN	509 m (1670 ft)
KEY ELEVATIONS	trailhead 1335 m (4380 ft), highpoint 1817 m (5960 ft)
	lake basin 1790 m (5870 ft)
HIKING TIME	4 to 5 hours
DIFFICULTY	easy
TRAILHEAD ACCESS	easy, but long
MAP	USGS The Wigwams

Opinion

Our planet loses more than an acre (0.4 hectare) of wilderness every 15 seconds. It's devoured by logging, housing construction, road building, and commercial development. Cherish the few remaining untouched enclaves. Like Two Mouth Lakes basin. Carpeted with meadows, beneath granite cliffs and domes, it's a miniature Sierra Nevada—at 1790 m (5870 ft), rather than 3660 m (12,000 ft).

The hike begins on an abandoned, overgrown road, but within 30 minutes you'll be on a pleasant trail. It climbs a creek canyon, crosses a granite ridge, then descends through subalpine forest to Two Mouth Lakes on the Selkirk Crest. The ridge suggests a cross-country detour northwest; experienced scramblers should accept the invitation.

Exploration possibilities beyond and above the basin add to its appeal as a backpack destination. The basin's equatorial-strength mosquito plague, however, can make it a miserable place even to dayhike. If you plan to stay overnight, do it in autumn. The greenery will be less epicurean, but only then is the basin fit for human habitation.

Remember that you're an uninvited guest here. Two Mouth Lakes basin is officially classified as habitat for rare mountain caribou and grizzly bears. If visitor impact becomes evident, the Forest Service might impose restrictions. Please tread lightly. Observe *Leave No Trace* guidelines.

Fact

before your trip

For current conditions, visit http://www.fs.usda.gov/activity/ipnf/recreation/hiking, or stop at the Bonners Ferry Ranger District office, in Bonners Ferry, Idaho. It's on the S side of town, on the W side of Hwy 2/95.

by vehicle

From Bonners Ferry, Idaho, follow the directions for Pyramid and Ball lakes (Trip 39). Pass the Kootenai National Wildlife Refuge. At the 10.5-km

Two Mouth Lakes basin

(6.5-mi) junction, turn left (W) onto Myrtle Creek Road #633 and reset your trip odometer to 0.

0 km (0 mi)
Starting W on Myrtle Creek Road #633.

3.1 km (2 mi)
Proceed straight on Road #633 where Burton Creek Road #2411 forks right.

11.6 km (7.2 mi)
Proceed straight where Road #1309 descends left.

15 km (9.3 mi)
Proceed straight where Road #2405 forks right.

16.1 km (10 mi)
Just after a descent, cross a bridged creek, then pass a left fork.

16.9 km (10.5 mi)
Proceed straight. Pass Myrtle Lake Trail #286 (right).

19.1 km (11.8 mi)
Cross a small, bridged creek. A granite dome is visible ahead (SW).

19.6 km (12.2 mi)
For **Two Mouth Lakes Trail #268**, park on the left, at 1335 m (4380 ft). Begin hiking up the old road (right). For Harrison Lake (Trip 41), continue driving on Road #661. The road crosses Slide Creek, then heads NE.

21.8 km (13.5 mi)
Arrive at a junction. For **Harrison Lake Trail #6**, turn right (S) onto Upper Myrtle Creek Road #2409. Reach the trailhead in 2.2 km (1.4 mi), at 1479 m (4850 ft).

on foot

Begin on barricaded **Road #658**. About 10 minutes from the trailhead, fork left onto a brushy, **skid road**. Ascend NW through alder and fir.

In about 20 minutes, pass the **trail register** and a sign stating this is trail #268. Soon pass an enormous hemlock. The skid road continues ascending moderately, curving S, then SW. It levels, then descends gently. Views open up.

About 30 minutes along, proceed onto the **actual trail**. Switchback right and begin an earnest ascent NW above Slide Creek canyon. The forest is primarily subalpine fir, spruce and hemlock. An impressive granite dome is soon visible S. Two boardwalks ease your passage through boggy areas. Cross a couple creeklets.

The trail gradually curves S near the head of forested Slide Creek canyon. A 152-m (500-ft) cliff is visible above (W). At about 1¼ hours, reach the trail's 1817-m (5960-ft) **highpoint**, on a granite ridge. Two Mouth Lakes basin is visible below (S).

The trail S into the basin is straightforward. But before descending, get a better view by turning right and briefly following the ridge NW. Stay just below the crest, on its S side. Granite slabs here allow comfortable lounging.

Proceeding on the main trail, reach the **lake basin** at 5.6 km (3.5 mi), 1790 m (5870 ft). **Two Mouth Lakes** are a bit lower. The upper lake is about 300 m (328 yd) farther SE, near the base of a granite slope.

From the initial foray NW along the granite ridge, experienced scramblers can continue **cross-country**. Carefully assess this route from the granite ridge before setting out. Head for the anvil-shaped peak. Follow its crest NE as you round the head of Slide Creek canyon (well above the trail). From the 2109-m (6919-ft) **highpoint**, descend the E-jutting ridge. Then work your way ESE to the **trail**. Turn left (N) and follow it back to the **trailhead**.

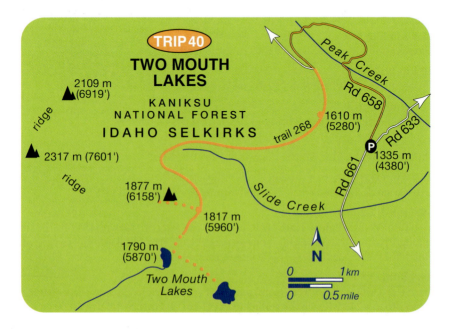

TRIP 41
Harrison Lake

LOCATION	Kaniksu National Forest, Idaho Selkirks
	W of Bonners Ferry
ROUND TRIP	9.7 km (6 mi)
ELEVATION GAIN	406 m (1332 ft)
KEY ELEVATIONS	trailhead 1479 m (4850 ft)
	Harrison Lake 1885 m (6182 ft)
HIKING TIME	3 to 4 hours
DIFFICULTY	easy
TRAILHEAD ACCESS	easy, but long
MAPS	USGS The Wigwams, Roman Nose

Opinion

A sapphire pool in a granite goblet (see page 23) is the reward. It's yours in return for a relatively short hike on a moderately demanding trail.

Others obviously agree Harrison Lake is one of the Idaho Panhandle's glory holes: the small campground here is worn bare from overuse. But why trundle a full backpack such a meagre distance? Give your knees and the lake a break. You'll have plenty of time to appreciate Harrison on a dayhike.

For some, it's enough to pull up a lakeside boulder and meditate on the yin and yang of rock and water. If you're more rambunctious, you can rock romp around the shore—feeling the beauty, instead of just observing it. Or you can really feel it, by jumping into the clear, cold lake. The sandy bottom allows easy entry for kids who want to get wet.

Scramblers will see opportunities to explore higher. You can aim for the beaky summit of Harrison Peak by starting where the trail crosses the peak's shoulder.

If you're planning a trip to Harrison Lake, also consider Two Mouth Lakes (Trip 40). The trailheads are quite close.

Fact

before your trip

For current conditions, visit http://www.fs.usda.gov/activity/ipnf/recreation/hiking, or stop at the Bonners Ferry Ranger District office, in Bonners Ferry, Idaho. It's on the S side of town, on the W side of Hwy 2/95.

by vehicle

From Bonners Ferry, Idaho, follow the directions for Pyramid and Ball lakes (Trip 39). Pass the Kootenai National Wildlife Refuge. At the 10.5-km (6.5-mi) junction, turn left (W) onto Myrtle Creek Road #633 and reset your trip odometer to 0. Then follow the directions for Two Mouth Lakes (Trip 40). At the 21.8-km (13.5-mi) junction, turn right (S) onto Upper Myrtle Creek Road #2409. Reach the trailhead at 24 km (14.9 mi), 1479 m (4850 ft).

Rd 2409

Myrtle Creek

P 1479 m (4850')

TRIP 41

HARRISON LAKE

↑
N

0 _____ 1 km

0 _____ 0.5 mile

trail 6

▲ Harrison Peak
2223 m (7292')

**KANIKSU
NATIONAL
FOREST**

IDAHO SELKIRKS

trail 217

Pack River

Harrison
Lake   1885 m
(6182')

on foot

Follow **Trail #6** (initially a barricaded road) S through alder. Soon hop over a creeklet and pass a **trail register**. In about 15 minutes, cross a bridged creek.

The heavily overgrown road now resembles a trail. It turns right (N) into a young, conifer forest. Shortly after, begin a switchbacking ascent. Within 7 minutes, the narrow, overgrown trail heads S. The grade eases. Cross lush, **avalanche paths**. Short, steep pitches break your momentum on this otherwise moderate ascent.

About 1¼ hours from the trailhead, turn right (W) and cross a **shoulder of Harrison Peak** at 1854 m (6080 ft). The trail then descends. A rocky cirque is visible SW. Jump a stream and follow cairns across rock slabs in subalpine forest. Right (N) is craggy, 2223-m (7292-ft) Harrison Peak.

Reach a **junction** at 2.75 mi (4.4 km). Bear right (SSW), rockhop a creeklet, then resume ascending on rock slabs. Left (SSE) is Trail #217. It drops SE to the Pack River Road trailhead, accessed from Sandpoint. When you return from Harrison Lake, watch for this junction; don't descend Trail #217. Instead, ascend onto rock slabs immediately after the creek crossing.

Reach the bouldery SE shore of **Harrison Lake** at 4.8 km (3 mi), 1885 m (6182 ft). It's hidden in a bowl, ringed by granite walls and talus slopes.

Shoulder-Season Trips

Fry Creek (Trip 48) flows into Kootenay Lake

TRIP 42
Slocan Lakeshore

LOCATION	Valhalla Provincial Park, SW end of Slocan Lake
ROUND TRIP	16 km (10 mi)
ELEVATION GAIN	150 m (492 ft)
KEY ELEVATIONS	lakeshore 538 m (1764 ft), highpoint 607 m (1990 ft)
HIKING TIME	5 to 6 hours
DIFFICULTY	easy
TRAILHEAD ACCESS	easy
MAP	Slocan 82 F/14

Opinion

The lumber mill in Slocan is a monument to hard work. And the trail that departs the village and follows Slocan Lake's southwest shore is a workers' trail.

Constructed in the 1920s, the shoreline trail conveyed loggers—and their horses loaded with supplies—to and from Evans and Beatrice creek valleys. Logging camps at Evans and Cahill lakes were beachheads of industry in the wilderness.

Today the lakeshore and the entire mountain range rising abruptly west of it are protected by Valhalla Provincial Park. So the lakeshore trail is now strictly recreational. It's a shoulder-season hike as rewarding as any in the West Kootenay.

Evans Creek is the ostensive goal of shoulder-season lakeshore hikers. But you'll miss little by turning around earlier, because there's no scenic climax. The entire trip is a scenic groove.

The trail itself is well-constructed. Short ups and downs are more interesting than taxing, though they add up to a noticeable elevation gain. Also, some sections are slick, so be sure-footed.

The atmosphere keeps changing: forest, mossy boulder fields, slabby rocks, grassy slopes. Views of the lake and the Selkirk Range are frequent. Water lapping on the shore is occasionally audible. Most of the way you'll be 15 to 30.5 m (50 to 100 ft) above the lake. At times you'll be on the water's edge.

Noise is the pebble-in-the-boot on this otherwise ideal hike. You'll hear vehicles plying Hwy 6, on the far shore, 1.1 km (0.7 mi) distant. You can ignore the subtle whoosh of cars, but bellowing trucks are annoying.

The lakeshore trail can be snow-free nine months a year. The optimal time to hike here is early spring, before most trails are open. But keep it in mind as an alternative in summer, when the peaks are cloud-cloaked, or when it's so hot all you want to do is swim.

Fact

by vehicle

From the Petro Canada station at the junction of Hwys 6 and 31A in **New Denver**, drive S on Hwy 6. Follow Slocan Lake's E shore 31.5 km (19.5 mi) to the

village of Slocan. Turn right (W) onto Giffin Road, which is signed for Drinnon Pass. Reset your trip odometer to 0.

From **Playmor Junction** (midway between Nelson and Castlegar, where Hwy 6 departs Hwy 3A) go N on Hwy 6. Proceed 46.5 km (28.8 mi) to the village of Slocan. Turn left (W) onto Giffin Road, which is signed for Drinnon Pass. Reset your trip odometer to 0.

0 km (0 mi)
Starting W on Giffin Road.

0.4 km (0.25 mi)
Turn right onto Slocan Street.

0.7 km (0.4 mi)
Turn left onto Fletcher Avenue. Cross Harold Street. Pass the motel and cafe.

1.1 km (0.7 mi)
Turn right onto Main Street. About 100 m (110 yd) farther reach the trailhead parking lot. There's a picnic table and BC Parks kiosk here, where Slocan River flows out of Slocan Lake. Elevation: 538 m (1764 ft).

on foot

Cross the bridge over the Slocan River. On the W bank, turn right (N) onto the signed, **dead-end road**. Follow it 0.4 km (0.25 mi) to the **trailhead** on the boundary of Valhalla Provincial Park.

Your general direction of travel will remain N. The trail follows the lakeshore all the way to the S bank of Evans Creek.

About 30 minutes beyond the trailhead, cross an expanse of **mossy boulders**. Close inspection will reveal at least six types of moss.

Reach a signed **junction** at 4 km (2.5 mi), 564 m (1850 ft). Right descends to a small, pebble beach. Only the S end of the beach is public, so follow the main trail left.

Ascend 43 m (140 ft)—skirting above **private property**, through scraggly trees—to the 607-m (1990-ft) **highpoint**. Then descend back to the lake. The trail is now out of the forest, within 5 m (15 ft) of the shore, traversing slabby rocks and mossy, grassy slopes.

Cross a small, bridged creek before reaching the **campground** beside the mouth of **Evans Creek** at 8 km (5 mi). Moderate-paced hikers arrive here in about 2¾ hours.

The unscenic trail to Beatrice Lake ascends left (W), soon crossing a hefty metal bridge to the N bank of Evans Creek.

Beatrice Creek

Evans Creek

Slocan Lake

New Denver

TRIP 42

SLOCAN LAKESHORE

N

607 m (1990')

0   2 km
0   1 mile

SELKIRKS

538 m (1764') P

6

Slocan

Hwy 3A

Galena-trail cable car spanning Carpenter Creek (Trip 43)

TRIP 43
Carpenter Creek Valley

LOCATION	between Sandon and New Denver, S of Hwy 31A
ONE-WAY TRIP	14.5 km (9 mi) Sandon to New Denver
	8 km (5 mi) Sandon to Three Forks
	6.5 km (4 mi) Three Forks to New Denver
ELEVATION LOSS	509 m (1670 ft)
KEY ELEVATIONS	376 m (1234 ft) Sandon to New Denver
	256 m (840 ft) Sandon to Three Forks
	120 m (393 ft) Three Forks to New Denver
HIKING TIME	4½ hours Sandon to New Denver
	2½ hours Sandon to Three Forks
	2 hours Three Forks to New Denver
DIFFICULTY	easy
TRAILHEAD ACCESS	easy
MAP	Nakusp 82 K / 4

Opinion

Every spring, hikers coax atrophied muscles into marching again. Carpenter Creek Valley is the ideal place to do it. Instead of an onerous task, it's an indulgence. Not only is the trail—rejoice!—entirely downhill, it's scenically engaging and offers insight into West Kootenay history.

The 21-km (13-mi) trail has three distinct sections. You can hike each separately. The optimal trip comprises two sections: Sandon to Three Forks (mid valley), and Three Forks to New Denver (lower valley), totaling 14.5 km (9 mi). The third section—New Denver to Rosebery (Slocan Lake)—is a dull hike, but runners or cyclists might appreciate it.

The first section begins at the mining boomtown of Sandon, midway up Carpenter Creek Valley. From there you'll walk a generally level path traversing the forested west slope of Payne Mtn. This is a railbed, formerly the K&S (Kaslo and Slocan) Railway, converted to trail by volunteers. At Payne Bluffs, you can survey the valley below before descending the steep pack-trail to Three Forks, at the junction of Sandon Road and Hwy 31A. The Galena trail then dives into lower Carpenter Creek Valley, where the forest is lusher and the lively creek is your vivacious companion. You'll cross it on a cable car. The descent is gradual all the way to New Denver. Though the highway is not far above the trail, passing vehicles are invisible and inaudible.

On both the K&S and Galena sections, you'll see artifacts—mostly railroad ties and rusty pieces of rail. You'll also pass a mine shaft, a cement flume, and the collapsed remains of a huge timber-building that once housed an ore concentrator. A few interpretive signs along the Galena trail describe historical details. Most hikers, however, will find these stimulate rather than satisfy their curiosity. So we offer the following, local-history snapshot.

Carpenter Creek tumult

The Slocan and Kokanee mountain ranges spawned mining booms—gold, silver, copper—in the late 1800s. Many Kootenay towns were originally mining settlements. The Payne mine was the starting gun that initiated the race to Sandon. Within a year, 750 mining claims covered the mountainsides above Carpenter Creek. Within two years, Sandon's population soared to 5,000. The nearby towns of Cody and Three Forks also flourished.

Within five years, the Kaslo and Slocan (K&S) Railway and the CPR's Nakusp and Slocan (N&S) Railway were serving the mines. The Silvery Slocan mining district became famous for galena, an ore rich in silver, lead and zinc. Some of it, called "float," was found above ground. The rest was mined from hard-rock veins.

In 1899, the local economy stumbled into decline, nudged by three forces: a miners' strike, low metal prices, and the lure of Klondike gold. Sandon was devastated by a fire in 1900 but was quickly rebuilt. The mining industry fizzled after 1910. The town was washed out by Carpenter Creek in 1933 and again in 1955. Today, Sandon comprises only a few buildings. No trace of Three Forks remains. Cody is barely noticeable.

We do not recommend or describe the New Denver to Rosebery section of trail. The path itself is monotonously straight, devoid of interesting turns and twists. It's walled in by mundane, immature forest. The trees even prevent you from seeing Slocan Lake where the path follows the shore. And traffic on the nearby highway is audible.

Fact

before your trip

To hike from Sandon to New Denver, you must arrange a vehicle shuttle or hitchhike between the trailheads. To hitchhike, follow the directions below to the New Denver trailhead, on Denver Siding Road. Park your vehicle there. Walk back out to Hwy 31A and hitch E (right) to Three Forks and, if you're very lucky, all the way to Sandon. You'll probably be dropped at Three Forks and will have to catch another ride—SE to Sandon—but that should be easy.

by vehicle

For the **New Denver trailhead**, drive E on Hwy 31A from New Denver. It climbs steeply, switchbacks, then straightens. Turn right (S) onto Denver Siding Road—a residential street marked by a blue-and-white hiker sign. Proceed about 75 m (82 yd), turn left toward the highway maintenance yard, and reach the trailhead parking area at 630 m (2066 ft).

For the **Three Forks trailhead**, drive 8.3 km (5.2 mi) E on Hwy 31A from New Denver, or 37.9 km (23.5 mi) W on Hwy 31A from Kaslo. Turn SE onto Sandon Road. The trailhead parking area is immediately on the right, at 750 m (2460 ft).

For the **Sandon trailhead**, depart Hwy 31A at Three Forks, heading SE on unpaved Sandon Road. At 5.6 km (3.5 mi) arrive at the mining boomtown of Sandon—now just a few buildings. Proceed straight (E) on Reco Road; do not cross the Carpenter Creek bridge. At 6 km (3.7 mi) reach the trailhead parking area (left), near the Historic Railway Trail kiosk, at 1006 m (3300 ft). Reco Road continues E, leading to the Mt. Carlyle trailhead (Trips 7, 8 and 9).

on foot

K & S Rail Trail, Sandon to Three Forks: 8 km (5 mi), 2½ hours

From the Historic Railway Trail kiosk, follow the gravel railbed. The elevation here is 1006 m (3300 ft). Your general direction will be NW all the way to Payne Bluffs junction.

About 5 minutes from the trailhead, reach a 3-pronged fork. Proceed on the middle, level, two-track road through lush forest. Within 20 minutes, at 2.3 km (1.4 mi), reach the end of driveable road. Beyond, the railbed narrows and is more overgrown. Pass rusty rails, the **Altoona Mine site**, and a cascade. About 35 minutes from the trailhead, cross a bridged creek. The railbed dwindles to a narrow trail traversing the slope. Bright-orange tiger lilies and flaming-red Indian paintbrush add a decorative fringe to the mixed forest.

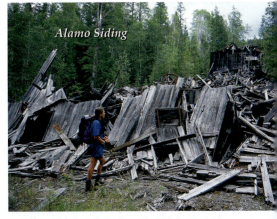

Alamo Siding

At 5.7 km (3.5 mi), about 1¼ hours from the trailhead, reach Payne Bluffs junction. Left descends W to Three Forks. Proceed straight 10 minutes through aspen and cedar to reaches trail's end at **Payne Bluffs**—a rocky, narrow perch overlooking Carpenter Creek Valley. Kane Creek valley is visible NW.

Turning left (W) at Payne Bluffs junction, the trail descends 260 m (853 ft) in 1.7 km (1.1 mi) to reach **Three Forks** at 750 m (2460 ft) in less than 30 minutes. This is the junction of Sandon Road and Hwy 31A. At the beginning of Sandon Road is the Three Forks trailhead parking area. From there, the Galena trail follows Carpenter Creek downstream to New Denver.

Galena Trail, Three Forks to New Denver: 6.5 km (4 mi), 2 hours

The Galena trail departs Sandon Road about 75 m (82 yd) SE of Hwy 31A. Start by the interpretive signs, just past the SE end of the trailhead parking area, at 750 m (2460 ft). Immediately descend to Carpenter Creek and cross a bridge to the S bank. In a couple minutes, pass a signed but unmaintained trail forking left to Sandon. Proceed straight.

After descending to a lower point beside the creek, the trail continues following it downstream (SW). In about half an hour, reach **Alamo Siding** at 655 m (2150 ft). In 1904, this was home to 200 people. Today there's an outhouse and table here, in addition to the ruins. Just beyond, a **cable car** conveys hikers to Carpenter Creek's N bank, where the trail continues SW. It stays level while the creek plummets into Denver Canyon.

At 588 m (1930 ft), about 1½ hours from Three Forks, reach a **junction** at a substantial wood bridge and descending steps. Bear right and cross the bridge for the New Denver trailhead at Denver Siding Road. Left is an alternative route to New Denver. It's not recommended except for the initial 37-m (120-ft) descent, which is a very worthwhile sidetrip. It leads to **Carpenter Creek**, constricted by narrow canyon walls into an awesome, thundering torrent. Visible on the far wall are remnants of a cement flume from the mining days. Check it out, then ascend back to the bridge.

Willow-herb

After crossing the bridge at the junction, follow the trail generally W. In 20 minutes, pass a highway maintenance yard. Bear right to reach the Denver Siding Road trailhead at 630 m (2066 ft). Hwy 31A is just beyond.

TRIP 44
Silver Avenue

LOCATION	Kaslo River Valley
	between New Denver and Kaslo, S of Hwy 31A
ROUND TRIP	4.4 km (2.7 mi)
ELEVATION GAIN	128 m (420 ft)
KEY ELEVATIONS	trailhead 902 m (2960 ft)
	Retallack Lodge 1030 m (3378 ft)
HIKING TIME	1 to 1½ hours
DIFFICULTY	easy
TRAILHEAD ACCESS	easy
MAP	Rosebery 82 K/3

Opinion

Forested mountainsides. The rollicking Kaslo River. A couple tiny lakes. And a few structures, several decrepit. That's all you see along Hwy 31A between Kaslo and New Denver. Vehicle traffic is usually light. Even in summer, when tourism spikes, the two-lane blacktop is not busy. We've driven it and seen no one, though we did share the road momentarily with a skittish bear.

Gripped between the Goat and Kokanee ranges, this slender valley is the definition of "remote." For about 20 years, however, starting in the late 1800s, pandemonium reigned. Silver was discovered here. Sandon sonic-boomed from a couple tents to a wild-west city. Thousands were soon working here: seeking fortunes, or proffering food, drink, clothes, equipment, housing, medical treatment, and entertainment to fortune seekers. Thousands more came and went: hauling in supplies and hauling out the precious ore. Trails were blazed. Wagon roads punched through. Railways constructed. The valley became a teeming transportation corridor.

We call it "Silver Avenue," because the shiny metal is ultimately responsible for the highway now serving us here; because the valley was once an important and famous avenue of discovery and wealth; and because today you can walk—with little more effort than you would on a metropolitan avenue—a path previously followed by the miners, merchants, barkeeps, prostitutes, con men, gamblers, engineers, carpenters, blacksmiths and horsepackers swept up in the silver rush.

Yes, this is merely a walk. Too short and easy to be a genuine hike, it never strays far from the highway. So it's ideal for gently nudging children into the wilderness. And it invites "I'm on a mission" drivers to stop their careening vehicles, and take a break from the West Kootenay's whipsaw roads.

No, you won't see mining relics. You'll simply see a beautiful valley that a century ago was the scene of a meteoric frenzy and is now eerily tranquil. It's a place where, knowing a little history, your imagination can carry you farther than your feet.

photos on page 246: *1 Kaslo River 2 Robb Creek trailhead 3 early July foliage*

If your feet are up to it, however, combine this walk with the Retallack Cedars trail (Trip 45)—a quick loop through a spectacular pocket of towering trees. In 10 to 30 minutes, you'll come away knowing how magnificent the West Kootenay was before most of the ancient forests were felled.

Fact

Bog orchid beside rail trail

by vehicle

In downtown **Kaslo**, drive NW on "A" Avenue. As it begins climbing, ignore North Marine Drive (Hwy 31N) on the right. Proceed uphill. Soon reach the intersection of "A" Avenue and Washington Street. Reset your trip odometer to 0 here. Turn left onto Washington, which becomes Hwy 31A. Follow it generally NW. At 24.2 km (15 mi) turn left (S) into the small, unpaved, pullout. This is the Robb Creek trailhead, at 902 m (2960 ft). There's a kiosk here and a bridge spanning the Kaslo River.

In **New Denver**, reset your trip odometer to 0 at the junction of Hwys 6 and 31A (Union Street and 6th Avenue). Drive E on Hwy 31A (6th Avenue). Follow it generally NE. At 8.3 km (5.2 mi) proceed through Three Forks and pass Sandon Road (right). At 22 km (13.6 mi)

Goat Range, from rail trail

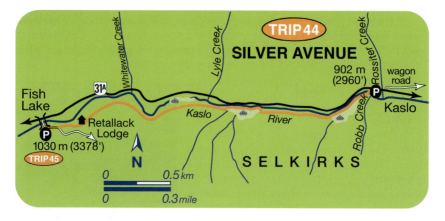

turn right (S) into the small, unpaved, pullout. This is the Robb Creek trailhead, at 902 m (2960 ft). There's a kiosk here and a bridge spanning the Kaslo River.

on foot

Cross the bridge spanning the Kaslo River. Hike W, upstream, above the river's S bank. This is a rail trail, formerly the K&S (Kaslo and Slocan) Railway. In 5 minutes, pass a weeping cascade at a mossy bank. The highway is often in view, but the creek muffles vehicle noise.

Within 10 minutes, see a long cascade across the highway, and soon another. At 15 minutes, 1.2 km (0.75 mi), enter a large, **clearing**. Proceed NW, across the dirt. The trail resumes at the K&S sign on the far side of the clearing.

While ascending, a marshy pond is visible left (SW) in the meadow below. About 30 minutes along, reach **Retallack Lodge** at 2.2 km (1.4 mi), 1030 m (3378 ft).

Decision time. You can turn around at Retallack and retrace your steps to the trailhead, or continue just beyond to the **Retallack Cedars** (Trip 45), where a 0.6-km (0.4-mi) trail loops through a cathedral grove of ancient trees. It's possible to tour the cedars in 10 minutes, but these venerable titans deserve at least 30 minutes of admiration.

From the lodge, reach the cedars in 5 minutes by proceeding on the road. Ignore the left fork at the top of the rise. Descend to the small, trailhead parking area (left). The signed trail departs here. Immediately ahead is a bridge over the Kaslo River. On the other side is Hwy 31A.

After hiking among the cedars, you can choose to extend the hike father. Cross the bridge over the Kaslo River and resume on the main trail. It continues generally WNW, paralleling the N side of the highway, 3.5 km (2.1 mi) to the picnic area at **Fish Lake**.

After hiking back to your vehicle at the Robb Creek trailhead, you have yet another option. From the trailhead, walk NNW across the highway and pick up the signed Wagon Road (now a recreation trail). It contours SE, paralleling the NE side of the highway. But you'll see little. We advise against.

TRIP 45
Retallack Cedars

LOCATION	Kaslo River Valley
	between New Denver and Kaslo, S of Hwy 31A
LOOP	0.6 km (0.4 mi)
ELEVATION GAIN	negligible
KEY ELEVATIONS	trailhead and cedar grove 1030 m (3378 ft)
HIKING TIME	10 to 30 minutes
DIFFICULTY	easy
TRAILHEAD ACCESS	easy
MAP	Rosebery 82 K/3

Opinion

King John put his stamp on the Magna Carta, binding the monarchy to the laws of England. Spanish sailors began using the magnetic compass to navigate. Eyeglasses were invented in Italy and soon adopted by Roman scholars. Meanwhile, the Retallack Cedars were saplings.

These 600-to-800-year-old trees still stand in what is now a cathedral grove. It's one of the few remaining in the West Kootenay and the easiest to visit. You'll find it a mere one minute off a paved highway. The grove is so beautiful and accessible, it served as a film location for *Snow Falling on Cedars*, which in 1999 was nominated for *Best Cinematography* at the Academy Awards.

A short, comfortable trail—suitable for anyone who can walk— loops among the trees and grazes the nascent Kaslo River. We urge you to stop here when driving between Kaslo and New Denver. It's possible to tour the cedars in ten minutes, but these venerable titans deserve at least 30 minutes of admiration. Shorten and slow your hiking stride to a leisurely, art-gallery stroll. Marvel at the riotous greenery. Relax into the serenity of this cool, moist, shady glen. The time will pass quickly.

Children will find this soccer-field-size terrarium fascinating if you prod their innate wonder. Suggest they be silent, listening carefully for a full minute, then ask them to tell you each of the sounds they identified. Encourage them to find and point out to you what they believe are the homes of forest creatures. Prompt them to mimic the graceful stance of ferns or Devil's club, or the rooted, balanced stature of the cedars themselves.

Fact

by vehicle

In downtown **Kaslo**, drive NW on "A" Avenue. As it begins climbing, ignore North Marine Drive (Hwy 31N) on the right. Proceed uphill. Soon reach the intersection of "A" Avenue and Washington Street. Reset your trip odometer

Retallack Cedars trail

to 0 here. Turn left onto Washington, which becomes Hwy 31A. Follow it generally NW. At 27.3 km (17 mi) turn left (S) at the sign for Retallack Lodge. The unpaved road immediately crosses a bridge spanning the Kaslo River. Just beyond is the small, trailhead parking area (right) at 1030 m (3378 ft). The signed trail departs here.

In **New Denver**, reset your trip odometer to 0 at the junction of Hwys 6 and 31A (Union Street and 6th Avenue). Drive E on Hwy 31A (6th Avenue). Follow it generally NE. At 8.3 km (5.2 mi) proceed through Three Forks and pass Sandon Road (right). At 18.9 km (11.7 mi) turn right (S) at the sign for Retallack Lodge. The unpaved road immediately crosses a bridge spanning the Kaslo River. Just beyond is the small, trailhead parking area (right) at 1030 m (3378 ft). The signed trail departs here.

on foot

The trail initially leads NW, above the SW bank of the Kaslo River. No further directions are necessary for this very short walk. If you must, you can turn back in a few minutes having at least glimpsed the great cedars. Ideally, devote 30 minutes to the loop. That allows you time to stop frequently and admire the complex, verdant understory, as well as the girthy trees.

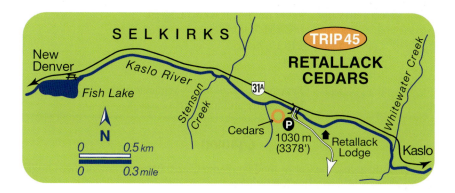

Giant cedars

TRIP 46
Kaslo River

LOCATION	Kaslo
LOOP	2.7 km (1.7 mi)
ELEVATION GAIN	111 m (364 ft)
KEY ELEVATIONS	lower trailhead 544 m (1785 ft)
	covered footbridge 655 m (2150 ft)
HIKING TIME	1 to 1½ hours
DIFFICULTY	easy
TRAILHEAD ACCESS	easy
MAP	*Kaslo & Area Trail Map*—available at the Moyie
	Info Centre and local businesses

Opinion

Bilbo Baggins, the Cat in the Hat, Santa Claus. It seems any of them might come sauntering across this folkloric bridge.

It's a startling, beet red. It arcs over the boisterous Kaslo River with whimsical grace. It's hidden in an evergreen forest, beyond earshot of civilization yet within easy walking distance of downtown Kaslo.

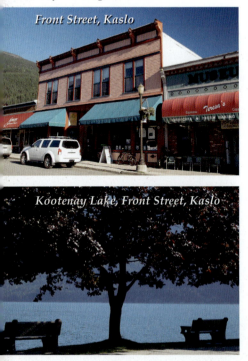

Front Street, Kaslo

Kootenay Lake, Front Street, Kaslo

The covered footbridge is the culminating sight on the short, easy, Kaslo River loop. You'll follow the river there and back. And upon returning to Kaslo, your fondness for this lakeside village will likely have grown.

Volunteers—members of the Kaslo Trailblazers Society—devoted 1090 hours to designing, constructing, and installing the bridge. Made from local timber, it's 34 m (112 ft) long. The beet-red stain is organic.

The result is enchanting because it's not merely practical. Any safe, lasting bridge linking trails on both sides of the river would have been celebrated. But they built more than a bridge. In old-world tradition, they created art.

After that first bridge, another was built downstream, closer to town. The result of 1700 volunteer hours, it's 38 m (125 ft) long, and allows walkers to avoid the highway while re-entering

Kaslo River bridge

the village. It's called *Unity Bridge* because donors worldwide contributed to the project. Visit www.kaslotrailblazers.org to learn more.

Before or after your river walk, be sure to visit the S.S. Moyie—the world's oldest, intact, passenger sternwheeler, and a national historic site. She was retired in 1957 after a 59-year career, much of it hauling freight and passengers up and down Kootenay Lake. You'll find her on the lakeshore, just below Front Street, between 3rd and 4th streets.

Ideally, visit the Moyie on a longer, river-walk loop—see "optional extension" below—by following the river down to the lake, then returning up Front Street, to the Moyie, then into the centre of Kaslo.

Fact

by vehicle

Drive to **Kaslo**, at the junction of Hwy 31A (from New Denver) and Hwy 31 (from Nelson).

From the **Balfour** ferry terminal, on the W shore of Kootenay Lake, it's a 45-minute drive to Kaslo. Just before entering the village, Hwy 31 crosses the Kaslo River. You'll cross this bridge on foot if you complete the loop walk. Just beyond the bridge, the first street left (NW) is "C" Avenue. It leads to 5th Street, where left (SW) leads to the trailhead. But you'll likely visit Kaslo first, so here are directions from the village.

Lower Trailhead: From "A" Avenue and 5th Street in Kaslo, drive SW (away from the lake) on 5th Street. It curves right (W) and becomes unpaved Higashi Way (formerly Railroad Avenue). Pass a few houses. Reach the trailhead parking area (map/sign, picnic table) at road's end, on the Kaslo River's N bank. The elevation here is 544 m (1785 ft).

Upper Trailhead: In downtown Kaslo, drive NW on "A" Avenue. As it begins climbing, ignore North Marine Drive (Hwy 31N) on the right. Proceed uphill. Soon reach the intersection of "A" Avenue and Washington Street. Reset your trip odometer to 0 here. Turn left onto Washington, which becomes Hwy 31A.

At 1 km (0.6 mi) turn left (S) into the signed, "Welcome to Kaslo" pullout. The elevation here is 730 m (2390 ft).

on foot

Round trip to covered bridge

If you want to see the covered footbridge without hiking the loop, start at the **upper trailhead**. Descend switchbacks to a picnic table just below the highway. Continue another minute to the Kaslo River's N bank and the **covered footbridge** at 655 m (2150 ft).

Complete loop

Start at the **lower trailhead**. Follow the trail upstream (WNW), along the **Kaslo River's N bank**, through a forest of primarily cedar.

At 1.2 km (0.75 mi) turn left (S) and cross the **covered footbridge** at 655 m (2150 ft)—15 m (50') above the river.

On the **Kaslo River's S bank**, turn left (E) and follow the trail downstream. Ignore the connector trail (straight / S) accessing True Blue Rec Area.

Reach the **second bridge** at 2.5 km (1.6 mi), on the W edge of Kaslo. Cross to the river's N bank, then walk Higashi Way left (WSW) to the parking lot at 2.7 km (1.7 mi).

Optional extension

When you reach the second bridge, instead of crossing, stay on the river's S bank. At **trail's end**, follow unpaved Spruce Street right (SE), past the recycling bins, to **Hwy 31**.

After turning left (NE) and crossing the highway bridge to the Kaslo River's NE bank, immediately turn right. Follow the levee downstream (SE) to Kootenay Lake. Bear left. Pass the campground. After rounding the peninsula, turn left (NW) and follow Front Street through downtown Kaslo. Turn left (SW) onto 5th Street. It curves right (W), becomes Higashi Way (unpaved), and leads to the lower trailhead at road's end—only a couple minutes beyond the second bridge.

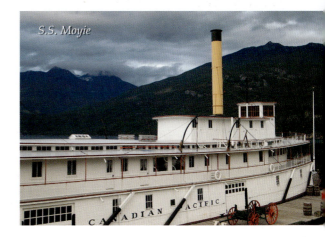

S.S. Moyie

TRIP 47
Kaslo Vista

LOCATION	Kaslo
ROUND TRIP	1 km (0.6 mi)
ELEVATION GAIN	155 m (508 ft)
KEY ELEVATIONS	trailhead 612 m (2007 ft)
	viewpoint bench 767 m (2516 ft)
HIKING TIME	30 minutes
DIFFICULTY	moderate
TRAILHEAD ACCESS	easy
MAP	Kaslo 82 F / 15

Opinion

Kaslo—with its lakeshore setting, embracing mountains, historic downtown, and frontier atmosphere—is certifiably idyllic. Thus the real-estate office window is a popular tourist site, attracting visitors who stare wistfully at the photos of local homes for sale.

Instead they should hike to *Kaslo Vista* for an aerial perspective of this unique, wilderness village. For most visitors, Kaslo will soon be and remain a memory. Better not to miss this unforgettable view of their dream town.

The trailhead is just a few minutes' drive from the post office. The trail climbs the forested skirt of Mt. Buchanan. As far as the viewpoint bench, it's short enough to be called a *walk*. Yet it's steep enough that afterward you can honestly say "I got some exercise."

And the view: ce'st magnifique! You'll see how Kaslo clings to Kootenay Lake and huddles beside the Kaslo River. You'll overlook the inland fiord separating the Selkirks (which cast an early shadow over Kaslo before sunset), from the Purcells (over which Kaslovians watch the sun rise). And you'll hear a buzz and throb that isn't apparent in town but up here is obvious. It's like a pinch, reminding you the utopian mise en cène before you is real.

Fact

by vehicle

In downtown **Kaslo**, drive NW on "A" Avenue. As it begins climbing, ignore North Marine Drive (Hwy 31N) on the right. Proceed uphill. Soon reach the intersection of "A" Avenue and Washington St. Continue straight on "A" Avenue. In 3 blocks, turn right onto Wardner Street. In 1 block, pass Park Street (right). Immediately turn left into the signed, trailhead parking area, at 612 m (2007 ft).

on foot

The trail departs the NW side of the parking area. Just ahead, bear right (NNE).

*Kaslo, Kootenay Lake,
Purcells beyond, from Kaslo Vista*

TRIP 47
KASLO VISTA

Mt. Buchanan
summit 1909 m (6262')

767 m
(2516')

Lardeau

31N

612 m (2007')

N. Marine Drive

Wardner Street

P

Kootenay Lake
532 m (1746')

31A

A Ave

New
Denver

K A S L O

N

4th St

0   100 m

Hwy 31

At about 3 minutes, fork left (W). Keep to the main trail, ignoring the fall-line "shortcuts." Steep switchbacks lead to a **viewpoint bench** at 0.5 km (0.3 mi), 767 m (2516 ft).

For an improved vista, continue 1 minute above. Kaslo and Kootenay Lake are visible below (SE). Distinctly pyramidal Mt. Loki (Trip 30), punctuates the Purcell Range beyond.

Purcells and Kootenay Lake, from downtown Kaslo

TRIP 48
Fry Creek Canyon

LOCATION	Purcells, N end of Kootenay Lake
	E shore, near Johnsons Landing
ROUND TRIP	10 km (6.2 mi)
ELEVATION GAIN	208 m (682 ft)
KEY ELEVATIONS	trailhead 567 m (1860 ft), highpoint 616 m (2020 ft)
	Fry Creek bridge 550 m (1804 ft), creekside
	campsite 643 m (2110 ft)
HIKING TIME	3 to 4 hours
DIFFICULTY	easy
TRAILHEAD ACCESS	easy
MAP	Lardeau 82 K/2

Opinion

"I suppose this is just another creek to you, but in Australia this would be one of the wonders of the world." That was our Aussie friend's comment upon seeing Fry Creek. But we had to admit that, no, even here, this isn't just any creek.

You know how certain phenomena, tornadoes for instance, are so powerful they seem alive? And not just alive, but purposefully menacing? You might get that feeling watching Fry Creek's spring rampage. The haystacks and hydraulics are alarming to behold, because you imagine yourself caught in them, gulping and swirling into watery oblivion.

The canyon itself is also a marvel. The north wall rises 1403 m (4600 ft) from the creek. Both walls, though forested, are sufficiently vertical to appear on the topo map as dark brown smudges. They maintain that sheer angle for 6 km (3.7 mi).

Dynamite was required to build the trail. Sections of canyon wall were blasted away to create ledges. As a result, hikers enjoy the exhilarating experience of being suspended just above the roaring, churning creek. Yet the trail is broad and level—quite safe, as long as you walk with awareness.

In spring, when higher-elevation trails are still snowbound, Fry Creek Canyon trail is clear, and the creek is at its most awesome. That's the optimal time to hike here. Bring along visiting friends, aging parents, or beginning hikers. This trip is as easy as it is entertaining.

Fact

by vehicle

In **Kaslo**, set your trip odometer to 0 at the junction of Hwys 31A and 31N. That's the intersection of "A" Avenue and North Marine Drive, just W of and uphill from downtown.

0 km (0 mi)

Starting N on Hwy 31N, from the junction with Hwy 31A in Kaslo. Head toward Lardeau and Duncan Lake.

Fry Creek Canyon

28.4 km (17.6 mi)
Pass the village of Lardeau. A BC Parks sign warns of the turn you'll be taking toward the Purcell Mountains and Fry Canyon.

34.5 km (21.4 mi)
Turn right (E) onto Argenta Road and reset your trip odometer to 0.

0 km (0 mi)
Starting E on Argenta Road from Hwy 31N. Cross a bridge over the Duncan River at 0.5 km (0.3 mi). Pavement ends.

1.2 km (0.7 mi)
Reach a 4-way intersection. Turn right (S) onto Argenta Road. It leads to Argenta, Johnsons Landing, Fry Creek Canyon trailhead, and the Earl Grey Pass trailhead (Trip 18). Left is unsigned. Straight leads to the trailheads for MacBeth Icefield (Trip 15), Monica Meadows (Trip 16), and Jumbo Pass (Trip 17).

5.8 km (3.6 mi)
The road ascends and narrows.

6.5 km (4 mi)
Reach a signed junction. Turn right (S) for Fry Creek Canyon and Johnson's Landing. Sharp left (N) leads to the trailhead for Earl Grey Pass trail (Trip 18).

10.6 km (6.6 mi)
Bear right where Salisbury Creek Road ascends left.

12.8 km (7.9 mi)
Slow down for a sharp turn left, then go right, crossing the bridge over Salisbury Creek.

17.9 km (11.1 mi)
Reach Fry Creek Canyon trailhead at 567 m (1860 ft).

on foot
   Right of the kiosk, the trail initially descends SSW. Just beyond, proceed through the **fence** opening. At 5 minutes, continue left (ESE), ignoring the right (S) fork.

Begin a moderate ascent. Pass the **park boundary sign**. Cross a bridged tributary. Overlook Kootenay Lake. The trail contours S. Within 30 minutes, proceed among huge boulders. Fry Creek is soon audible.

After hiking about 45 minutes, reach 616 m (2020 ft). Continue straight (SSE) at the signpost. Ignore the right (NW) fork descending 10 minutes to private property on the bushy, treed lakeshore at 532 m (1746 ft).

Reach another signed junction just ahead. Left (SSE) enters Fry Creek Canyon. Right (SSW) quickly drops to **Fry Creek bridge**, at 550 m (1804 ft), where you can gaze into the abyss below: deep pools, bedrock cascades, roaring water. Beyond the bridge is private property.

After detouring to the bridge, resume SSE on the main trail. Follow it upstream into **Fry Creek Canyon**. It deepens and constricts, becoming a chasm. For several kilometers, the trail is essentially a catwalk between the swift torrent and the vertical wall. Step carefully. A stumble could land you in the creek with little hope of recovery.

About 1½ hours from the trailhead, reach a small, treed **campsite** beside the creek, at 5 km (3.1 mi), 643 m (2110 ft). Most hikers turn around here.

Up canyon, the rapids are smaller, less engaging, and the forest is scraggly. The trail strays from the creek and soon deteriorates, though BC Parks sometimes clears blowdown as far as the **confluence of Fry and Carney creeks**, at 9.5 km (6 mi), 854 m (2800 ft).

A mining road, abandoned long ago, follows Carney Creek N. It's plagued with blowdown. The Carney Creek drainage, however, is rife with beautiful, mature cedars.

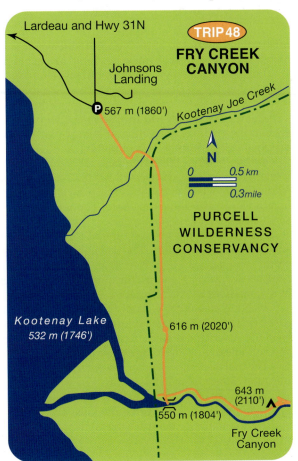

TRIP 48

FRY CREEK CANYON

Lardeau and Hwy 31N

Johnsons Landing

🅿 567 m (1860')

Kootenay Joe Creek

N

0 — 0.5 km
0 — 0.3 mile

PURCELL WILDERNESS CONSERVANCY

Kootenay Lake
532 m (1746')

616 m (2020')

643 m (2110')

550 m (1804')

Fry Creek Canyon

TRIP 49
Kokanee Cedars

LOCATION	Selkirks, W of Kootenay Lake between Nelson and Kaslo
CIRCUIT	2 km (1.2 mi)
ELEVATION GAIN	122 m (400 ft)
KEY ELEVATIONS	trailhead 1174 m (3851 ft), lowpoint 1052 m (3451 ft)
HIKING TIME	1½ to 2 hours
DIFFICULTY	easy
TRAILHEAD ACCESS	easy
MAP	Forest Service brochure

Opinion

Ancient forest is often referred to as *old growth*. It's a dishonourable, misleading descriptor, implying unproductive excess, even malignance. *Old growth* suggests a ghastly, cancerous lump in need of surgical removal.

Loggers are always standing by, eager to operate with a chainsaw, so perpetuating the *old growth* perspective is ecologically foolish. That's why we call this the *Kokanee Cedars* trail, choosing to ignore the official name *Old Growth trail*.

Come. Pay homage to the monarchs who reign supreme in this small, enchanting enclave. Marveling at beings vastly greater than oneself can be deeply moving—humbling yet uplifting.

At one point in this wilderness arboretum, you'll stand among a dozen, western red cedars, each at least 2.5 m (8.25 ft) in girth. One goliath is more than 600 years old, which means it started growing during the Renaissance. Western hemlocks are also numerous here. Though impressively large, they appear small compared to the giant cedars.

Beneath the soaring, forest canopy, a lush understory flourishes. Lady ferns and devil's club are prolific. The deep-green atmosphere is soothing. Elsewhere on the mountain, it might be brilliantly sunny, blazing hot, or fiercely windy. Here it's always dark, moist, still, quiet. The only sound is the gurgle and swish of Kokanee Creek, which you'll cross twice on bridges.

Walking among the Kokanee Cedars will give you a sense for the Hamill Creek trail (Trip 18), where backpackers enjoy nearly two days in ancient forest. Here the advantage is quick, easy access. The trailhead is very close to Nelson and en route to Kokanee Glacier Provincial Park.

The trail is short, well groomed. After the initial, brief descent into the gorge, elevation change is negligible. It's an easy walk even for kids wearing Crocs.

Regardless how they're shod, fledgling hikers will enjoy this trip as much as any in the book. So do bring the kids. The world needs more people who revere ancient forests and reject the myth of *old growth*.

Ancient cedar

Fact

by vehicle

In **Nelson**, from the middle of the orange bridge spanning Kootenay Lake's west arm, drive Hwy 3A NE 20 km (12.4 mi). Or, in **Balfour**, from the turnoff to the Kootenay Lake ferry terminal, drive Highway 3A SW 11.7 km (7.3 mi). From either approach, turn E onto the unpaved road signed for Kokanee Glacier Provincial Park. Reset your trip odometer to zero.

0 km (0 mi)
Starting E on the unpaved road to Kokanee Park, from Hwy 3A.

4.2 km (2.6 mi)
Cross the Busk Creek bridge.

7.2 km (4.5 mi)
Proceed straight on the main road. Ignore the descending left fork.

10.2 km (6.3 mi)
Cross the Sunset Creek bridge.

11.5 km (7.1 mi)
Reach the trailhead parking area (left), at 1174 m (3851 ft). It's signed *Old Growth Recreation Trail*. The road ends 4.5 km (2.8 mi) farther at the Gibson Lake trailhead (Trips 22, 23, 24, 25, 26), in Kokanee Glacier Park.

on foot

Constructed steps ease your descent into Kokanee Creek gorge. Quickly reach a **fork**. Go left. Right leads to a viewpoint. In a few minutes, pass an information **kiosk**. Your general direction of travel is S. The trail drops to 1119 m (3670 ft).

Proceed through a huge, **split boulder** cleaved by water repeatedly seeping into cracks and freezing. Devil's club floats in the forest understory. Lady ferns contribute to the primeval atmosphere. Within 15 minutes, approach the E bank of **Kokanee Creek**.

Entering Kokanee Cedars

Cross a **lush slide** path where the trail plows through head-high greenery. Another slide path is visible across the creek. About 30 minutes from the trailhead, having descended 82 m (270 ft), reach a **junction**. Either way loops back to this point. Go left.

Just 7 minutes farther, pass a **dozen giant cedars**. Immediately beyond is the **biggest cedar in the grove**. It's at least 15 m (50 ft) around. Though 600-plus years old, it's still robustly healthy. A **boardwalk** circles its double-wide trunk.

About 5 minutes from the junction, bear right, passing a faint left spur that ascends to intersect the road well S of the main trailhead. About 8 minutes beyond the double-trunk cedar, the trail curves W. Cross a **bridge** built atop a single, massive log. Reach the trail's 1052-m (3451-ft) **lowpoint**.

Soon cross another log bridge over Kokanee Creek's main channel. On the W bank the trail curves N, heading back toward the trailhead. Big cedars are now less prevalent. Stumps indicate second-growth forest.

After re-crossing the creek on another one-log **bridge**, you're again on the E bank. Quickly reach familiar ground: the **junction** where left (N) returns to the trailhead.

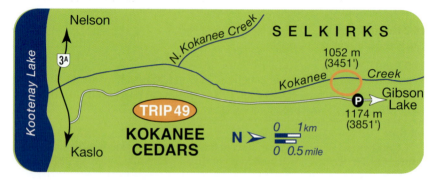

TRIP 50
Pilot Peninsula

LOCATION	Kootenay Lake, E shore
	S of Kootenay Bay ferry terminal
ROUND TRIP	12.8 km (8 mi)
ELEVATION GAIN	235 m (770 ft)
KEY ELEVATIONS	trailhead 540 m (1770 ft)
	highpoint 604 m (1980 ft)
HIKING TIME	3 to 5 hours
DIFFICULTY	easy
TRAILHEAD ACCESS	easy
MAP	Crawford Bay 82 F/10

Opinion

Like beads of sweat on straining, bulging muscles, water trickles down from the Purcell and Selkirk summits. Rivulets gather speed and volume, cascading into the inland fiord called *Kootenay* Lake—a great, languorous vein of deep, cold, clean water that influences every aspect of life in this valley. Yet there's only one trail allowing hikers to stride the lakeshore for a significant distance: on Pilot Peninsula.

The peninsula—hikeable year-round regardless of weather—juts 7 km (4.3 mi) into 110-km (68-mi) long Kootenay Lake. Crawford Bay is on the east side of the peninsula. Pilot Bay, on the west side, is the centerpiece of a small provincial park. Several trails crisscross the peninsula. The least taxing is also the most rewarding. It links the north end of Pilot Bay with a beach near the peninsula's south tip. The trail roughly follows the lakeshore for 6.4 km (4 mi), grants occasional views, passes an inviting campground on Sawmill cove, and accesses a couple small, stony beaches. A few stately cedars and hefty ponderosa pines grace the forest en route.

The provincial park campground, on a point in Pilot Bay, is just 1.8 km (1.1 mi) from the trailhead. Though it's off the main trail, dayhikers who make the short detour will be glad they did. The setting is lovely, and the variety and number of birds is remarkable. Geese splash-land in Sawmill Cove. Loons warble contentedly. Tree swallows zoom overhead.

South of Sawmill Cove, the trail exits the provincial park but remains easy to follow. After passing the spur to Boomer's Landing beach at 3.5 km (2.2 mi), the trail narrows on slopes that drop steeply to the lakeshore. It's slippery here when wet, so be careful.

Though it's possible to complete a circuit on Pilot Peninsula, don't. Re-hike the lakeshore trail: from the beach at the peninsula's south tip, back to the trailhead. Your other options—the Upper Levels and Homestead trails—are longer, steeper, less scenic.

Fact

by vehicle

From Hwy 3A, at the Kootenay Bay ferry terminal, on Kootenay Lake's E shore, turn SE onto Pilot Bay Road. It starts behind the ferry-terminal restrooms. Pavement ends at 2 km (1.2 mi). Turn left onto a signed spur at 3.4 km (2.1 mi). Reach the road's end, trailhead parking area at 3.5 km (2.2 mi), 540 m (1770 ft).

on foot

The trail starts left (N) of the kiosk. After a brief NE ascent, it veers right (SE) then undulates gently. **Pilot Bay** is soon visible below (right).

In 20 minutes, approach the N side of **Sawmill Cove**. Cross a tiny bridge over a creeklet. Just beyond, proceed straight where a right spur leads W to a beach on the cove. About 70 m (82 yd) farther, cross another small bridge in a cedar grove. Pass the S side of Sawmill Cove about 30 minutes from the trailhead. A lovely bog here sustains luxuriant fern and cow's parsnip beneath towering birch and cottonwood.

Reach a signed **junction** at 1.8 km (1.1 mi). The main trail continues left (SE). Right (NW) climbs then drops; enters the **campground** (7 sites, pit toilets) in about 10 minutes; then ends on an elevated point between cobblestone beaches. The view of Sawmill Cove is better there than from the main trail. Look for lavender penstemons on the point. Also watch for a variety of colourful birds, including tree swallows (white and bright green), bald eagles, loons, and Canadian geese.

Proceeding SE on the main trail from the 1.8-km (1.1-km) junction, reach a fork in just 30 m/yd. Right (S) ends in 150 m (165 yd) on a **small**, **stony beach**

Kootenay Lake

with a view SW, across Kootenay Lake, to the Nelson Range. The main trail ascends left (SE), allowing glimpses of the lake for the next several minutes before again confining you to the trees.

Reach a fork at 3.5 km (2.2 mi), 550 m (1800 ft). The main trail continues left (SE), ascending gently. Right (S) descends to **Boomer's Landing** in a couple minutes. It's another stony beach with a view S of Kootenay Lake. Returning from Boomer's, ignore the steep path ascending right; go back to the main trail.

Proceeding SE on the main trail from the 3.5-km (2.2-mi) fork, reach the **next fork** in just 150 m (165 yd). Don't go left (NE). That trail ascends through viewless forest to a junction well inland, where right on the Upper Levels trail eventually leads back down to the peninsula's S tip. Right (E) is the more scenic option. You'll climb 46 m (150 ft), top out at 591 m (1940 ft), then traverse a slope 53 m (175 ft) above the shore. The lake is visible through the trees. Water lapping on the rocks is audible.

Near 4 km (2.5 mi) the trail narrows on a **steep, airy slope** that drops sharply to the lakeshore. Near 4.8 km (3 mi), 542 m (1780 ft), cross a **bluff** where the forest opens and allows a dramatic view of the lake. Pass a notably large ponderosa pine. A minute beyond, bear left following a yellow, wooden arrow on a tree. A brief ascent leads to the next fork. Go left again, following another yellow, wooden arrow on a tree. Ignore the faint right spur.

Ascend steeply to 604 m (1980 ft) and reach a **fork**. Left veers N. Proceed straight (E) and descend slightly. The trail soon parallels the lakeshore, staying about 24 m (80 ft) above the water. Watch closely for the next **junction** (easy to miss in this direction, despite the brown signpost) where a left fork ascends inland to the Upper Levels. Proceed straight (SE), gradually descending to a **beach near the peninsula's S tip**. Total distance: 6.4 km (4 mi). Wing-booted hikers will arrive here in 2 hours.

You can return to the trailhead via two routes. (1) Retracing your approach (roughly following the lakeshore) is the quickest, least strenuous, and most scenic option. (2) If there's plenty of daylight left, you want a more rigorous workout, and you prefer change even if it's for the worse (cheerless forest, no lake views), go back only as far as the Upper Levels trail junction (brown signpost, a few minutes from the S-tip beach) and turn right. Ascend well inland to a junction where left eventually enables you to descend back to the lakeshore trail near Boomer's Landing.

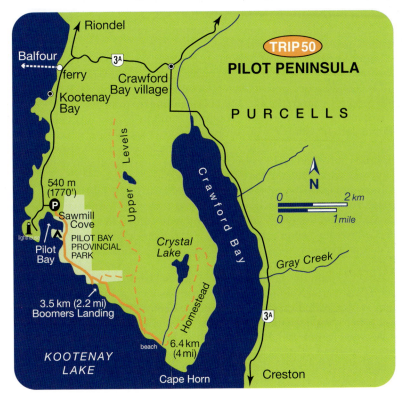

TRIP 51
Pulpit Rock

LOCATION	Nelson
ROUND TRIP	3.6 km (2.2 mi)
ELEVATION GAIN	338 m (1109 ft)
KEY ELEVATIONS	trailhead 565 m (1853 ft), Pulpit Rock 903 m (2962 ft)
HIKING TIME	1½ to 2 hours
DIFFICULTY	moderate
TRAILHEAD ACCESS	easy
MAP	Kokanee Peak 82 4/11

Opinion

Nelson is a Christmas tree ornament of a town. A wealth of restored heritage buildings and homes, and a hillside-spilling-to-lakeshore setting give it a charm rivaled by few small cities in North America. You must look to European villages for comparison. And after admiring Nelson from Baker Street, you should overlook it from Pulpit Rock.

Hiking to Pulpit is the best way we know to quickly justify our always-substantial carb intake at the Kootenay Bakery Cafe, because the trail is steep. It's also a good place to mingle with Nelsonites, many of whom often nip up here for a quick, vigourous workout.

Pulpit Rock is the most popular trip in this book, because it's very short, snow-free most of the year, and a couple-minute drive from downtown. So don't expect solitude. More likely you'll overhear fellow hikers' conversations. You'll certainly hear traffic and city noise wafting up from below.

Expecting the experience to be more urban than wild, you won't be disappointed. It's simply a burst of athletic exercise during which you'll see nothing but forest until the top. Then, suddenly, you'll look down between your knees at Nelson and Kootenay Lake's west tentacle. If you're fit, you can tag the rock within 30 minutes of leaving your car.

In summer, this sun-blasted slope gets hot. You'll need a water bottle, perhaps two, and you'll want a hat if you intend to lounge atop the rock. Summer, however, is when you'll have more to admire than the aerial view of Nelson. Prowling about, you'll find wildflowers galore, including purple lupine, orange tiger lilies, white yarrow, yellow stonecrop, and red Indian paintbrush.

About 17 minutes beyond Pulpit Rock is Flagpole. This grassy, flowery bench is a superior vantage: more spacious as well as more scenic. Yet most hikers are so fixated on Pulpit they never explore beyond. At Flagpole, it's possible to chew on the view in privacy.

Beyond Flagpole is the CBC Tower, high on Mt. Nelson. Resist the summit's allure. The effort/reward ratio is poor on that taxing ascent. Invest your precious hiking time elsewhere: on a premier, West Kootenay trail.

Nelson and Kootenay Lake's west arm, from Flagpole

Fact

by vehicle

In **Nelson**, follow Nelson Avenue to the N edge of town. Proceed onto the orange bridge spanning Kootenay Lake's west arm. Reset your trip odometer to 0 at the far (NW) end of the bridge.

0 km (0 mi)

Starting N on Hwy 3A, from the NW end of the orange bridge.

0.3 km (0.2 mi)

Turn left (W) onto Johnstone Road.

2.7 km (1.7 mi)

Arrive at the paved, trailhead parking lot (right) at 565 m (1853 ft).

on foot

The trail departs the left (SW) end of the parking lot. It initially leads WSW.

Begin a steep, stair-stepping, switchbacking ascent. Soon cross an unpaved road at 600 m (1968 ft). The trail continues squirming sharply up the S shoulder of Mt. Nelson. Your general direction of travel is WNW.

Bear left (S) at a **signed fork** and soon after reach **Pulpit Rock** at 1.8 km (1.1 mi), 903 m (2962 ft). Swift hikers arrive here within 30 minutes.

The outcrop is small, affording room for only a few people. If it's occupied, look for a private perch in the surrounding vegetation. Visible far below (E) is the west arm of Kootenay Lake and the city of Nelson. Beyond is the Nelson Range.

Beyond Pulpit Rock

At the **signed fork** just shy of Pulpit Rock, right (NNW) leads 1.1 km (0.7 mi) generally N to Flagpole, then continues 3.3 km (2 mi) farther N to the CBC Tower at 1700 m (5576 ft), near the 1733-m (5686-ft) summit of Mt. Nelson.

Flagpole—a grassy, flowery bench—is a moderate, 30-minute round trip from Pulpit Rock, affords a greater panorama, yet is lightly visited. The CBC Tower is a long trudge in forest.

Heading to **Flagpole**, in about 12 minutes fork right (NNE) at 1032 m (3385 ft). About 4 minutes farther, fork right again. Continue ascending. Then descend the right spur 1 minute to the open bench at 1220 m (4002 ft).

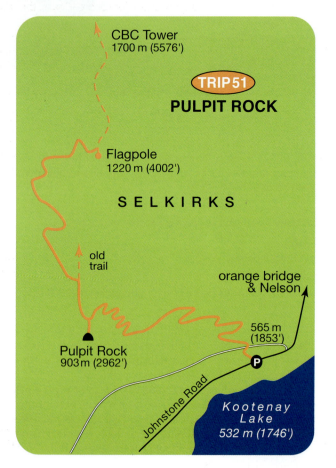

CBC Tower
1700 m (5576')

TRIP 51

PULPIT ROCK

Flagpole
1220 m (4002')

S E L K I R K S

old
trail

orange bridge
& Nelson

565 m
(1853')

Pulpit Rock
903 m (2962')

Johnstone Road

K o o t e n a y
Lake
532 m (1746')

TRIP 52
Sproule Creek

LOCATION	W of Nelson
ROUND TRIP	10 km (6.2 mi)
ELEVATION GAIN	262 m (860 ft)
KEY ELEVATIONS	774 m (2540 ft), trail's end 1037 m (3400 ft)
HIKING TIME	3 to 4 hours
DIFFICULTY	easy
TRAILHEAD ACCESS	easy
MAP	Kokanee Peak 82 F / 11

Opinion

Sproule Creek trail isn't spectacular, but it's pleasant and convenient. Located a few minutes from Nelson, it's hikeable most of the year. It can even be enjoyable on a gloomy or drizzly day. Though the hiking is easy, the trail is long enough to give you a workout and provide a sense of escape.

In the 1920s, Sproule Creek canyon was a logging corridor served by a wagon trail, a small-gauge railroad, and a flume. Timber was milled in the canyon. Rough lumber was transported to a planer mill near the Kootenay River. Wildfires devastated the canyon in the 1930s.

The forest was recovering its previous stature, spawning immense aspen and cottonwoods, when the canyon was again logged in 2006 despite protest. The impact was significant, but creekside it's not as evident as feared. The trail remains, and it still invites you on a beautiful walk through the woods.

You'll cross the creek frequently and follow the bank for all but the final kilometer. Being continually within sight and sound of the water is refreshing, relaxing—an opportunity to sooth jangled emotions, practice walking meditation, or seek your muse.

Fact

by vehicle

From the junction of Hwys 6S and 3A in **Nelson**, drive W on Hwy 3A. In 8.5 km (5.3 mi) turn right (NE) onto Taghum Frontage Road, across from the Shell station. Reset your trip odometer to 0.

0 km (0 mi)
Starting NE on Taghum Frontage Road.

0.5 km (0.3 mi)
Turn left (N) onto Sproule Creek Road, which is mostly paved.

3 km (1.9 mi)
Bear left, staying on the main, paved road.

4 km (2.5 mi)
Pavement ends. Fork left. Ignore the right fork to a house. Parking is left, on the E bank of Sproule Creek, immediately before the vehicle bridge. Elevation: 774 m (2540 ft).

Sproule Creek

on foot

Walk across the vehicle bridge spanning Sproule Creek. Above the W bank, opposite the driveway for house 6544, turn right (N) onto the signed trail. A minute beyond, cross a bridge to the E bank and hike upstream (N).

Within 5 minutes, bear left on the **Hill Bypass**. Within 10 minutes, proceed straight where the Westside Loop forks left. Stay on the E bank. The trail gradually bends NW—your general direction of travel the rest of the way.

Cross a bridge over the **creek's E fork** at 1.7 km (1.1 mi). Bear left (NNW) on the main, creekside trail at 850 m (2788 ft). Ignore the E fork trail ascending right (NE). It's rough and ends soon.

The trail is now beside the creek, overhung with cedars and firs. Cross two more bridges in the next 10 minutes. The logging road is nearby (left / W), paralleling the trail for 1.5 km (0.9 mi).

At 3.2 km (2 mi), the **road crosses the trail** and bends SE to descend along the E bank. Soon after, the trail crosses a bridge to the creek's NE bank.

Near 4.5 km (2.8 mi), pass a stand of stately cottonwoods. After hiking about 1½ hours, reach **trail's end in a grassy clearing** at 5 km (3.1 mi), 1037 m (3400 ft).

TRIP 53
Syringa Park

LOCATION	W of Castlegar
ROUND TRIP	6 km (3.7 mi)
ELEVATION GAIN	90 m (295 ft)
KEY ELEVATIONS	trailhead 460 m (1510 ft), overlook 550 m (1804 ft)
HIKING TIME	2 hours
DIFFICULTY	easy
TRAILHEAD ACCESS	easy
MAP	Castlegar 82 F/5

Opinion

Big lake. Sandy beach. Southwest slope. Forested campground. Nearby city. No wonder Syringa Provincial Park throbs with sun-starved humanity every summer.

Of course, the park is quiet in spring and fall. That's the time for a contemplative walk along the shore of Lower Arrow Lake. And a short, scenic, shoulder-season hike on the forested slopes above.

The forest trail is sidewalk smooth. Though rarely steep, it climbs to impressive viewpoints overlooking the south end of the Columbia River system, which stretches 230 km (143 mi) north to Revelstoke.

The trees are tilt-your-head-back-and-stare-up-at-'em tall: ponderosa pines, and Douglas firs. You can recognize Doug firs by their deeply fluted or channeled bark. The cinnamon-hued pondies have jigsaw-puzzle bark, and needles in brushy bunches.

Regardless when you're here, pack full water bottles; the forest is dry. It's summer, and you want to take your kids hiking? Do it early morning or late evening, otherwise they'll wilt. Or keep to the sandy lakeshore, where it's easy to cool off. From the campground, you can walk surprisingly far NW along the water's edge.

Fact

by vehicle

From **Nelson**, at the junction of Hwys 6S and 3A, drive SW on Hwy 3A toward Castlegar. Pass Playmor Junction at 21 km (13 mi). Proceed SW on Hwy 3A. At 36.5 km (22.6 mi) ignore Pass Creek Road (right / N). At 37 km (23 mi), where straight (SW) crosses the Columbia River to enter Castlegar, bear right (W) on Broadwater Road, toward Robson and Syringa Park. Reset your trip odometer to 0.

From **Castlegar**, at the junction of Hwys 22 and 3, drive N on Columbia Avenue. Cross the Columbia River bridge and reset your trip odometer to 0.

Syringa Park campground beach,
Lower Arrow Lake

0 km (0 mi)
On the N side of the Columbia River bridge, starting W toward Robson. Proceed on Broadwater Road through Robson.

11.3 km (7 mi)
Pass Keenleyside Dam.

16.7 km (10.4 mi)
Enter Syringa Provincial Park

16.9 km (10.5 mi)
Pass the E trailhead (right). It's just beyond the yellow gate at the beach parking area (left).

18.2 km (11.3 mi)
Bear left on pavement, where unpaved Deer Park Road ascends right. There's a pullout just beyond, on the left, at 460 m (1510 ft). Park there if space is available. Otherwise proceed past the gate house, the RV sani-station, and the campground entrance, to the large, paved, day-use parking lot at road's end.

on foot

You can start hiking in three places. The **E trailhead** is near the yellow-gated beach parking area, just inside Syringa Park's E boundary. The **middle trailhead** is on Deer Park Road, above the pullout and gate house. The **W trailhead** is at the large, paved, day-use parking lot at road's end.

From each trailhead, a trail ascends generally N. The two end trails curve, traverse the slope, and intersect at the top of the middle trail. Looking down on this trail system from the air, it would resemble a wonky, three-pronged pitchfork. Most people begin on the middle trail, as described below.

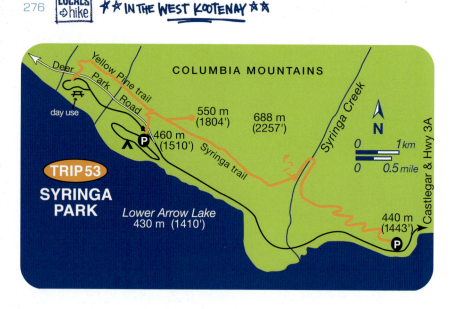

COLUMBIA MOUNTAINS

Deer Park Road

Yellow Pine trail

day use

550 m (1804')

688 m (2257')

460 m (1510')

Syringa trail

Syringa Creek

N

0   1 km
0   0.5 mile

Castlegar & Hwy 3A

TRIP 53

SYRINGA PARK

Lower Arrow Lake
430 m (1410')

440 m (1443')

The **middle trail** initially ascends cement steps from Deer Park Road. Enter forest of primarily white-bark pine, ponderosa pine, and Douglas fir. The grade eases after the first steep switchback. Lower Arrow Lake is soon visible below.

Within 10 minutes, having ascended to 497 m (1630 ft), reach **rock outcroppings** and the junction where all three trails intersect. There's a map/ sign here and a wooden bench. You have three options.

(1) Go left (W) on the **Yellow Pine trail**. Gradually descend to the W trailhead and the day-use parking lot at the end of paved road, where your total distance will be 2.6 km (1.6 mi). Follow the road a short way E to return to the pullout below the middle trailhead.

(2) Go right (E) on the **Syringa trail**. It stays higher longer and affords more views. Finally switchback down to the E trailhead, across the road from the yellow-gated beach parking area, where your total distance will be 3.3 km (2 mi). Follow the road 1.3 km (0.8 mi) W to return to the pullout below the middle trailhead.

(3) Go right (E) on the **Syringa trail**. After enjoying the viewpoints, **return to this junction**, then descend the middle trail if you're in a hurry, or follow the Yellow Pine trail to enjoy a bit more hiking.

The third option, with the Yellow Pine extension, is best. It allows you to hike most of the trail system, descend more gradually, and spend very little time walking on road. It's described below.

Proceeding right (E) on the Syringa trail (from the junction where all three trails intersect) ignore a very steep, left spur. In a couple minutes, reach a fork. Left (N) switchbacks 0.5 km (0.3 mi) to

Syringa trail

Lower Arrow Lake

an **overlook** at 550 m (1804 ft). It's on a slabby bluff adorned with statuesque ponderosa pines. The view extends W, up Lower Arrow Lake valley.

Resuming E on the main trail (from the overlook fork), in another 7 minutes enter a cool, lush **gully** where birch trees flourish. The trail contours at about 518 m (1700 ft), winding in and out of shallow ravines.

After a slight elevation gain, reach a fork marked by a wood post. The main trail (right / E) soon begins a switchbacking descent S to the E trailhead. Left ascends NE (initially on smooth, solid rock, then on steep, loose rock) to a viewpoint at the edge of **Syringa Creek canyon**.

TRIP 54
Christina Lake

LOCATION	Monashees, Gladstone Provincial Park E of Grand Forks
ROUND TRIP	12.8 km (8 mi) to climactic viewpoint
ELEVATION GAIN	306 m (1004 ft) to climactic viewpoint
KEY ELEVATIONS	trailhead 500 m (1640 ft) climactic viewpoint 650 m (2132 ft)
HIKING TIME	4 hours
DIFFICULTY	easy
TRAILHEAD ACCESS	easy
MAP	Grand Forks 82 E/1

Opinion

Spring hiking can be cathartic. You start out straining beneath the weight of winter. You return buoyed by the promise of summer. That's why West Kootenay hikers should make an annual spring pilgrimage to Christina Lake, where a long trail traverses a sunny, west-facing slope high above the lake's northeast shore.

Though much of the lake is crowded with homes and cabins, the northeast shore is not. Here, the only evidence of humanity is a comfortable, well-maintained hiking trail. It ascends moderately, then undulates. A few spurs drop sharply to the water's edge. Occasionally, a superb lake view opens up. Ultimately the trail descends gradually to the lake's north end.

Though we encourage you to hike to the climactic viewpoint at 6.4 km (4 mi), you can turn around at 2.5 km (1.6 mi), where a fine vista from a bench among ponderosa pines offers a sense of completion. This shorter hike requires only two hours round trip.

Most of the Christina Lake trail is forested—a pleasing mélange including ponderosa and cedar. Yet you'll frequently overlook the lake and see the gentle mountains above the west shore. In April, yellow glacier lilies are profuse on grassy slopes. So are ticks; check yourself carefully after your hike. In spring, Queens Cup (white, six petals) brightens the forest. You also might glimpse lupine and Nootka rose. You'll certainly see ferns.

Don't fixate on hiking all the way to Troy Creek campground, on the northwest shore. Dayhikers who follow the main trail beyond 9 km (5.6 mi) will likely regret it, because the scenery deteriorates and the lake remains hidden. Upon reaching the signed junction at 6 km (3.7 mi), we urge you to ascend the right (north) spur just ten minutes to a climactic viewpoint where nearly the entire lake is visible.

Christina Lake, from climactic viewpoint

Fact

by vehicle

From **Castlegar**, drive SW on Hwy 3. After passing the sign for Boundary Forest District, the highway descends. Just after Christina Lake is visible right (SW), slow down at the sign for Alpine Road / Texas Point. The highway soon levels. Follow signs directing you left into the pullout. Loop back, cross the highway, and proceed W onto East Lake Drive. Reset your trip odometer to 0.

From the N edge of the town of **Christina Lake**, drive N on Hwy 3 about 5 km (3.1 km). Slow down at the sign for Alpine Road / Texas Point. Turn left (W) onto East Lake Drive. Reset your trip odometer to 0.

0 km (0 mi)
Starting W on East Lake Drive, departing Hwy 3.

0.7 km (0.4 mi)
Alpine Road is left. Fork right, following the sign for Texas Creek.

1 km (0.6 mi)
Stay right on East Lake Drive, cross the bridge, then bear left.

3.7 km (2.3 mi)
Bear right.

4.5 km (2.8 mi)
Reach the Texas Creek Campground entry gate. Elevation: 500 m (1640 ft). If you're not camping, park here.

on foot

Ignore the signed trail just before the campground. Skirt the gate. Enter the campground. Follow the first, paved lane right (E) past campsites. It gradually curves left (N).

About 5 minutes from your vehicle, reach campsites 34 and 42. **Deer Point trail** starts here, right of the toilets.

Begin a gradual ascent ESE. In 1 minute, ignore the right (S) spur. Just 8 m/yd farther, fork left (E) to continue on Deer Point trail through a mixed forest of birch, cedar, Douglas fir, and ponderosa pine.

The trail quickly gains 73 m (240 ft). At 7 minutes, fork left. This short spur rises over bedrock to a **viewpoint bench**. Just 2 minutes farther, **rejoin the main trail** and bear left.

A minute farther, bear left again, ignoring a right fork. Continue ascending. After reaching 670 m (2198 ft), the trail descends 50 m (164 ft). Cross a creek. At 2.5 km (1.6 mi), about 40 minutes from your vehicle, reach a wizened **log bench** affording a **lake view**. Seeking only a short hike, turn around here. Just beyond (SE) is a bridged stream.

After hiking about 52 minutes, cross a creek at 597 m (1958 ft). At about 65 minutes, attain another view of the lake. Just 1 minute farther, immediately after rockhopping a creeklet, reach a **signed fork** at 5.2 km (3.2 mi). The left (W) spur is worth a quick detour—descending 15 m (50 ft)—to a superb view from an outcrop. Texas Point is visible left (S).

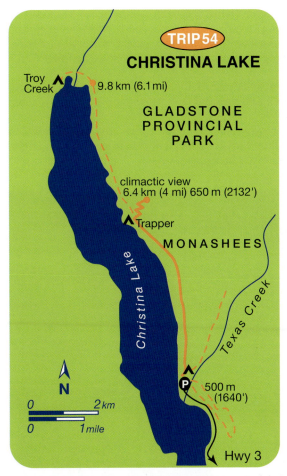

TRIP 54

CHRISTINA LAKE

Troy Creek

9.8 km (6.1 mi)

GLADSTONE PROVINCIAL PARK

climactic view
6.4 km (4 mi) 650 m (2132')

Trapper

MONASHEES

Christina Lake

Texas Creek

500 m (1640')

N

0   2 km

0   1 mile

Hwy 3

Resuming on the main trail, cross a bridged creek about 5 minutes farther. About 8 minutes beyond that, cross the wide, cedar **bridge spanning Trapper Creek** at 5.7 km (3.5 mi). Total hiking time: about 1¼ hours.

Just 20 yd/m farther, a signed left (W) spur drops steeply to Trapper campground, on the lakeshore. Proceed on the main trail 1 more minute to a **signed junction** at 6 km (3.7 mi), 592 m (1942 ft). Left (NW) is the main trail, which we don't recommend because it's disappointing (skip below for a summary). Instead, ascend the right (N) spur. A final, 10 minutes of effort will earn you a commanding view of nearly the entire lake.

The spur, marked with orange blazes, is a narrow-but-adequate route. In 3 minutes, enjoy a prefatory view. Pass several impressive Douglas fir trees and a spectacular ponderosa pine. In 10 minutes, at 6.4 km (4 mi), 650 m (2132 ft), attain a **climactic view** from an open, grassy **promontory**. Here you can overlook the N end of the lake and see down-lake all the way S to the town of Christina Lake.

Main trail beyond 6 km (3.7 mi)

From the signed junction at 6 km (3.7 mi), where the right (N) spur ascends to a climactic viewpoint, the main trail continues up-lake (NW). We don't recommend proceeding, because the effort/reward ratio is poor. Nevertheless, here's a summary.

At nearly 6.5 km (4 mi), a faint, left fork descends W to the lakeshore at Deer Point. For the next 0.5 km (0.3 mi), the main trail crosses **open, rocky slopes** with scrubby vegetation and a few ponderosas. At 7.7 km (4.8 mi) rockhop a creeklet.

Traverse a **rockslide** at 8 km (5 mi). The trail is now about 54 m (177 ft) above the lake. Beyond 9 km (5.6 mi), it descends steadily. Reach level ground behind **Christina Lake's N shore** at 9.8 km (6.1 mi). Quickly arrive at a junction. Left is the main trail, leading generally W. Right (N) follows Sandner Creek upstream.

The entire N shore is privately owned. Only after the trail rounds the NW shore and reaches **Troy Creek campground** at 11.3 km (7 mi) are hikers granted lake access.

Nearly all the ancient cedars that once graced this area were felled and hauled away by the first settlers. Massive stumps remain in what is now a tight, maze like, oppressively-dark forest of scrawny trees.

TRIP 55
Cascade Gorge

LOCATION	Kettle River, S of Christina Lake
ROUND TRIP	8 km (5 mi)
ELEVATION GAIN	45 m (148 ft)
KEY ELEVATIONS	trailhead 475 m (1558 ft)
	Kettle River trestle bridge 455 m (1492 ft)
	Cascade Gorge bridge 480 m (1574 ft)
HIKING TIME	2 to 2½ hours
DIFFICULTY	easy
TRAILHEAD ACCESS	easy
MAP	Grand Forks 82 E/1

Opinion

Few rivers in the Pacific Northwest are truly wild. The Kettle River, unrestricted by dams, is among the untamed.

Originating in the Monashees, the Kettle flows out of B.C. into Washington. It returns to B.C. but makes a hairpin turn near Christina Lake and again exits into Washington, finally merging with the Columbia River at Lake Roosevelt.

Just before that hairpin, as if knowing it will soon leave its home and native land forever, the Kettle gives a fantastic, whitewater salute. It becomes a roaring dynamo as it plummets through Cascade Gorge. The water thunders with thrilling—some might say "terrifying"—intensity.

The Kettle's dramatic homage to Canada is your destination on an easy hike along a 4-km (2.5-mi) stretch of the Trans Canada Trail—a 21,500-km (13,330-mi) path crossing every province and territory, and linking the Atlantic, Pacific and Arctic oceans. When completed, it will be the world's longest recreational trail.

Another appeal of this short segment of the TCT are two bridges. You'll cross the first shortly after leaving the trailhead. It's an impressively long, high, trestle bridge spanning a very broad, languid Kettle River seemingly exhausted from its vigourous performance in Cascade Gorge. The second bridge—our recommended turn-around point—spans the Kettle immediately above Cascade Gorge.

Because the TCT is a multi-use trail, you're not required to walk it. Mountain bikes are welcome. The advantage of a bike is that it can speed you through the mundane stretch between the trestle bridge and the gorge.

Kettle River trestle bridge

Cascade Gorge

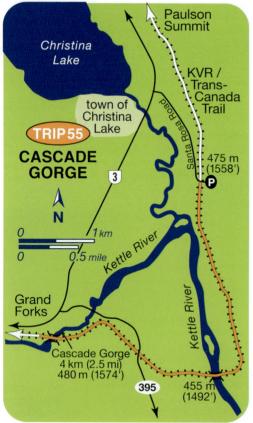

Christina Lake

town of Christina Lake

TRIP 55

CASCADE GORGE

Paulson Summit

KVR / Trans-Canada Trail

Santa Rosa Road

475 m (1558')

P

0 ——— 1 km

0 ——— 0.5 mile

N

Kettle River

Kettle River

Grand Forks

Cascade Gorge
4 km (2.5 mi)
480 m (1574')

395

455 m (1492')

Just north of the town of Christina Lake is Gladstone Provincial Park. The Christina Lake trail (Trip 54) begins there. We suggest you camp at Gladstone. On consecutive days, hike along Christina Lake and hike (or bike) to Cascade Gorge.

Fact

by vehicle

In the **town of Christina Lake**, set your trip odometer to 0 at Christina Lake village (West Lake Drive). Drive 0.5 km (0.3 mi) N on Hwy 3. Turn right (E) onto Santa Rosa Road. At 2 km (1.2 mi)—just before the first switchback—turn left into the spacious, trailhead parking lot. Elevation: 475 m (1558 ft).

on foot

Ignore the trail departing the NE corner of the parking lot (beside the kiosk) and heading N. Instead, cross Santa Rosa Road to where the trail leads S.

Immediately bear left, ignoring the driveway on the right. Cross bridged Chandler Creek. Within 5 minutes, the Kettle River is visible below. The trail proceeds generally SSE.

At 15 minutes, bear left, staying higher, ignoring the overgrown road forking right. The trestle bridge spanning the Kettle River is now in view ahead (S).

A gentle descent leads to the E end of the **Kettle River trestle bridge** at 455 m (1492 ft), about 20 minutes from the trailhead. A staircase descends to the riverbank on the downstream side. Cross the bridge to the far (W) bank.

Heading W now, the trail pierces private property, granting you insight into rural B.C. culture. After veering right (NW), cross Hwy 395. Continue through pleasant woods. After the trail curves left (W) and ascends, watch right. You'll soon glimpse the gorge below.

About 1 hour after departing the trailhead, stop when you see a low, cement wall below the right side of the trail. It's apparent where others have detoured off trail here, to overlook **Cascade Gorge** from the bedrock precipice. Follow one of the bootbeaten paths, but be cautious approaching the edge of the abyss. There's no fence to prevent you from falling.

Resuming on the main trail, 2 minutes farther W is **Cascade Gorge bridge**, at 4 km (2.5 mi), 480 m (1574 ft). It spans the Kettle River immediately above the maelstrom. There are toilets and picnic tables on the SE bank, left (S) of the trail.

On the far (NW) bank, the trail continues E, but it pulls away from the river and parallels Hwy 3. Better to turn around at the bridge and retrace your steps back to the trailhead.

Kettle River. Trans-Canada Trail (KVR rail trail) upper right.

Your Guides

Kathy and Craig are dedicated to each other and to hiking, in that order. Their second date was a 20-mi (32-km) dayhike in Arizona. Since then they haven't stopped for long.

They've trekked through much of the world's vertical topography, including the Nepalese Himalaya, Patagonian Andes, and New Zealand Alps. In Europe, they've hiked the Scottish Highlands, Spain's Costa Blanca and Els Ports mountains, Mallorca's Serra de Tramuntana, the Alpes Maritimes, the French, Swiss, Austrian, and Italian Alps, and Italy's Dolomiti. In North America, they've explored the B.C. Coast, Selkirk and Purcell ranges, Montana's Beartooth Wilderness, Wyoming's Grand Tetons, the Colorado Rockies, the California Sierra, and Arizona's Superstition Wilderness and Grand Canyon.

Visit Kathy and Craig's website: www. hikingcamping.com. You'll find their articles are often mini-guidebooks, and their photo gallery is constantly growing.

In 1989, they moved from the U.S. to Canada, so they could live near the range that inspired the first of their refreshingly unconventional books: *Don't Waste Your Time in the Canadian Rockies, The Opinionated Hiking Guide*. Its popularity encouraged them to abandon their careers—Kathy as an ESL teacher, Craig as an ad-agency creative director—and start their own guidebook publishing company: hikingcamping.com. They now migrate annually to southern Utah, where they wrote *Hiking From Here To Wow: Utah Canyon Country*. Their most unusual book, *Heading Outdoors Eventually Leads Within*, explores the interior dimension of hiking.

Though the distances they hike are epic, Kathy and Craig agree that hiking, no matter how far, is the easiest of the many tasks necessary to create a guidebook. What they find most challenging is the need to spend twice as much time at their computers—writing, organizing, editing, checking facts—as they do on the trail.

The result is worth it. Kathy and Craig's colorful writing, opinionated commentary, and enthusiasm for the joys of hiking make their guidebooks uniquely helpful and compelling.

Where Locals Hike in Utah canyon country

Join Kathy & Craig in Utah for five days—spring or fall.

We're inviting a few, keen hikers to join us in the other-worldly wilderness that inspired us to write our best-selling guidebook, *Hiking from Here to WOW: Utah Canyon Country.*

Each group will be small (six hikers max), screened by us for their on-trail compatibility. All will be accomplished, athletic, ambitious, adventurous.

If you're among them, you'll enjoy an affordable yet luxurious, hiking-focused vacation. Together we'll walk canyon and slickrock routes that are not in our guidebook, or any other.

These hikes would take a determined visitor weeks of exploration to locate and refine. They're our favourite passageways in the complex, fascinating land where we live when not in the Canadian Rockies.

But we haven't, and never will, write about these places. They're too precious to publicize. We'll only share them—in person—with a few friends and guests.

Intrigued? Write us. We'll send details about our Utah canyon-country guiding. – Kathy & Craig nomads@hikingcamping.com

photos page 288: *1 Serra Bernia, Costa Blanca, Spain 2 Aravaipa Canyon, Arizona 3 Campell, Costa Blanca 4 Bellestar, Spain 5 Costa Blanca 6 Superstition Mountains, Arizona 7 Romero Pools, Arizona 8 Facheca, Costa Blanca 9 Els Ports, Spain 10 Mediterranean coastal walk, Spain 11 Serra del Penyal, Costa Blanca 12 Roosevelt Lake, Arizona*

1

2

3

4

5

6

Don't Waste Your Time in Winter

While the Canadian Rockies are buried in snow, you could be hiking with us in Spain or Arizona, where the weather's ideal. After exploring these winter-hiking havens for years, we now offer our readers the opportunity to come along. Interested in joining our next group? Write us, Kathy & Craig, at nomads@hikingcamping.com.

7

8

9

10

11

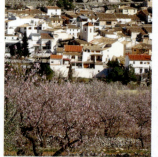

12

Other Titles from hikingcamping.com

The following titles—boot-tested and written by the Opinionated Hikers, Kathy & Craig Copeland—are widely available at outdoor shops and book-stores. Visit www.hikingcamping.com to read excerpts and purchase online.

Don't Waste Your Time in the™
Canadian Rockies
The Opinionated Hiking Guide
all-new ULTRALIGHT GEAR 7th edition

ISBN 978-1-927462-02-7 The Rockies are so vast, with so many trails, you need a guidebook that truly guides. Counsels you about each trail. Advises you where to hike, where not to hike, and explains why. Ensures you invest your precious hiking days wisely, for maximum reward. *Don't Waste Your Time* does this and more. A lively, stimulating departure from the dull-guidebook tradition, it dazzles with 560 colour photos, and a graphic, easy-to-read map for each hike. And this meticulous, 677-page opus is now ultralight gear. Take only the trail directions with you, leave the rest behind. Average trail weight: 67 grams (2.4 oz) per hike. Finally, a hiking guidebook fit for adventure, not just the armchair. Each of the 145 trips in *Don't Waste Your Time* is rated *Premier, Outstanding, Worthwhile*, or *Don't Do*. The book covers Banff, Jasper, Kootenay, Yoho and Waterton Lakes national parks, plus Mt. Robson and Mt. Assiniboine provincial parks. It includes 84 dayhikes, 41 backpack trips, and 20 shoulder-season trips. 7th edition June 2016.

• A zip-open, hardshell case (24 x 16.5 x 6.4 cm) holds the *Opinion* book and the nine *Fact* booklets.

• The *Opinion* book contains all the trip descriptions, and most of the photos. Use it at home, in the car, at the trailhead. It provides everything you need to know to choose your next hike. But leave it behind when you go hiking.

• The nine *Fact* booklets contain the trail directions, including the maps. Pack the one booklet you need, so you can refer to it while hiking. The booklets' average trail weight is just 67g (2.4 oz) per hike, so you can always have this essential piece of gear with you in the backcountry.

• Each *Fact* booklet is much lighter than any smartphone, tablet or eReader. Not restricted by battery life, the booklets never die. Flipping back-and-forth to compare hikes is easy. Photos are impressively big. Text is easy on the eyes.

• Trip descriptions in the *Opinion* book are insightful, engaging, inspiring. They illuminate each trail, empowering you to choose the optimal one for your interests, ability and mood. The authors' discerning advice can boost a day on the trail from "hmm" to "Wow!"

Trail directions in the *Fact* booklets are divided into *By Vehicle* and *On Foot* sections. The instructions are carefully crafted—precise, clear, complete—ensuring you spend your weekend or vacation striding instead of searching.

Where Locals Hike
in the Canadian Rockies
The Premier Trails in Kananaskis
Country, near Canmore and Calgary

ISBN 978-1-927462-04-1 The 58 most rewarding dayhikes and backpack trips within two hours of Calgary's international airport. All lead to astonishing alpine meadows, ridges and peaks. Though these trails are little known compared to those in the nearby Canadian Rocky Mountain national parks, the scenery is equally magnificent. Includes Peter Lougheed and Spray Valley provincial parks. Discerning trail reviews help you choose your trip. Detailed route descriptions keep you on the path. 320 pages, 180 photos, trail maps for each hike, full colour throughout. 5th edition, April 2017.

Done in a Day: Banff
The 10 Premier Hikes

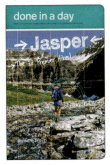

ISBN 978-0-9783427-0-8 Where to invest your limited hiking time to enjoy the greatest scenic reward. Choose an easy, vigourous, or challenging hike. Start your adventure within a short drive of town. Witness the wonder of Banff National Park and be back for a hot shower, great meal, and soft bed. 136 pages, 90 photos, trail maps for each trip, full colour throughout. Updated first edition June 2011.

Done in a Day: Jasper
The 10 Premier Hikes

ISBN 978-0-9783427-1-5 Where to invest your limited hiking time to enjoy the greatest scenic reward. Choose an easy, vigourous, or challenging hike. Start your adventure within a short drive of town. Witness the wonder of Jasper National Park and be back for a hot shower, great meal, and soft bed. 128 pages, 75 photos, trail maps for each trip, full colour throughout. Updated first edition June 2011.

Index

Trips begin on bold page